The Boy from
Baby House 10

The Boy from
Baby House 10

*From the Nightmare of a
Russian Orphanage to a New Life
in America*

Alan Philps and
John Lahutsky

St. Martin's Griffin
New York

THE BOY FROM BABY HOUSE 10. Copyright © 2009 by Alan Philps and John Lahutsky. All rights reserved. Printed in the United States of America. For information, address St. Martin's Press, 175 Fifth Avenue, New York, N.Y. 10010.

www.stmartins.com

Book design by Kathryn Parise

The Library of Congress has cataloged the hardcover edition as follows:

Philps, Alan.
   The boy from Baby House 10 : from the nightmare of a Russian orphanage to a new life in America / Alan Philps and John Lahutsky.—1st ed.
        p. cm.
      ISBN 978-0-312-57697-4
      1. Lahutsky, John, 1990– 2. Developmentally disabled children—Russia (Federation)—Biography. 3. Cerebral palsied children—Institutional care—Russia (Federation)—Biography. 4. Adopted children—United States—Biography.
5. Intercountry adoption—United States—Biography. I. Lahutsky, John, 1990–
II. Title.
      HV874.82.L34P55 2009
      362.196'928360092—dc22
      [B]
                                                                                          2009017119

ISBN 978-0-312-65648-5 (trade paperback)

First St. Martin's Griffin Edition: February 2011

10 9 8 7 6 5 4 3 2 1

The names and identifying characteristics of some people have been changed.

To the children who never made it

Contents

Preface   xi

1   The Half–Open Door   1

2   A Voice in the Silence   17

3   Pineapples and Peacocks   38

4   Beyond the Reach of Angels   51

5   A Superhuman Feat   58

6   Nobody Cares   65

7   The Mother's Tale   80

8   The Rat   88

9   Message from the Gulag   97

10   The Sour Grape   105

11   A Narrow Escape   119

12   Babes in the Wood   128

13 Cognac and Chocolate   137

14 Groundhog Day   147

15 The Blame Game   151

16 Narrow Escape (Reprise)   156

17 The Empire Strikes Back   162

18 Christmas Pudding in July   184

19 The Caged Bird   195

20 One of Us   199

21 Candle Power   211

22 Potentially Very Good News   221

23 Ticket to Santa Barbara   228

24 An Evil Trick   231

25 A Prisoner of the Caucasus   237

26 A White Lie   243

27 Unforgiven   248

28 Reunited   254

29 A Bit of Sleuthing   259

30 The Sister's Tale   267

31 The Vanya Effect   275

Epilogue: The Boy from Bethlehem   280

How This Book Came to Be Written   285

Preface

I willed myself to keep climbing. Though my legs are weak, my arms are strong, probably as strong as anyone else's in my Boy Scout troop. The men and boys below were shouting, "Come on, John! You can do it." I stretched out my left arm, gripped the rope, and pulled myself up. I told myself, Yes I can do it.

I could tell that none of the other boys had been expecting me to try to climb the rope netting. I had watched them one by one grapple their way to the top and seen they did not find it easy as they swayed backward and forward, like sailors on the rigging in a high wind. I worried that my legs would get tangled in the ropes and the instructor would have to rescue me. Or I could fall off and be left hanging foolishly in my harness. The other boys had all had their turn and the instructor looked at me and said, "John, do you want to try?" I could tell he would not mind if I said no. I looked him in the eye. "I'll go for it."

The instructor strapped me into a harness and tightened the fastenings around my waist and shoulders. Then he put a helmet on my head and adjusted the strap. I reached up and grasped the coarse rope netting and pulled myself up. As my feet left the ground, my whole body lurched backward and I fought to hang on. One hand after the other I pulled myself upward. I broke into a sweat and started to breathe heavily. I heard the voices below me shouting, "Keep going, John!"

I maneuvered my right hand to grab the next rope, and an image flashed into my mind—a small boy, naked, sedated, behind steel bars in a locked room. That boy too was trying to climb. He was trying to climb over the bars of a crib, but they were too high. He tried and he tried until he collapsed, exhausted, on a bare plastic mattress.

I stopped a moment to catch my breath, and I heard voices below shouting, "Don't stop. You can do it." It was as if they were encouraging the little boy in my head. Yes, I can do it, I thought, as I gripped the rope, gritted my teeth, and pulled myself up with all my force. I'd do it for the sake of that little boy, who was utterly alone.

That boy, you see, was me, my six-year-old self, when I was in another country and spoke a different language and my name was Ivan, or Vanya for short.

I reached the top of the netting, to a burst of applause from my fellow Scouts. I turned and smiled at them. It had been tough—but nothing compared to what my six-year-old self had overcome.

My Scout troop does not know about my past. What would they say if they knew?

What follows is my story. I am told I may be the only child to have survived the worst type of institution in the Russian children's gulag and gone on to live a normal life in America. These institutions created by Stalin continue to devour children to this day. That's why I feel my story has to be told.

As my mom says, if it saves just one child from the hell I went through, it will be worth it.

I, like thousands of other Russian children, was categorized at the age of five as ineducable and condemned to "permanent bed regime"—a living death in bare cribs. I hope my success in an American high school—despite having had no education at all until I was nearly ten—will prove how wrong those Russian experts are to write off children as "imbeciles."

My friends who knew me in Russia often ask how I survived when so many of the children like me died before the age of seven. I cannot answer that question.

This book has been a long time in the making. For years after my coming to America, my mom used to send reports on my progress to a British couple, Alan and Sarah, whom I had known when I was in Baby House 10 in Moscow. We sent photos to them: my first visit to Disney World, being greeted by Mickey Mouse; my citizenship party, where I wore a stars-and-stripes top hat and Mom wrote on the back "All American John"; and me in a tuxedo dressed as my hero, James Bond; and later, me in my Scout uniform.

In 2006, Mom sent them something different—an article from our local newspaper, in which a journalist interviewed us about how we found each other, our life together now, and my early childhood in Russia. Alan e-mailed back to say that, judging from the article, it was obvious I knew only a fraction of my extraordinary story. The next year, Alan and Sarah came to stay with us here in the United States, and we shared memories of our time in Moscow when Alan was a newspaper correspondent, Sarah was accompanying him as a "trailing spouse," and I was in the care of the state. I had many questions: What happened to my birth family? How did I come to be in Baby House 10 and why was I sent from there to an adult mental asylum at the age of six? Why had it taken so long to rescue me?

The more I heard, the more eager I was to know everything. I wanted to know why Russian doctors made no distinction between mental and physical disability and how they could condemn children with mild physical disabilities to a living hell. As we sat talking, Alan said my story would make a great book. I leaped at the idea. You must write it, I told him. You and Sarah and Vika and all the others should tell their parts in my story. The world should know.

Since I have been in America, I have learned a lot about Russia. I recently gave my history class a presentation on the fall of the czar, the rise of Lenin, and Stalin's takeover. This has brought me some insights into the system that tried to destroy me.

The story begins when I was only four years old. My memories of early childhood are vague, as most people's are. Being locked away, I was not aware that at times I was the still center of a whirlwind of efforts to rescue me, which culminated in my mom's responding to my cry for help.

To write this book, Alan has been back to Moscow to interview most of the people who came into contact with me during that time, and has used diaries, photographs, videos, and official documents. I contributed more as my memories of my life after the age of six became clearer.

What I witnessed in my places of incarceration is seen through my eyes. But much of the rest of the story is told by two people very dear to me: Vika, a young Russian woman who devoted months of her life to trying to save me, and Sarah, whom I would not leave in peace until she had found me a life outside a murderous system.

　　　　　　　　　　　　　　　　—*John Lahutsky*
　　　　　　　　　　　　Bethlehem, PA, September 2008

The Boy from
Baby House 10

1

The Half-Open Door

November–December 1994

"Can I have a toy, please?"

Vanya's request hung in the air unanswered. The room was full of children, but there was no movement except for Nastya the caregiver, who was noiselessly wiping the surfaces with a damp cloth. Vanya followed her every move, desperate for a response. But she kept her back turned to him as she shuffled to the ledge where tiny Valeria was lying immobile in a bouncing chair that never bounced. Valeria was staring but not seeing anything, and there was no contact—not a touch, not a word, not a glance—between caregiver and child as Nastya wiped around her, as if she were one of the wooden toys on the shelf. When the cloth came close to her foot, the little girl flinched and a look of fear passed over her face.

Vanya hoped Nastya would turn around after she had finished dusting the ledge and he could catch her eye. But no, she moved to the playpen where blind Tolya was feeling his way around for toys that were not there. She tut-tutted as she noticed the rail had been gnawed by the children.

Nastya bent down to wipe the tray of the baby walker in which Igor spent his days, unable to move around because the baby walker was tethered to the playpen with a knotted rag. Igor arched his back and started banging his head against the bars of the playpen behind him, and Vanya could see the boy was trying to attract Nastya's attention. But she ignored him too.

Vanya did not dare ask Nastya for a toy a second time. He was afraid of what she might do. When she began her shift, she was silent and grumpy; but then after her break, she would start shouting at the children, or worse. Once she had thrown Igor from the changing table into the playpen. Afterward, Vanya had noticed a great big bruise growing on his head.

Vanya was alarmed to see the blank expression on the face of his friend Andrei, who was sitting opposite him at their little table. Even more alarming, he was rocking backward and forward like the children in the baby walkers did. This could go on all day, but Vanya needed a friend to talk to—he was the only other child in the room who could speak. Vanya had to do something. He could not wait any longer for Nastya to turn round. She was folding clothes in the opposite corner of the room, "Can we have our toy, please, Nastya?" he said to her back.

His question was met with silence. Vanya braced himself for one of her outbursts. He held his breath as he watched her turn slowly from the pile of clothes. She shuffled a few steps toward a high shelf and took down a battered matryoshka, a nest of Russian dolls. He could barely contain his excitement as she carried the toy toward him.

"Have this one. Share it with Andrei." She slammed the wooden toy down on the table between the two boys. Andrei stopped rocking, but his expression remained blank.

Vanya quickly discovered that some parts of the matryoshka were missing or broken. But having any toy, even a broken one, was better than nothing. Taking his time, he lined all the dolls up in order of size in front of Andrei. Then he took them apart and put the pieces back inside one another. He repeated the process, but still there was no response from Andrei.

"Come on, Andrei. It's your turn now," he said in an urgent whisper.

Andrei continued staring in front of him. But Vanya refused to give up.

"I'll roll one toward you and you catch it." The doll wobbled across the table, bumped into Andrei's chest, and fell on the linoleum floor. Andrei made no attempt to catch it.

Vanya looked anxiously to see if Nastya had heard the doll crashing to the ground. But no, she was still busy folding pairs of tights.

"Andrei, you didn't even try. Now this time really try."

He held up the doll in front of his friend's face. Andrei turned his head slightly and gazed with dull eyes at the doll. "That's better. Now I'm going to roll it to you again."

Once again Andrei remained immobile and let the doll roll off the table. This time Nastya did hear it.

"So you're throwing your toy on the floor? I told them you weren't fit to have toys." With an angry swipe, she took away the remains of the doll, and Vanya watched in shock as she placed it back on the high shelf. She sat down at her desk to fill out forms.

Vanya stared at the tabletop, now as barren as the rest of the room. He looked up at Andrei, who refused to meet his gaze. He had started rocking again. Igor was crashing his head against the bars of the playpen with ever increasing ferocity. Between the crashes, Vanya could hear the sound of little Valeria mewing on the ledge.

His eyes alighted on the radiator under the window. He smiled at its chunky shape and the memory of the rough surface of the metal and the comforting warmth it gave off. He longed to slide off his chair and crawl over and touch it, but only his favorite caregiver, the one he called Auntie Valentina, allowed him to move around the room. Nastya would shout and scream if she saw him crawling on the floor.

He remembered the wonderful morning when the door had opened and a man came in with a big box. He announced he had come to mend the radiator. Vanya managed to attract the man's attention by asking who he was, and he was allowed to sit and watch. The man told him he was the plumber, and he opened his box to reveal tools of different shapes and sizes.

In all his four years, Vanya had never seen so many fascinating objects. The plumber noticed his interest and gave him a lug wrench to hold. Then he took a wrench and started unscrewing the radiator. Vanya watched his every move and asked the name of each tool, repeating the word so he could remember it. The plumber smiled, and when he had finished with the wrench, he gave it to Vanya to hold. Luckily, Valentina was on duty that day, and she did not pull Vanya away. He smiled to himself as he recalled a really exciting moment. Water was flowing from the pipe and there was a big pool on the floor. Valentina was sent to fetch a rag. Then the plumber asked him to hand back the wrench, as he needed it urgently.

Vanya closed his eyes and replayed the whole scene in his mind. Now he was the plumber, and Andrei was his helper and held the wrench for him. He would say, "Andrei, quick. Hand me the wrench. The water's leaking!" And Andrei would pass him the wrench, and he would use all his strength to tighten the nut. And the water would stop dripping and Valentina would clear up the mess. He would pack up his tools in the shiny metal box and go off to mend another leaky radiator. How wonderful that would be!

Nastya's chair scraped backward and she stood up abruptly. Vanya had spent so many days watching her every move that he knew her sudden sense of purpose meant she was about to go on her break. She went to her bag, which was hanging on a hook on the wall, and took out a pack of cigarettes. She hunted for a lighter in the pocket of her coat. She did not look in the mirror; not like Tanya, who put on lipstick before she went out.

As he watched her, Vanya's heart was beating fast. He had noticed that the connecting door to the next room was ajar. It was normally closed. What a stroke of luck—Nastya was going out and she hadn't noticed. Suddenly all his senses came alive with the possibility of adventure. With Nastya out of the way, he could crawl over to the door and peep into the next room, the one the caregivers called Group 1. He knew there were other children there. Perhaps there would be a child like him he could speak to. He looked at Andrei, who had his blank face on again. Even if there were no children, there might be a friendly caregiver he had never met before. She might say a kind word to him that he could save up to remember later during the long nap.

Cigarettes in hand, Nastya hesitated before leaving and scanned the room. Vanya lowered his gaze and held his breath. Maybe she could read his thoughts and had guessed his plan. What was she doing? Why was she hanging about? Now she was going toward the interconnecting door. Vanya's heart was in his mouth. She was going to notice that the door was open and she would close it and there would be no chance of adventure. To his relief, he saw Nastya take her bag off the hook. Miraculously, she had not noticed that the interconnecting door was open. Vanya's eyes followed her as she went out into the corridor, and he heard the key turn in the lock.

Now the children were on their own, there was no time to waste. Vanya slid off his chair, landing with a thump on the floor. He was not allowed to crawl; they told him the floor was dirty and he could get sick from it. He shut his mind to the thought he might get hit if Nastya caught him. Using all the strength in his arms, he pulled himself along the shiny floor. Halfway across the room, he heard a beautiful sound coming from the direction of the open door. Someone was singing. He speeded up.

He reached the door, and pushed it a fraction so that he could see inside. Dazzled by the midday sun streaming though the net curtains, he could just make out a tall silhouette framed in light. He screwed his eyes up. The silhouette bent down and resolved itself into the figure of a young woman who was putting a baby gently back in a crib. What tenderness she showed to the baby, what infinite care she lavished, all the while singing her haunting melody. She picked up another child, and Vanya noticed she was dressed differently from all the other women in the baby house. She was not wearing a white coat but had jeans on her long legs, and her hair was loose, not tied back.

For once Vanya lost his tongue. He watched the scene silently, unwilling to break the spell. He wanted to remember every detail, so that he could recall it as he lay restless in his crib in the afternoon.

The young woman was walking around the room, cradling the baby, and suddenly her eyes met his. She did not break off her singing, but flashed a smile at him. Vanya had been expecting to be shouted at and told to get back to his room, but not a word was said between them. Emboldened, he crawled an inch farther in to the babies' room. He wished he could live in there. It was so different: Could it be a dream? he wondered, until a harsh voice barked behind him. "Get back in here, Vanya. You're not allowed in there." Vanya recognized the voice Nastya had after her break. He shuffled back into Group 2. Nastya pulled shut the interconnecting door, grabbed him under his armpits, dragged him across the floor, and plunked him back on his chair.

"Don't try that again," she snarled into his face, forcing Vanya to breathe in the sickly smell from her mouth.

It was time for the midday feed. Women from the kitchen brought in two large aluminium saucepans and a tray piled high with bowls and feeding bottles full of brown soup, and set them out on a table by the door. Vanya scrutinized the tray to see if there was a special treat for him—a piece of bread. None of the other children had bread, but his favorite caregiver, Auntie Valentina, always brought him a hunk of bread when it was her shift. Today was Nastya's day, and she had never given him bread. But perhaps the cook had remembered him and slipped a slice among the bottles.

Nastya doled out ten portions of thin potato puree and vegetable soup into a line of bowls. Vanya and Andrei were always served first, and they were expecting their bowls at any moment. Andrei had even stopped rocking. But Nastya turned to Vanya and snapped, "After your disgraceful behavior this morning, you will be served last. And your friend can wait too."

Crestfallen, Vanya watched as Nastya took a bowl, squatted down beside Igor's baby walker, pushed the bowl against his chin to force his head back, and shoveled in food with a big spoon. At his first gulp, Igor let out a yelp. Vanya knew that the hot food was burning his mouth. But Nastya continued without saying a word, tipping big spoonfuls of potato puree down his throat. Igor squirmed, trying to turn his head away. "So you're not hungry today," said Nastya. She stood up and returned the bowl to the table.

She picked up Tolya from the playpen, dumped him in a chair, and fetched another bowl. Vanya watched as the blind boy felt his new surroundings, trying to get his bearings. As his fingers explored the chair, Nastya pushed his head back and started loading the mixture into his mouth. Vanya watched the spoon move faster and faster while all the time Tolya was struggling to get the food down. Whenever he turned his head away to give himself time to swallow, Nastya jerked it back and continued shoveling the food down. Almost as fast as she could push it in, it welled out of his mouth and down his chin onto a piece of rag. The bowl was soon emptied and she moved on to the next child.

Next she took one of the bottles of brown soup and shuffled over to the ledge where Valeria was lying. She shoved the nipple into the tiny girl's mouth and upended the bottle. Valeria was so weak that Vanya could barely hear her sucks. "Hurry up," Nastya said, turning away from the girl as she surveyed the room. The rhythm of Valeria's sucks slowed and died away, with the bottle still almost full. Nastya removed it impatiently and moved on to the next child.

Vanya watched with growing hunger as Nastya rushed through the lunch routine. He really needed a hunk of bread today. Perhaps if he asked nicely . . . No, today was not the day to ask for treats. Sure enough, when she slammed two bowls down on the table in front of the boys, along with two big spoons, there was no bread. "Don't make a mess," she warned. In silence Vanya and Andrei spooned the cold slop into their mouths, without even the comfort of something to chew.

While the boys were still eating, Nastya took the children one by one to the changing table and, without making eye contact or saying anything, stripped the children of their wet tights and soiled rags, and replaced them with dry ones. Then she walked past Vanya and Andrei as she deposited each one in a crib in the adjoining room. This was the beginning of the afternoon nap.

Vanya dreaded the boredom of the long afternoons confined to his crib. As his turn loomed, he racked his brains in search of a way to delay the inevitable. When Auntie Valentina was on duty she would let him sit with her for a while when she had put the others down for their nap. She would teach him a song or a poem. But today was Nastya's day. She had already whisked Andrei off. As he made a big show of not having finished his lunch, scraping every last drop of puree from his bowl, he thought of a way to start a conversation with her. As she bent down to pick him up, he asked, "Did you buy your carpet?"

Nastya looked stunned. "How do you know about my carpet?"

"I heard you talking about it with the doctor. You said you'd seen a carpet in the market and you were going to buy it after your shift."

"Yes, I did go and buy it. I did."

"Is it beautiful?"

"Yes, it is." There was pause as she picked him up.

"What's a market, Nastya?"

"A place where you buy things. But now it's your nap time."

"But I'm not sleepy." Nastya did not respond. She was in too much of a hurry to get him into his crib. As she shut the door behind her, Vanya was left staring at the cracks in the wall through the bars in his crib. With his finger he traced the lines in the paintwork, hopping over the bars as he followed each crack to the end of the crib. He felt crushed by the great expanse of time stretching ahead of him. He knew it would be dark before he was rescued. The other children were restless and moaning in cribs placed against the four walls of the room.

He shut his ears to the unhappy sounds of the other children and concentrated on going over in his mind his big adventure from the moment Nastya had left the room and he had slid off the chair. He conjured up an image of the young woman with her long hair tenderly holding the baby and singing to it. He remembered her smiling at him and imagined her singing to him now. He asked himself again, Who was she? Why was she dressed differently from the other caregivers? Why hadn't she shouted at him or hit him for leaving his group? He turned over in his mind what had happened but remained just as puzzled as when he started.

When he had replayed the scene in his head several times, he searched for something else to think about. He conjured up an image of the nest of dolls. He was playing with them again, but this time they were not broken and cracked and no pieces were missing. He imagined lining them up on the table, from the tiniest one as small as his finger to the largest, which was as big as Valeria in her bouncing chair. There were so many they could barely fit on the tabletop. They formed a great wall at his end of the table, and he was hiding behind them from Andrei. That made Andrei laugh.

Then he started rolling them down the table. But this time Andrei did not have his blank face on. He was lunging left and right to catch the dolls—all of them, the little ones that skittered along the tabletop and the big ones that wobbled and meandered from side to side. Andrei caught each one and sent them back up the table, where Vanya let them fall dangerously off the edge and then caught them before they crashed to the floor. And Nastya never heard a thing!

There was no chance of Nastya's letting him have the matryoshka again today. But what about tomorrow? Tomorrow was Tanya's day. He was not sure about Tanya, but he could ask her. And then the day after that would be Auntie Valentina's day. She would be sure to let him have the dolls. That was something to look forward to.

Two days later, Vanya was sitting at his little table, eagerly waiting for his favorite caregiver to come on duty. Tanya had already taken off her white coat and was looking at her watch, eager to be off. The door opened and in came the beloved figure of Auntie Valentina in her shabby coat, carrying an umbrella and a bulging plastic bag in her hand.

Vanya watched as Valentina hung up her coat and started to rummage in her plastic bag. She took out a paper package and placed it in front of him. Trembling with anticipation, he peeled back the greaseproof paper. It was a thick slice of salami.

She whispered to him, "I have a banana for you later." His face lit up.

"Auntie Valentina, you're my favorite caregiver, you know," he said, his mouth full of meat.

"Get on with you, Vanya," she said as she went to the bedroom. She came back carrying Kiril, the boy who was always hanging in the baby bouncer. She held him on her lap and dressed him slowly, first in T-shirt and tights, and then pants and sweater. Her face was preoccupied.

"Auntie Valentina, why are you sad today?" Vanya asked.

"Kiril is leaving us. He's off to the internat."

Vanya had heard this word but wanted to find out what it meant. "What's an internat?" he asked. Valentina did not answer. Just then the door opened and in bustled Svetlana, the woman who was always carrying papers. There was a brief exchange during which Valentina slid Kiril's arms into an outdoor coat, kissed him tenderly on the top of his head, and handed him over to Svetlana. The door slammed and he was gone.

Vanya remembered this had happened before. Svetlana had come for a child and never brought him back. Maybe she would come for Andrei next, and he'd be left without a friend. He pushed that thought out of his mind. He looked around to ask Valentina to tell him what this internat was. But she was busy changing another child, and her look said, Don't ask me that question.

Minutes later, the interconnecting door to the babies' room opened and the deputy head doctor came in carrying a little blond girl. "You've got a spare crib now. This one's for you," she told Valentina, consulting a brown card. "Kurdyaeva is her name. Born premature. Her mother gave her up at birth. She's fifteen months old now and still can't sit unaided. Obviously very retarded. Definitely one for you."

Valentina settled the girl in one of the walkers tethered to the playpen on Vanya's side of the room, and went to sort out the paperwork.

"Hello. I'm Vanya. What's your name?"

The girl fixed him with an intelligent gaze and burbled, straining to say something, but all that came out was a strangled *m-m-m* sound. Vanya could see she was desperate to join him and Andrei at their table.

"And this is Andrei," he said. "Look, Auntie Valentina has given us a toy each today."

He started demonstrating his toy—half of a broken plastic telephone. Vanya had the base and Andrei was holding the receiver, which was missing its cord. The girl got excited as Vanya's fingers rotated the dial, which made a chirruping sound. Her look said, Let me play. With an attentive audience, Vanya demonstrated how the dial turned and showed her the face on the front of the toy. He was so engrossed that he did not notice a figure standing over them.

"Oh, Masha, you like that, do you?" said an unknown voice. A hand reached down, snatched the telephone from him, and gave it to the girl. Vanya was left with his jaw hanging open. The person now had her back to him and was crouching down, fussing over the new arrival. "Now, Masha we must practice your speaking. Say Mama. *M-m-m-m*." Masha obediently repeated *m-m-m*.

Vanya was enthralled at the spectacle. His eyes followed the young woman as she stood up and bounced over to Valentina. "Please forgive my rudeness. I'm Vika. I'm a volunteer. I've been helping my friend who works in the baby room. I've become very close to Masha. Is it okay if I come to visit her now that she's moved to Group 2? I can help you as well."

"Oh, I can always do with help here. As you see, I'm all on my own with a dozen children to feed and change for twenty-four hours at a stretch. And I'm not as young as I was," said Valentina, laughing. "You can stay and help me give them lunch if you like."

As they talked, Vanya realized that this was the young woman he had gazed at through the interconnecting door while she was singing to the babies—the one he had not stopped thinking about ever since the day of his adventure. And now that she was in his room, he could barely contain his excitement. As he watched her clumsily spooning slops into

Masha's mouth, with half of it falling on the floor, he was glad just to have her nearby. He practiced saying her name to himself—Vika, Vika.

"We've never had a volunteer before," said Valentina as they shared the work of feeding the children. "Outsiders aren't usually allowed in here."

"I'm not sure I'm really wanted. In fact, some of the staff think I get in the way."

Valentina smiled kindly. "Surely not, dear."

As the young woman and Auntie Valentina chattered away, Vanya watched and listened with rapt attention. He was being ignored and all the attention was being lavished on Masha, the new arrival, but he did not mind. He had resolved to make Vika his friend.

When Vanya woke up the next day, it took him a while to recall why he felt happy. It was not because Auntie Valentina was coming on duty. Her shift was yesterday. Then he remembered Vika. She was not like the women in white coats whose shift patterns he had memorized. Vika could appear any day. He had first seen her on Nastya's day, and then she had appeared on Valentina's day, so it seemed to him as he lay in his crib that she might easily appear today. All day he looked up every time the door opened, hoping to see her sweet face; but each time, he was disappointed, until it got dark and he knew for sure she was not coming.

The next day she did not come. He found comfort in whispering her name to himself. Then suddenly he heard himself crying, "Vika, Vika," as he saw her head poking around the door. "Have you come to see Masha?"

"You've remembered my name. Remind me—what's yours?"

"I'm Vanya."

"Oh, yes. You were showing Masha the telephone. And yes, I have come to see her." She strode across the room, swooped down on Masha, pulled her out of the baby walker, and held her in her arms. Masha's face, normally so sad, broke into a smile.

"Who are you? Who gave you permission to come here?" Vanya's heart skipped a beat as Nastya emerged from the bedroom. In all the excitement, he had forgotten she was the one on duty. Vika turned to face the caregiver, still holding the girl in her arms.

"Sorry. I should have introduced myself. I've come to see Masha."

"Do you work here?"

"N-n-no."

"Then you shouldn't be here."

"But I've been helping with the babies in Group 1. I've been coming for months."

Nastya's officious attitude softened as she saw an opportunity. "Well, I could do with a break. You can look after the children for ten minutes."

The door shut, and then to Vanya's delight, Vika sat down on a little chair at his table with Masha on her knee. She turned the girl to face her, looked her in the eyes, and started making the sound *m-m-m*. "Come on, Masha, you can do it." Masha was silent. Vika put her lips against the child's cheek and repeated the sound. Still she was silent.

"Come, Masha, you used to do this so well when you were with the babies." Masha continued to gaze happily at her, but no sound came out.

Vika sighed. She tugged off Masha's socks, planted her bare feet on the floor, and put her hands on the tabletop, while supporting the child under the shoulders. "You must make your legs strong," she said. The girl sagged.

Vika looked desperate. Vanya's face took on a similar expression as Vika scoured the room for anything that could stimulate Masha. Her eye alighted on a baby chair with a horse's head in front and a pair of handlebars. She dragged it from the corner to Vanya's table, placed Masha on the seat, and put her hands on the bars. In this position, she could hold herself upright. "Clever girl! You're riding a horse." Masha's eyes brightened. For the first time, she looked alert as she gripped the handles.

Vika made a galloping-horse noise. She encouraged Vanya to join in.

Then she started clapping her hands and clicking her tongue. He hadn't had so much fun for ages.

"What's all this noise? You've stirred them up. I'll never get them to sleep this afternoon." Nastya was back from her break and determined to end the party. "And why have you taken her socks off?" she demanded. "She'll catch cold."

"Look how happy she is. This chair really helps her. Maybe you could sit her in it from time to time . . ."

"As though I haven't got enough to do with all the changing, washing, and feeding."

With that, Nastya pulled Masha out of the horse chair and put her back in her assigned place in the tethered baby walker. Masha let out a terrible howl.

"Anyway, why are you wasting your time on her?" She tapped her finger twice on her head, in a crude gesture meaning imbecile.

Vika realized she might not be allowed back to see Masha and made a last attempt to get on good terms with the caregiver. "I could help you serve lunch if you like," she offered.

"No. I can manage on my own. Isn't it time you were going? And don't bother to come again."

Vika kissed the top of Masha's head, picked up her bag, gave a little wave to Vanya, and was gone. Once again Vanya was surrounded by silence.

All afternoon, as he lay awake in his crib, he thought about Vika. Nastya had told her not to come back. He was never going to see her again. He felt his loss like a great weight on his chest, making it hard to breathe. Then he imagined himself leaping out of his crib and striding into the dayroom and standing in front of Nastya and declaring, "Isn't it time you were going? And don't bother to come back!" Then Auntie Valentina would come on Nastya's days. How wonderful that would be.

He tensed up when Nastya came to take him out of his crib. He kept his eyes shut when she changed him. When he was sitting at his table again, he stared at her with hatred when her back was turned. He was feeling so upset that when the door opened, he did not react in his usual way and turn to see who was coming in. Too late, out of the corner of his eye, he saw someone go past in jeans and a sweater. His heart leaped as he thought it must be Vika. He turned on his chair and was disappointed to see there were two women not wearing white coats, but neither was Vika. One had long hair like Vika's, but it was blond; the other was talking in a funny-sounding voice.

They had come in with a caregiver he had only seen twice before in Group 2, but he remembered she was called Zhanna. She seemed uncomfortable, and he sensed she wanted the visitors to leave. But the woman with the short hair kept asking questions. Finally Zhanna ushered the two women toward the door, saying the children were about to have supper. Vanya was surprised by this, as supper only happened after Nastya had her afternoon break, and she had not had it yet. As they approached the door, Vanya seized his opportunity.

"Please come again," he said to the woman with short hair.

To his delight she turned back and came over to him. She gave him a car and, when he asked if she had one for Andrei, she put her hand in her bag and took out another one. He had never played with a toy car before, and neither had Andrei. They both moved their cars around the tabletop, smiling at each other. They were so engrossed with the cars that he almost forgot to ask the woman her name—Sarah—and to make her promise to come again. She said she would.

Before supper was served, Nastya whisked the cars away and put them on a high shelf. The next morning when Vanya awoke, the first thing he thought of was his car. He sat up, stretched out his hand, and imagined moving his car along the rail of the crib. Then he imagined it moving in a great arc along the wall.

"Nastya, can I have my car now?" he asked when she entered the bedroom.

"Car? What car?"

Vanya started to feel uneasy. He grabbed the bars and pulled himself up. "You know, the car Sarah gave me."

"Sarah? I don't know any Sarah."

Now Vanya started to panic. "You know, the one with the funny voice who gave me a car. And she gave one to Andrei too."

Nastya stooped to pick up a child. "I don't remember any cars," she said casually. "You must have dreamed it."

2

A Voice in the Silence

October 1994–June 1995

Sarah met Vanya quite by chance. In fact, she almost missed him completely. It was at the end of a long day—her first visit to Baby House 10, when she was plunged unprepared into a world that seemed to belong in the time of Charles Dickens.

As she recalls more than a decade later, she had no particular idea of what she was going to do with herself when she arrived in Moscow in the fall of 1994. "I was the trailing spouse of a newspaper correspondent, with two children at school. I wondered how I was going to fill the next four years. One day I was dragged along to the newcomers meeting of the International Women's Club. This was an excuse for foreign women to dress up and eat Dunkin' Donuts—just arrived in Moscow—at the American ambassador's residence. There was a queue halfway to the Kremlin. Inside, we were offered the chance to sign up for icon painting, Indian cookery, yoga, Russian literature, and other worthy activities.

Among the Gucci-clad oil company wives, I came across a couple of British women in leggings selling T-shirts from boxes. They represented the welfare group, which had set itself the huge task of helping Russians whose lives had been destroyed by the collapse of Communism. They desperately needed Russian speakers as interpreters, and I could not turn them down. Little did I know that the consequences of this encounter would take over my life so that at the end of the four-year posting I would not be ready to leave."

Thus it was that one overcast and snowless day in December, Sarah was picked up at her apartment by Louisa, an American friend, who needed an interpreter for a visit to a baby house. Moscow was looking its worst. The changes that would transform the city into a neon-lit boom-town had barely started, and there was still no snow to hide the city's broken pavements and potholed roads.

The back of Louisa's gleaming red Jeep Cherokee was piled high with children's winter coats and boots, potties, packages of pencils and felt-tipped pens, all bought with money raised by the welfare group, as well as a box of cookies beautifully baked and iced by Louisa herself.

As Louisa navigated her way across the Moscow ring road, zipping across four lanes of traffic to slide into the U-turn lane in the center of the highway, she was aware of being an object of wonder. She was the only woman driver on the road, and probably the only one in the whole of Moscow at the wheel of a powerful and expensive SUV. She stuck out even more with her long blond hair. As they drove up Novoslobodskaya Street, a battered Lada strained every sinew to overtake the Jeep, and four thickset men in leather jackets leered at the American woman who dared to challenge male supremacy on the road.

Fighting her way through the traffic, Louisa explained that Baby House 10 was the most central of the orphanages, but the hardest to gain access to, due to the eccentricity of its head doctor, who was very suspicious of outsiders. She thought the foreign women were all missionaries for an American religious cult and had convinced herself that the last interpreter was giving her the evil eye. Since then, the head doctor had obstructed all visits by the group, declaring the place to be under quarantine whenever anyone called for an appointment. This time, Louisa told Sarah, they were going unannounced.

The car stopped at a high gate with flaking green paint at the end of a potholed alley. They opened a small side gate to enter the baby-house grounds. Sarah recalls a desolate scene: Under bare linden trees were a couple of large wooden playpens, with fretted roofs decorated in the Russian peasant style. They had once been pretty adornments to the baby-house grounds, but now they were rotting away. Scattered among the trees were a swing without a seat, a sandbox open to the elements, and abandoned plastic carts and trolleys, all lacking wheels or handles. The baby house itself was a two-story building of yellow stucco. It had once been an elegant mansion, but its pilastered façade was marred by an outgrowth of sheds, storerooms, and coalbins that betrayed its use as a state institution.

This baby house was home to 62 children, ranging from newborns to five-year-olds. But Sarah could not see or hear any of them. Her first impression was that rather than a place filled with gurgling babies and happy toddlers, it was a dead end. The main street—packed with shoppers, hawkers, and beggars—was only fifty yards away, but the baby house could have been in a different world.

Sarah and Louisa walked up the steps onto a porch, whose generous space was crammed with broken furniture, old strollers, and plastic toys that could never be mended but that no one took the responsibility to throw away.

Beside the door, a young woman in a white coat and heavy makeup was sitting on a bench, staring into the distance as she smoked a cigarette. She showed no interest in the two foreign women as they pulled open the outer door. They passed through a tiny lobby and pushed open a second door to enter the baby house. There was an institutional smell— stale air, boiled cabbage, and urine. An older woman in a white coat with thick glasses and a stethoscope around her neck was walking toward them, carrying a sheet of paper. She recognized Louisa and accepted the box of cookies.

"We've brought you the coats and boots you asked for," Louisa said.

"You need to give them to Adela. I'll try and find her." She left the foreigners standing in the corridor. There was still no sign of any children, but Sarah could hear the muffled sound of a child crying.

She walked cautiously down the corridor in the direction of the sound, reading the signs on the doors—HEAD DOCTOR, DEPUTY, SPEECH THERAPIST, MASSAGE. These rooms were silent. She tried one door. It was locked. She worked her way up the corridor and found the source of the sound. It was coming from a room marked ISOLATOR. There was a glass panel in the door. Inside, she could see three cubicles. In the farthest cubicle was a little boy about two years old. She watched as he shook the bars of the crib, jumping up and down. He looked like he had been crying forever, exhausted now with only the strength for occasional sobs. There was no teddy bear in the crib. There were no pictures on the walls. The cubicle was bare.

Sarah recoiled in shock and could not stop herself approaching a soft-faced woman who was coming out of the office marked DEPUTY.

"Excuse me. What's the matter with the little boy?" asked Sarah. "He seems terribly upset."

"His mother left him here this morning. She can't cope with him anymore," said the woman. "She's a student. She needs a break so she can finish her studies. We told her to come back in a couple of years. He'll be easier to manage then."

"But why is he in there all by himself?"

"They have to spend three weeks in isolation. They could infect the other children."

"But he doesn't look ill . . ."

"That's the rules—three weeks' quarantine. Then he's assigned to a group."

"But he has no toys."

"Toys aren't allowed. They can spread germs," said the deputy.

Sarah wanted to question further, but Louisa was approaching and she did not look happy. "Didn't I tell you not to ask awkward questions?" she whispered. "They won't let us back in."

At that moment, the woman in thick glasses appeared through the front door from outside, followed by an old woman with a smudge of soot on her forehead and wisps of gray hair straying from under a green mobcap. In her hand she was carrying a coal bucket and a thick pair of gloves, blackened by years of use.

Sarah's first thought was that this droll woman must be a cleaner. Only when she was introduced did it become clear that this was no menial but Adela, the head doctor of the orphanage, responsible for the lives of 62 young souls.

"The boiler needs repair," Adela said, taking off her workman's gloves. Her eyes darted fretfully between the visitors and her deputy.

"Adela, we've brought you the coats and boots you asked for," Sarah said. "They're in the car. If you get someone to open the gate, we'll bring the car in."

Despite her elevated position, Adela took it upon herself to pull back the bolt and drag the gate over the rough ground. Louisa drove in and parked by the main door, the Jeep's gleaming red bodywork shaming the baby house's ancient car, an off-white Volga station wagon with a red cross painted on the side. The staff hung back by the entrance, a knot of women in white coats, as Adela unloaded the donations and carried them inside.

When all the goods were counted and signed for, Louisa asked if there was anything more the baby house needed from the welfare group. Adela stared at the floor and muttered, "We've got everything we need." There followed an awkward silence. The woman in thick glasses piped up: "Adela Vladimirovna. What about a washing machine? Ours has been broken for months."

"Yes, yes. That's what we need. You sort it out with Louisa."

There was one bag of donations left over. Sarah saw an opportunity. "Here are some toys, Duplo and things like that. Can we give them to the children?"

Another woman in a white coat stepped forward. She introduced herself as Zhanna, the chief defectologist, and was clearly a person of some authority. Sarah was left wondering what her sinister title could mean.

The defectologist led the foreigners along the corridor and up a flight of stone stairs with a cold, brown-painted handrail on steel rods. At the top of the stairs was a furnished area with a carpet, red plastic sofas, and an anemic plant on a stand. No one was sitting there and there was still no sign of any children. At last they came to a heavy door marked GROUP 3. Inside, a dozen boys and girls ages four and five were milling around. They were dressed in ill-matched clothes from the communal cupboard, wearing tights of fawn or faded blue. One girl stood out: Clearly the staff favorite, she was wearing a polka-dot dress, had a big white bow in her hair, and was walking around clutching a doll. Sarah noticed that some of the children had rashes on their faces and the boys had bruises and scratches.

A lone caregiver in a white coat was sitting at a desk, her back to the children, writing in a notebook.

There was a playhouse, and some molded plastic animals were scattered on the floor. More interesting toys were displayed in a glass cabinet. They were clearly just for show. A boy was hitting another with an indeterminate bit of plastic. The caregiver raised her eyes from the desk, twisted her head over her shoulder, and shouted to the boy, "Stop that." She did not say hello to the visitors.

The children gathered around the foreigners, slipping their hands into the bags they were carrying, saying, "Give me, give me."

As the children scrambled for Louisa's cookies, the defectologist made a sweeping gesture to include every child in the room and said, "They are oligophrenics, all of them."

Sarah asked her what the word meant. "You know, mentally retarded," she said. She pointed to a mixed-race girl in a tartan shift. "Take that one, for example. Her mother's a drug addict and her father's gone back to Cuba. The grandmother used to visit, but not even she comes anymore. She could be dead for all we know."

The girl's face crumpled as she heard these shocking words, but the defectologist did not appear to notice. She pointed to a boy in a purple shirt and pink shorts. "We've had him since birth. He was found at the railway station. His mother gave birth in Moscow and then disappeared back to Latvia. And this one, his mother lives in an internat. She got pregnant by the janitor."

In the months to come, as Sarah visited more and more baby houses, she learned that this heartless attitude toward the children was the norm. But on that December day, the defectologist's callous words made an indelible impression. "I could not believe she was discussing the children as if they couldn't hear her or were too stupid to understand. She had such a pleasant and motherly face, but she seemed to have lost all her maternal instincts when it came to the children in her care. The message I got was that these children were all cursed at birth and would never overcome their flawed origins.

"I picked up a little girl. She had short hair, cut in an unflattering style. I sat her on my knee and gave her a Duplo horse and rider. I expected the sweet smell of my daughter who was the same age. But instead there was a strong whiff of dirty child, unwashed clothes, and neglect. I remember wondering, How come this big institution didn't even have a washing machine to keep the children's clothes clean?"

Having asked permission from the defectologist, Sarah and Louisa opened the bags of toys in the middle of the floor. The children stampeded to ransack this treasure trove. They pulled apart the brightly colored figures and reassembled them, hungrily absorbing the pleasure of the colors. They pulled handles and pressed buttons, setting off a cacophony of rings, buzzes, and hoots.

The happy chaos unleashed in Group 3, Sarah soon sensed, did not fit in with the strict regime of the baby house, and within minutes the defectologist signaled it was time to go. As she left, she told the caregiver, "I'll be coming back later to pick up the toys and put them in my room. These are educational toys and they can only play with them under my supervision. We don't want them broken."

Sarah opened her mouth to protest, but Louisa jabbed her in the ribs. The caregiver slipped out after them, saying, "It's time for my break." She whipped out a key and locked the door on the twelve children and skipped down the stairs. Sarah opened her mouth to say, But who's looking after the children? and then bit her tongue.

As they were being led to the stairs, they came to a door marked GROUP 2. "Are there more children in here?" Sarah asked. "Maybe we could give them the rest of the toys."

"Oh no. It's only the bad cases there—the incurables. They don't need toys. They're not capable of playing with them." Something in her attitude made Sarah determined to see inside that room. "Can we meet them, please?"

Reluctantly the guide opened the door. They were greeted by silence. After the loud stampede of the previous room, this one seemed at first sight to be empty. Then they saw there were about a dozen children in the room, but none were moving. "These are the lying-down ones. They're all very sick," said the guide.

In a raised playpen, a little blond girl was lying immobile.

"What a pretty thing. How old is she?" Sarah asked. She looked about a year old.

The defectologist turned and asked the same question of the caregiver, who checked on a list of names stuck to the wall and answered: "Ivanova—she's four. She's got damage to the central nervous system."

"But she's following us with her eyes."

"That's just a reflex. It doesn't mean anything," the defectologist insisted.

Tethered to the playpen with pieces of cloth was a row of baby walkers, with three children sitting in them. They were lined up like racing drivers at the starting grid, but they were never going anywhere. Their heads were lolling back. They had obviously been sitting there for hours.

Next to the playpen was a little girl in a bouncing chair, placed on a ledge. She was too weak to make it bounce. Her enormous liquid eyes stared out from under long lashes. "That's Kovalchuk. She's got a heart problem."

"Doesn't she have a first name?" Sarah asked, stretching out her hand to touch the girl's cheek. She flinched and turned her head away.

"She's got nothing up here," the caregiver said, tapping her head. "Her mother gave her up at birth."

In a second playpen, a boy was crawling around with a plastic stick with a wheel on the end.

"Who's this one?"

Again the caregiver consulted the wall chart.

"That's Simonov. He's blind."

Blind doesn't mean you're retarded, Sarah thought. And why don't they use his first name? She opened her mouth to voice these thoughts but saw Louisa glowering at her and kept them to herself.

Inside the playpen was a glass mirror with a hard wooden frame. Why did a blind boy need a mirror beside him? And what could be more dangerous than a glass mirror in a playpen? The whole place was absurd—a mirror for a blind boy, baby walkers that were tethered so the children could not learn to walk, a bouncing cradle that did not bounce, babies that dreaded being stroked, four-year-olds the size of one-year-olds.

It got harder and harder to keep silent. Sarah felt anger boiling up inside her. Despite the warning looks, she wanted to scream at these women, Why are these children just lying there? Why is no one paying any attention to them? Why do you think they don't need what all children need? Don't you have children of your own?

Just as Sarah was struggling how best to voice these thoughts in Russian, all the time ignoring the ever sterner looks from Louisa, a blond-haired boy in the playpen started to bang his head against the frame. Sarah felt the firm push of the defectologist's hand on her back steering the visitors toward the door. It was then that she heard the words, "Please come again."

She turned round, startled to hear a child speak in this room of silence. Where was the voice coming from? She looked down to her left and saw beside the door was a small table with two little boys sitting at it. They looked about three years old. Ignoring the glare of the defectologist, she knelt down. "Hello, you two. I didn't see you." The boy with the voice piped up again: "Look. We've got a toy today."

In front of him was a plastic toy with four big buttons that you press, and an animal pops up—the sort of thing you give to a six-month-old.

She searched in her bag and found a little metal car. "This is more for a boy of your age."

The boy with the voice looked delighted as she rolled it up and down the table in front of him. He was eager to do it himself.

The two boys were dressed in blue jeans and sat like little old men at their table. She noticed their feet were compressed into tights that were far too small for them, forcing their toes to curl up underneath. They reminded her of Chinese women with bound feet.

"Do you like your car?" she asked.

"Yes, but have you got another one for Andrei?" He pointed to his friend, a handsome little boy with a bruise on his forehead.

"Luckily for him I do have another one."

The talking boy smiled a charming smile, with a slight squint.

"What's your name?" he asked.

"Sarah."

He repeated what was to him a strange foreign name with perfect pronunciation. The defectologist was making impatient noises.

"I must go now."

"You will come again. Please come again," he looked her in the eye.

She promised to come again. "But what's your name?"

"Vanya, my name is Vanya."

February 1995

Weeks passed and Sarah had not found time to go back and see Vanya as she had promised. It had been Christmas and then New Year's, and then a succession of family birthdays. The joy of her daughter Catherine's sixth birthday—the games of musical bumps and blind man's bluff, the magician from the British embassy, the Barbie-doll cake made by Louisa, and the pile of presents—all this was marred by the thought of Vanya in the silent room. Just one of Catherine's presents would have provided him with stimulation for a week.

She had been regularly visiting other baby houses as interpreter, and each visit took its emotional toll. "Every visit revealed more ill-treatment of small children. Afterward I felt so drained that all I could do was slump down and watch the comforting rubbish on the satellite TV channels. It was much easier to concentrate on how to make a meal from one chicken breast, two green peppers, and a banana than to process what I had seen."

But even daytime TV could not blot out the memories of a highly articulate child in that silent room for the incurables. Every baby house had one or more rooms like his, for children who had never learned to walk. These rooms were kept secret from visitors, and the staff's attitude suggested they thought the children in them were less than human. Sarah had never met a child in one of these rooms who spoke as fluently as Vanya. And she had never met a child who asked for a toy for his friend. On every visit to a baby house, children would beg for toys and sweets, but always for themselves. And the question nagged at Sarah, How had he managed to develop such emotional maturity?

One morning in February, she was churning these questions over in her mind while standing by the window in her apartment, watching the cars stream past along the Moscow ring road. Her children were at school and Alan was in the *Daily Telegraph* office next door. "Today is the day," she decided.

The baby house was not difficult to get to; the problem was Adela. Sarah knew if she put a foot wrong, she would never be able to go back. So she had to have a plan: She needed to find something to take to Vanya. Unlike Louisa, she did not have a store of home-baked cookies. Feeling like a thief, she scoured her children's room. At the back of the cupboard she found a discarded toy—a piece of chipboard, a hammer, nails, and colored bits of wood. Sarah stuffed it in her bag.

She felt awkward arriving in an expensive car and decided to go on foot, thinking it would only take twenty minutes.

Forty minutes later she was still slipping and sliding along the icy pavements. The new Russia was spreading all around: The baby house was an island in the middle of a giant building site where old houses were being demolished to make way for flats for the new rich. The demolition work only reinforced the isolation of the baby house from the rest of Moscow. Giant metal hoardings supported on concrete blocks had taken over half the alleyway that led to the orphanage gate, and it was a real obstacle course to avoid slipping into a trench or tripping on hidden rubble.

As Sarah picked her way along this path, she noticed a woman in front of her who was finding it even more difficult than she was to stay upright. Sarah slowed down to watch the woman lurch from side to side. It was 10:30 in the morning and this woman was already drunk. From the direction she was heading, she must work at the baby house and would soon be in sole charge of a dozen babies or toddlers. The woman staggered through the gate and disappeared.

As Sarah rounded the corner of the baby house, she could hear a male voice shouting—a rare sound in this world of women. There was an ambulance parked in front of the entrance.

The ambulance driver was yelling at a member of the staff who was standing on the porch at the top of the steps. From what she could make out, he was refusing to take a child to the hospital.

"Why are you wasting my time?" the driver was shouting. "Did you really think I'd take her? I've got enough to do without bothering about orphanage kids."

The woman tried to stand her ground in the face of the man's aggression. "But she's turning blue, she's dying. It's her heart."

"What hospital is going to admit her? None. You should know that by now," the ambulance driver roared.

She sneaked up beside one of the staff who was silently watching the scene from behind a pillar and asked, "What's happening? Where's Adela?"

"Oh, she's inside somewhere."

Sarah slipped inside under cover of the commotion. She stole past the locked rooms and knocked on the door marked HEAD DOCTOR. "Who's there?" came a timid voice.

"It's me, Sarah, the Englishwoman. What's going on outside?"

There was silence and then a key turned. The door opened a crack. Sarah caught a glimpse of Adela's panic-stricken face. Then the door shut again. Adela had hidden herself in her office to avoid the confrontation with the driver.

"Adela, let me in." The door opened and this time Adela whisked her inside. She was literally trembling with fear. She locked the door again.

The whole story came tumbling out. During the night, Valeria, the girl on the ledge in Group 2, had turned blue and could barely breathe. In the morning, Adela had called for an ambulance. An hour went by and the ambulance still had not come. Valeria was getting shorter and shorter of breath. They had transferred her to the isolator on the ground floor. Adela had had to ring again to beg them to come. And now that the driver was finally here, he took one look at Valeria and refused to take her because she came from a baby house and he would have to search all over Moscow to find a hospital that would admit her.

Outside, an engine burst into life. Adela and Sarah looked out the window of her office and saw the ambulance trundling out of the gate, empty. In the isolator, Valeria was fighting for breath, her status as the lowest of the low brutally confirmed.

Sarah had an idea and asked Adela if she could use her phone. She rang Alan in the *Daily Telegraph* office.

"Alan, there's a crisis here."

"Tough. There's a crisis in Russia every day. The army's threatening to mutiny and Yeltsin's disappeared again on one of his binges."

She ignored him and pressed on. "Do something useful for a change. A little girl here needs your help. She's dying. You can get a list of heart surgeons in Moscow, can't you? And then bring it here. We need to arrange a heart operation urgently. A male voice carries more authority."

Adela was perched on the edge of a small sofa, staring at the floor, fretting that the intervention of these foreigners might get her into trouble. Half an hour later, Alan arrived with a list of heart surgeons and began to call them from Adela's office. Strangely, the surgeons did not object to being bugged by a foreigner. This was the time when Russia was exhausted and foreigners had money and perhaps the answers to all its problems.

Within an hour, a Professor Ilyin, a pediatric cardiologist, had agreed in principle to do the operation. Adela sat stunned. As she listened to the conversation, she seemed astonished that the humble phone in her office could be used to reach such towering figures of surgery. Adela was truly a woman in the Soviet mold: The phone was an instrument used by senior people to issue orders or reprimands to her. It was not a means of two-way communication. Least of all was it a tool of aggressive intrusion, as used by reporters to disturb the calm of the powerful.

Thus Valeria was promised a heart operation. She had been lifted from the bottom of the heap by the intervention of—as Sarah put it—"a couple of nobodies." What's more, Alan and Sarah had won Adela's trust; and though she was still deeply suspicious of westerners, not once did she bar the door to them, even when their unlikely friendship was put to the test during the challenges of the years to come.

The new relationship between Adela and the two foreigners was sealed with a glass of kefir, which she invited them to drink by way of thanks. Knowing they were English, Adela declared herself to be a fan of Vivien Leigh, the actress. Alan won her heart by relating that his mother had once stood next to Vivien Leigh at the glove counter in Harrods and reported that her skin was so fine as to be transparent. Adela was thrilled as much by the story as she was impressed by Alan's Russian accent, learned as a schoolboy from an émigré count.

But in an instant her mood changed. She began to tell them about an island of devil-worshippers, which bore an uncanny resemblance to Britain. The island had been punished by God and had been swallowed up by the sea. Thus the earth had been cleansed. Adela shot her guests a look that seemed to say, "You are my friends, but I'm not so sure about your country."

She asked Alan, "Are there many unbelievers in England?"

"Adela, there's a church on every street corner," he said, neglecting to mention that they were almost all empty.

She clearly was not convinced. She launched into a story that seemed to have no connection with what they were talking about. A hundred Russian pilgrims had recently managed to travel to the Holy Land without passports, tickets, or visas. They just boarded a plane at Moscow

airport and miraculously it flew to Jerusalem, where they were welcomed with open arms. She ended the anecdote as suddenly as she had
begun it, with no explanation. As time went by, Alan and Sarah became
adept at decoding her riddles. In this case she was saying, in her timid
way, that God created miracles every day, but only for Russian Orthodox
Christians, not Anglicans, Baptists, or Catholics. She was struggling
with the idea that two emissaries from the island of devil-worshippers
had been instrumental in creating a medical miracle before her eyes.

Over the coming months, Sarah often wondered how Adela had
reached the heights of head doctor of a baby house, in charge of a huge
staff. Many years later, Sarah was told she had got the job by default when
the previous incumbent—a man—was accused of philandering with the
cleaners. Adela was given his job thanks to being a loyal member of the
Communist Party. Perhaps her many years of service to the godless Communist Party were now weighing on her conscience.

"Can I say hello to Vanya now?" Sarah asked when they had finished
their glasses of kefir and Alan had rushed back to his office to write
about the mutiny. "I have a little present for him."

"Yes, but first I want to show you something," Adela said. "None of
the other baby houses has one. Come with me."

As she followed Adela down a dark corridor, Sarah wondered what it
could be that Adela was about to reveal. The children needed so much.
Maybe a walking frame for Vanya? Or physiotherapy equipment for those
children who spent their lives lying down? They stopped in front of what
looked like the door to a storeroom.

Adela unlocked the door, and it took a while for Sarah's eyes to get
accustomed to the darkness inside. A flickering flame behind red glass
cast the dimmest possible light. One could just make out the dull gleam
of brass. But what assailed her senses most strongly was the rich smell of
incense. This room may have started out as a storeroom, but now it was
consecrated ground, a chapel, with an oil lamp suspended from the ceiling in front of an icon of the Virgin Mary. Gold paint glimmered from
the religious paintings on the walls, in contrast to the drab uniformity of
the rest of the baby house.

"How wonderful," Sarah said, swallowing her disappointment. "I've never seen a chapel in a baby house before."

Adela had revealed her secret: All her energy had gone into setting up this chapel, which she saw as the fulfillment of all the children's needs. At last her priority was clear—saving the children's souls.

Adela crossed herself in front of the altar. "Every Tuesday the priest comes to bless the children. He comes from far away. He has to get up at five in the morning to get here. He brings his congregation with him," said Adela proudly. "All the children are baptized."

Her expression changed. Sarah got the impression she felt she had said too much. She had lived all her life under Communism, which had taught that westerners were all CIA spies. As quickly as she had decided to open up the chapel—and her heart—she closed the door and locked it.

"It's still okay for me to visit Vanya, isn't it?" Sarah asked.

"Yes, you know the way," she mumbled, disappearing back into her office.

Vanya's face lit up when he saw her. "Sarah," he said. "I knew you'd come back."

"I'm just sorry it took me so long. And I've brought you something I thought you'd enjoy."

She knelt down by Vanya's table and unwrapped the toy hammer set. He took the hammer in his hands and within seconds he was holding each nail steady between finger and thumb before banging it into the chipboard. He hit the nails, not once stopping, his head bent over the chipboard, greedy for the activity.

When it was time to go, Sarah said, "I'll try and come again soon."

"I won't stop thinking about you," Vanya responded.

June 1995

In the weeks following the incident of the ambulance and the blue girl with heart problems, Sarah was accepted into the bizarre world of Baby House 10. "Looking back, I can see I shamelessly played the role of the

Englishwoman with the Russian soul, and the staff went along with this because the welfare group could provide much-needed supplies at a time when Russia was on its knees. The other baby houses were far more demanding. They soon wised up to the generosity of foreign donors and asked for big TVs for the staff, video recorders, new curtains, carpets, and new furniture for the director's office. Adela asked meekly for sugar, dried milk, washing powder, and a vegetable knife for the kitchen. Under Adela's direction, I was amazed to learn the kitchen had just one knife to prepare food for more than sixty children.

"The other baby houses also received gifts as payback for foreign adoptions. None of this happened in Baby House 10, where smart-suited scouts from adoption agencies quickly gave up trying to do business with Adela. I never saw any of the prettier children plumped up on preadoption diets as happened in other baby houses.

"A Moscow bank had even agreed to sponsor a program for a psychologist to train the staff of several Moscow baby houses in modern ways of childcare—a crash course in seventy years of missed expertise. The mere thought of a visiting psychologist, even a Russian one, scared Adela out of her wits and she refused to take part in the program, despite the offer of financial help. Any idea that involved the words experiment or research was ruled out.

"Thanks to my new relationship with Adela, I felt able to bring some foreign medical specialists to look at the children. Adela never condoned these visits, but she didn't stop them either. I believed that a western diagnosis would lead to a change in attitude."

Just how naive Sarah was became clear in the summer of 1995. Two Australian physiotherapists had come to Moscow for a conference, and it did not take much persuading to make them give up their only free morning to come to the baby house. "We'll forget Red Square, then," said one. They were deeply shocked at the condition of the children in Vanya's room and could not understand why Andrei and Vanya had not been encouraged to learn to walk. In fact, they observed, the compression of their feet in too tight clothing seemed designed to stop them ever learning. They even doubted the diagnosis they had been given of cerebral palsy. Outside the baby house, one of them could not hold back her tears. "There's no reason why those two boys should not have learned to walk. It's just neglect."

The next task was to get a doctor in to examine the children. The welfare group found a New York pediatrician working in Moscow, Dr. Ronald Swanger, who agreed to visit the baby house.

The visit almost didn't happen. Sarah was not available to interpret for him; and when Dr. Swanger appeared, Adela was waiting at the top of the steps and told him to go away, saying the place was under quarantine. Sarah took him back the next day. This time, the door was not barred to him; but Adela hid in her office, preferring to take no part in this groundbreaking event and not wanting to hear what he had to say. As usual, one of her deputies was left to show the visitor around.

The staff had never seen anything like Dr. Swanger. To them he must have looked like a clown, with his oversized glasses emphasizing the cheeky look in his eyes. He broke all the rules of adult behavior. He sat on the floor and stuck out his tongue at the children, who responded with weak smiles.

With his theatrical presence and exaggerated gestures, he charmed the staff like a film star. Where was his white coat? Where was his dignity? There he was sitting cross-legged on the floor and allowing the children to rifle through his medical bag. He had only had to touch them, and their faces lit up. Under his influence, the deputy head doctor surrendered her dignity and sat on the floor too.

Speaking softly, he offered an optimistic, can-do approach, utterly at odds with the fatalistic prognoses handed out in the baby house. Every child in the rooms of the incurables had potential and could have a better life—an operation here, a protein drink there, or a mother's love.

A little boy with Down syndrome he declared very bright, and all he needed was a home environment. He asked the deputy head doctor, "Couldn't you contact his mother and tell her how well he is doing?"

Many of the children needed small operations—cleft palate or cataracts. There was always an excuse why the operations had not been done. This boy had had chicken pox and could not be operated on. That boy had his heart on the wrong side.

The one child that Dr. Swanger had been briefed on was Valeria, the "blue girl" whom the ambulance men had refused to take to a hospital. Since Alan and Sarah's intervention, Valeria had been admitted to a hospital for an assessment and was now back in the baby house awaiting a slot for her operation. Dr. Swanger had discussed her case with Dr. Ilyin. The surgeon managed to carry out medical marvels in an ill-equipped theatre, without disposable rubber gloves or the right antibiotics. But even the finest medical care in the world would not help her if she had no reason to live.

"There's only one way she will survive," Dr. Swanger said. "When she comes out of intensive care, she has to have twenty-four-hour observation by someone who cares about her—someone who will stimulate her, feed her, and look after her." This sounded as if she needed the one person not available to her, a mother.

Sarah noticed with growing sadness that the American doctor's seeds of wisdom were falling on stony ground. The staff was following him with rapt attention, as if he had come to entertain them, but no one was bothering to write down his suggestions.

His calm and nonjudgmental tone was tested to the extreme when he met a four-year-old girl called Anna, who was paralyzed from the waist down thanks to a spinal injury. Despite having no language in common, they laughed and joked together. Dr. Swanger gave her his otoscope so that she could examine his ears, before he did the same to her.

His face registered shock when he examined Anna's back. She needed a corset because her constant slouching position was making her back worse. The deputy head doctor said she did have a corset, but it was too hard, and she did not like wearing it. Without a word, he took out a pen and notebook and sketched a pattern for a simple corset that could be made at home and stop her back deteriorating. Above all, he said, she needed a wheelchair—something never seen in the baby house.

Dr. Swanger said a cheery good-bye to Anna and headed upstairs to Group 2, the second room for the incurables.

"Anna's such a clever girl. She reminds me of Vanya. Do they know each other?" Sarah asked the deputy head doctor as they walked up the stairs.

"They are in different groups."

"But they'd so enjoy each other's company. They could talk together."

"No. That's not possible. Neither of them can walk. It would be too much of a strain on the staff. We have to share out the difficult cases among the groups."

As they entered, Vanya looked up from his table, delighted to see a fresh face, particularly a male one.

"So who's this young man?" asked Dr. Swanger.

"Pastukhov. Born premature. He has cerebral palsy, as you can see," said the deputy head doctor.

Sarah slipped out of interpreter mode. "Dr. Swanger. This is Vanya. We've become good friends. I wish you spoke the same language. He loves to talk."

"Hi, Vanya. I'm Ronald."

With great concentration, Vanya got his mouth around Ronald. The doctor knelt down beside him.

"Young man, you've got a squint. We should sort that out."

He turned to the deputy head doctor. "It's only a simple operation. It should be done as soon as possible."

"We've been meaning to take him," she said, searching for a pretext. "But he's been in poor health."

"And you're not walking?" Dr. Swanger looked puzzled and started to examine Vanya's feet. He peeled off the socks tied on with ribbons to reveal the integral feet of his romper suit, which were far too small. "I think it would be a good idea for this child to go barefoot. With physiotherapy he could learn to walk."

Sarah dutifully translated this revolutionary idea. She told him she had never seen a member of staff encouraging a child to walk. Like the Australian doctors, Dr. Swanger could not see justification for the diagnosis of cerebral palsy.

Dr. Swanger continued. "Couldn't he be adopted?"

There was no response. It was only many years later, in a chance conversation with this same woman, that Sarah finally got an answer. The deputy head doctor admitted with no trace of remorse that she had dissuaded Adela from putting Vanya up for adoption when he was two. She had reminded Adela that Vanya had not met his milestones. She said she was sure that the signs of cerebral palsy would soon appear. It would be wrong to deceive adoptive parents, she had argued. Adela, ever weak, had given in.

With these few words, Vanya's fate was sealed. He ended up in the room for the incurables, where only one thing was certain—the fatalistic attitude of the staff would turn him into a disabled child.

None of Dr. Swanger's suggestions was acted on. There was no communication with Valeria's mother, no corset for Anna, no eye operation for Vanya. The life of the baby house continued as usual. All that remained was the memory of an exotic American doctor who had come and put on a bit of a show.

3
Pineapples and Peacocks

1994–95

Strange as it may seem, no one in the baby house thought to tell Sarah or Vika about the existence of the other. Sarah did not know it, but by the time she started coming to Baby House 10, Vika had already been visiting for some months. It took Vanya to bring them together. But this did not happen until he was in mortal danger, far away from the baby house.

It was 1994, and the iron discipline of Soviet times was weakening, opening up possibilities that had not existed since before the start of Communism. Maybe this was why Vika had no difficulty coming regularly to the baby house, even though Adela risked being reprimanded if the authorities found out.

"I had just become a Christian and I was looking for meaning in my life," Vika recalls. "I had finished a five-year degree in physics. But instead of looking for a job, I enrolled in a New Testament study course. I did not tell my priest that I planned to volunteer at a baby house. I was afraid he would not bless my actions. He would have preferred me to work inside the parish, even in the church itself. But I believed that Christians should do something in the community. I kept my visits a secret.

"I became friendly with a woman who worked as a caregiver in the baby house. I went there with her. No one tried to stop me, but no one encouraged me either. My friend was working with the newborns, Group 1. I became very attached to a little girl called Masha. The specialists gave up on her. Before the age of one, they had written her off as an invalid and an oligophrenic. But I could see she just needed love and encouragement. She had such an intelligent face. She started trying to speak."

As Vika was directing her attention toward Masha, she herself became the focus of someone's attention. A little curly-headed boy began to poke his head around the door from the next room, she recalls. "He invented a game. He would look in, and then a voice would summon him back. He wanted me to notice him, but he was never allowed to leave his room. That rule was strictly enforced."

Vika's friend quickly became embittered. She could not do anything for the children. She could only feed and change them. The baby-house regime did everything to stop the staff and children getting attached to each other. When her friend grew very close to a little girl, they were split up. The baby house was always moving children from one group to another, parting them from familiar caregivers and friends. The most damaging form of division was when the baby house sorted the children into healthy and sick. The sick ones were sent to Group 2. Once, Vika's friend pointed to Group 2 and said, "All those children are going to die." At the time, Vika did not understand what she meant. "I thought she had gone crazy," Vika recalls. Her friend quit soon after.

One day Vika was shocked to find that Masha had been moved to Group 2. Her first impression of that room remains with her to this day. "The atmosphere was one of oppressive silence, like a hospital ward full of dying people. As soon as Masha entered that room, she started losing all her skills. In Group 1, she had learned to grab and to chew, although a little later than normal. And she was even using a spoon to feed herself. But the caregivers in Group 2 got impatient with her and said she was taking too much time feeding herself, and they stuffed a bottle in her mouth. They tied her into a chair so that she could not move. One of the caregivers said to me, 'What's the point of teaching her skills? Whatever you do, she won't catch up by the age of four, and she'll be doomed.'

"There was only one sign of life in that room, and that was the curly-haired boy, who introduced himself as Vanya. He learned my name, and he greeted me with a smile whenever I came to visit Masha. I could not understand how he could smile in such an appalling place."

Vika remembers how he used to pester her in the nicest possible way to take him out of the room. He quickly understood that she was taking Masha into the yard, and he set himself the goal of going outside too. But Vika ignored his requests. She thought he needed her less than Masha did.

Every time Vika brought Masha back from their walk, Vanya would ask her, "Can you take me outside now, Vika?" She always said no. Then one day she caught sight of his despondent face and gave in. He could not suppress a shriek of delight as Vika lifted him out of his chair.

Outside, it was a day of hazy sunshine, with high thin clouds. As she carried him out the door, it was obvious that Vanya was not used to sunlight, and he shielded his eyes with his hands. It was as if he had worn a blindfold all his life and someone had just ripped it off. He looked around the messy play area with eyes full of wonder.

Vika decided to give him a nature lesson and teach him the names of trees. She carried him up to a linden tree and drew his attention to its dark trunk and light green leaves. "Now, Vanya, this is a linden tree. You see the leaves? They are shaped like a heart. They get sticky in summer." She helped him touch a leaf, and he was fascinated by it.

She looked around the baby-house grounds for another tree. "What other trees do you know?"

Vanya was silent. Vika prompted him—a fir tree, an oak, a maple? She was shocked when it became obvious that he did not have a clue what she was talking about.

Vanya would be going to school at some point. He had to know his trees and his flowers. She put him down on the ground while she looked for flowers, but only weeds and sickly grass grew in the soil under the trees in the yard.

She turned around to see Vanya stretching his hand toward a solitary yellow flower, a splash of gold in the shade under the trees. She picked the flower and handed it to him. He held it by the stalk and gazed into the intricate pattern of the petals. "It's a dandelion. It looks like the sun, doesn't it?" she said.

"Sun," Vanya repeated. "What's the sun?"

With these three short words, Vanya had revealed a terrible truth. For Vanya, "outside" was another planet he had never visited because he had never been outside before. All he knew was what was contained within the four walls of Group 2.

"I was stunned," Vika says. "I pointed to things around us and drew a blank. He had no concept of the sky, of the clouds that were gathering above us, the grass we were sitting on, the swings that hung idly beside us, or the gate that separated him from the world outside. Increasingly desperate, I searched for something, anything that he could recognize. Only the drab Volga station wagon that was parked outside the front entrance elicited a name—car—for he had once played with a toy car."

Vika was overwhelmed by the task she had set herself. Where to start his education? "We'll start with colors," she announced to him.

She got up and set off to search the play area for something colorful, leaving Vanya on the grass.

The clouds were thickening and the atmosphere was getting more oppressive. One scarlet poppy grew in the thin soil. In the sandbox, she found a blue bucket. Ignoring the raindrops, Vika continued to scour the ground for color. Suddenly there was a crack of thunder, and the heavens opened up with a deluge of giant raindrops, and Vika ran back to where she had left Vanya. As she rounded the corner of the baby house, Vika could make out the figure of Vanya kneeling on the ground, his head thrown back, his arms outstretched, a look of delight on his features as the water streamed down his face and soaked his shirt.

He was like a boy in a drought-stricken country, embracing the long-delayed monsoon. But this boy was from Russia, a wet country, and he had never experienced rain because he had never been allowed to.

Vika ran toward him, picked him up and danced with him, sharing his delight. "Rain, Vanya, this is rain."

"Rain," he repeated, thrusting his head back to catch the full force of the shower. "I love you, rain."

It was at that moment in the rain that Vika realized that Vanya was as much in need of help as Masha. Here was a boy who was a self-starter, who had taught himself to speak in a world of silence, yet he was being shamefully neglected. At age five, he did not know summer or winter, how old he was, or what city he lived in. If he did not know these things, how was he ever going to cope with school?

There was only one caregiver who shared Vika's concerns about Vanya, and that was Valentina. She alone among the caregivers did not subscribe to the view that all physically handicapped children were mentally retarded. She had acquired her knowledge of child rearing from her mother, who had been brought up before the Bolsheviks declared war on the family. She had no qualifications, but she instinctively understood more about what Vanya needed than all the specialists in the baby house, who had been trained to create a Communist workers' utopia where disabled children were hidden away.

None of the specialists considered they had any work to do in Group 2. They had already written off the children. And yet Valentina would teach Vanya poems and songs from before the revolution that she had learned from her mother and grandmother. She delighted in the funny things he would say. When she got home from work, her husband would ask, "What did your little Vanya say today?" Despite the numbing burden of her twenty-four-hour shifts, she would force him to stand against the wall and make him walk. The other caregivers put diapers on him, but she taught him to use a pot.

Over the months, Vika learned to time her visits to coincide with

Valentina's shifts. She worked one day in four. She was the wife of a colonel in the Russian army and had worked in military hospitals all around the Soviet Union. When her husband retired, she had to go out to work to supplement his meager pension, and found a job at the baby house. She always maintained her own standards, even though the pay was paltry and the work backbreaking.

One day in late December, she had asked Vika to arrive before the end of afternoon nap time, as she needed her help in carrying out a plan. "It's a surprise for Vanya." Four days later Vika arrived, late as usual, to find that Valentina had rescued Vanya early from his afternoon nap. He was sitting in his underwear, and Valentina was taking a neat parcel of brown paper from her bag.

"Vika, you're just in time. I was getting worried," Valentina said. "Vanya and I need you to sit with the other children." Vanya was so excited he could not sit still. Turning to him, Valentina said, "Look what I've made you. It took me half the night."

She unwrapped the brown paper to reveal an olive-green shirt. She held it up to show to him. Vanya had never had any of his own clothes.

"Look. It's an army shirt. My husband is a colonel. He has three stars. But you can have one star—a major."

The shirt had two breast pockets, a row of brass buttons, and in pride of place on each shoulder, a shiny five-pointed star denoting his newly acquired rank.

Vanya's eyes lit up as she dressed him in the green shirt and lovingly did up the buttons.

From her bag she took a pair of smart trousers, ironed with a crease. "These are from my grandson. He's grown out of them." She helped his thin legs into them. She pulled out a pair of suspenders. "These are from my husband. I've cut them down for you," she said, clipping them on his trousers. She brought out a green tie and smoothed it down his front. Finally, she brushed his brown curls into a rather severe style, in keeping with the uniform. "How smart you look with your broad shoulders." She hugged him to her ample bosom. "My little major."

"At your service, comrade major!" Vika said, and saluted him.

Obviously he did not know what a major was, but he loved the way he looked. It was his first experience of nice clothes.

Valentina had brought some paper and a pen from home. She set the paper down in front of him and curled his fingers around the pen. "You're writing out orders for the soldiers." The two women stood back to admire him. How smart he looked!

At that moment, looking even more distracted than usual, Adela came in, her eyes scouring the room. She appeared not to notice Vika's presence. "Chairs," she muttered. "We need more chairs. The party's about to begin."

It took her a moment to recognize the boy sitting at the table, holding a pen and drawing on a sheet of paper. "What have we here? Good God—a student!" She clapped her hands together. "Vanya, how grown up you look!" After admiring him for a second, she hurried out of the room, dragging two chairs behind her.

Valentina divulged her secret. She was going to take Vanya to the New Year's party. Vanya would sing the song she had taught him— "The Little Fir Tree."

"What about Andrei and Masha? Can they come too?" Vanya asked.

"Children from Group 2 aren't invited," said Valentina, "but you and I are going anyway. And you're going to walk there."

She took him by the arms and helped him stand up and shuffle to the door and into the corridor. Valentina ordered him to put one hand on the wall, while she held the other. Their progress was painfully slow as he moved one foot and then the other. They could hear an accordion playing a Russian folk dance at the end of the corridor. Vanya was too excited to bother with trying to walk. He tried to sink to the floor and crawl, but Valentina held him upright.

"Majors don't crawl," she insisted. He looked up at her, pleading to be carried, but she was unbending. "If you want to go to the party, you walk."

Vika watched their slow progress down the corridor. It was clear that

Valentina was the grandmother that Vanya had never had. All the experience of her own children, she poured into this little boy who had been so let down by the experts. At last they reached the end of the corridor and entered the room kept for special occasions. It had been transformed. A Christmas tree, almost as high as the ceiling, stood in the corner, decked with gold and silver tinsel. The dusty cacti on the window ledges were hidden under sweet-smelling fir tree branches. The children were sitting in rows on little wooden chairs, the special sort lacquered black, red, and gold.

The staff had also undergone a transformation. The accordion was being played by Adela's friend, a blond-haired actress who was dressed as the Snow Maiden in an ice-blue frock covered in sparkling silver embroidery. She swayed and swooped with her bulky instrument, as light and brilliant as a butterfly. The elderly caregivers found their dancing feet. As the Snow Maiden approached them with her irresistible rhythms, they put their hands on their hips, shook a leg, and appeared to lose two decades.

The music stopped. The staff seemed to be looking around for someone, but Adela was nowhere to be seen. The Snow Maiden stepped in as master of ceremonies. "Who's going to recite a poem?" she asked. A little girl with a big white bow in her hair stood up and said a few lines in a soft voice.

"Anyone else?" she prompted. The children sat immobile on their chairs.

Valentina spoke up. "Yes—Vanya has something." The staff exchanged puzzled looks as Valentina helped Vanya make his way to the tree. It was obvious the staff were thinking, Wasn't this a boy from Group 2? And what was that smart uniform he was wearing? Valentina settled herself on a chair, with Vanya on her knee. "Vanya will sing 'The Little Fir Tree,'" she announced.

Everyone was silent, waiting to hear "a little fir tree grew in the forest . . ." But Vanya was taking his time. What eventually came out of his mouth was something completely different.

"Kitty, kitty, where are you?

Why did you piss in my shoe?"

Titters broke out all round. Vanya smiled at everyone, happy to have created a small sensation. He continued.

"Sorry, said the kitten, ever so.

I really, really had to go."

All the staff laughed. Valentina looked embarrassed and gave him a scolding. "Vanya, why did you recite that poem? You should have sung 'The Little Fir Tree.'" She was blushing. She had taught him the naughty kitten rhyme, but she never for a moment thought he would recite it in front of all the staff.

It was an extraordinary event in the life of the baby house. A gate-crasher, a boy consigned to live in silence among the speechless, had just starred at the annual party. While the "normal" children sat silently on their chairs, waiting to be invited up, one of the "invalids" had taken it upon himself to entertain the staff. This helpless boy had demonstrated his gift of making a personal connection with everyone he met. But more important than that, he had blown apart the system the baby house was founded on—the division of children into sick and healthy, educable and ineducable, those with potential and the doomed. Some of the staff who tittered at his rhyme were too steeped in the institutional way of thinking to see the truth. Uniquely, Adela did see his potential, but she felt too powerless to do anything to help him.

Ten days later, Valentina's early morning routine was disturbed when Adela burst into Group 2 in a state of anxiety and wanted to know why Vanya was not up and ready, as the commission was waiting for him. The word commission gave her a jolt. This was the commission from Psychiatric Hospital No. 6, which assessed all the children at the age of four and gave them a label that decided their fate for the rest of their lives. For some reason, Vanya's assessment was two years overdue. Now that he was nearly six, there was no escape.

Valentina dressed him quickly and wanted to sit him down and give him porridge and a drink. But Adela was standing over them flapping, saying they could not keep the commission waiting. She would not even let Valentina brush his hair. She said, "There's no time for any of that," picked up Vanya, and hurried out.

Valentina rushed to the doorway and stood watching as Adela, with Vanya over her shoulder, broke into a lopsided run down the same corridor along which he had so proudly walked in his major's uniform to make his grand entrance for the New Year's party. But on this day, he was facing backward as she carried him into the room. As they entered, Vanya jerked up his head and gave Valentina a beseeching look. Valentina stretched out her arms toward him, and the door shut.

Valentina was not important enough to be invited to take part in Vanya's assessment, even though, of all the staff in the baby house, she knew him best. The Christmas tree, the decorations, and the tinsel had been replaced by two tables placed end to end, behind which sat five women, all dressed in white coats.

Adela placed him on a chair in front of them and retreated to the back of the room. Vanya sat rigidly before the line of strangers, paralyzed by fear. His hair was a mess—some of it plastered to his face and the rest sticking out wildly. His eyes moved from side to side, scanning the faces in front of him in search of someone he could make contact with. He turned his head toward Adela, but she was busy fussing over a samovar, preparing tea for the members of the commission.

Adela's deputy stepped forward with a thick cardboard file with Vanya's medical history. What she read out made him sound like a hopeless case—born at six months, then had to be resuscitated, cerebral palsy, mother an alcoholic, abandoned by parents at eighteen months.

Before she had finished, one of the commissioners got up from behind the table, and without saying a word to Vanya, started clicking her fingers beside his head, above his head, and behind him. Then she repeated the action.

The deputy continued her report. Despite regular massage, she said, the boy had never learned to walk.

At this point, Vanya spoke up. "I walked here for the New Year's party."

The members of the commission exchanged surprised glances. But Adela's deputy said he was talking rubbish and that he could not actually walk on his own and had to be held up.

The head of the commission asked one of her team to examine Vanya's feet. She rolled up his trousers and started pinching the muscles in his legs. She tried to push his feet up and down. She ignored his yelps. She said there was no muscle tone in his legs and the tendons were too tight, so he would never be able to walk.

There was a speech therapist on the panel, an older woman, and she asked why there was no speech therapist's report in his file. She proceeded to give Vanya some tests. Without introducing herself, she held up pictures in front of him and asked him to identify them.

First there was a picture of a birch tree, and the speech therapist asked him what sort of tree it was. "It's a linden tree," Vanya answered, recalling the only tree that grew in the baby-house grounds.

The next picture he recognized too. It was a matryoshka doll. But he did not understand the woman's question: What is it made of? He thought and thought. And then he said, "I make dolls with Andrei."

It got worse. The woman showed him a picture of a traffic light and asked him which color meant go. He had never seen a traffic light, as he had never been out in the street.

Then there was a picture of a loaf of bread, which he did not recognize either as he had only seen slices of bread. Then came a pineapple, an ant, a turnip, the Kremlin towers, a fishing rod, and last of all, a peacock.

Finally the woman put the pictures down and asked him what day it was. Vanya replied, "It's Auntie Valentina's day."

He could not understand why the woman looked disapproving. She asked, "What's tomorrow?" He said, "Tomorrow is Nastya's day," and even volunteered that the day after was Tanya's day. The last question was, "What city do you live in?" Again there was long pause. He said, "I live here, in the baby house."

"And where is that?"

"Nearby."

That was the end of the test. The members of the commission started talking among themselves. The words "imbecile," "ineducable," "pronounced cretinism," and "undeveloped speech" were spoken. The head of the commission seemed eager to cut short the discussion, declaring, "He's destined for the internat." A young doctor on the commission stood up to her and suggested a home for children with cerebral palsy, where he could get some education. But the head of the commission slapped her down.

The head of the commission declared the assessment over and told Adela to take Vanya away. Adela left her place by the hissing samovar, picked Vanya up, and only then, when his fate had already been sealed, did she say a word in his favor. "He knows a lot of songs and poems," she said timidly. "He can recite them if you like." But nobody paid any attention. They were already looking at the next child's file.

Two weeks passed and Vika was still ignorant of the commission's visit and Vanya's ordeal. She had been busy with preparations for Orthodox Christmas, which is celebrated on January 6 in Russia. On her next visit, she found Valentina in a bad state. She had been crying. There was terrible news about Vanya. Valentina had heard it from the caregiver she had taken over from that morning. "Have you heard where they're sending your darling boy?" the caregiver had goaded her.

It was obvious from the expression on Valentina's face that she knew nothing.

"His papers have arrived. He's been assigned to an internat, along with all the worst cases."

Valentina told Vika she had been in shock since she had heard the news that Vanya would be sent to an asylum. Vika too was appalled. "But he won't get an education there. How could they do this to him?"

"He's going to a dark place," Valentina said. "Now that his papers have arrived, there's nothing we can do to save him. It's too late."

"I told her there was something I could do," Vika recalls. "I went and fetched Vanya from his crib. He was so excited to see me. He wanted to start a game straightaway, but he picked up on my sadness. He did not protest as I carried him over to the window. I pointed up to the sky and told him that Heaven was up there. Heaven, he repeated, with a serious look on his face.

"Now, Vanya, God is in heaven. What should you say to God?"

"What should I say? Tell me."

"If you are in trouble, Vanya, you must pray to God and He will send you a guardian angel to watch over you."

Over the next few weeks, Vika continued to visit Vanya, carrying the knowledge of his fate in her but unable to do anything. He became increasingly aware that something terrible was about to happen to him. Every time Vika had to go, he asked with an anxious look, "You are going to come again? You will come again, Vika?"

4

Beyond the Reach of Angels

February 1996

"Why are you putting this coat on me?" Vanya asked. "Am I going to the hospital?"

"You'll find out soon enough," Nastya grunted as she buttoned him into an ill-fitting, oversized coat.

The first sign that something different was about to happen had come immediately after lunch. As usual, Nastya put the other children back in their cribs; but she left Vanya sitting on his chair. Vanya tried to understand why he was being dressed to go outside. None of the doctors had come into Group 2 that morning to tell Nastya that he was going to the hospital. That was the only reason that children in Vanya's group ever left their room, except of course when Vika came to take him outside.

Now Nastya was pulling off his slippers and trying to force his feet into boots. The boots were too small. The zippers were broken but still they would not fit. Nastya swore under her breath as she shoved and shoved. His toes were now curled under his feet, so she shrugged and gave up.

In the final indignity, Nastya picked up a pink synthetic-wool hat and pulled it over his ears.

"But I'm not a girl," Vanya said. Nastya ignored him. She left him, fully clothed and sitting on his chair.

"Don't move. I'll be back in a minute."

Vanya thought, how could I move in this heavy coat and these boots? I could get off the chair, but I couldn't crawl around.

While he waited for Nastya to return, he thought of the last time he had been dressed up—not brutally by Nastya like today, but lovingly by Auntie Valentina. What a lovely shirt she had made for him, with those gold stars on the shoulders. She had called him "my little major." After the party, she had undressed him and carefully folded up his new clothes. He had hated to see her put the clothes away in her bag. But both of them knew the clothes would disappear if they stayed in the baby house.

His daydream was disturbed by the voice of Andrei calling his name from the communal bedroom. The door was open, and by leaning forward, Vanya could see Andrei's face peeping through the wooden bars of his crib.

"Andrei," he shouted. "She's put a coat on me, and boots and a hat. I think I'm going to the hospital. Don't forget to think about me. I won't stop thinking about you."

Andrei let out a cry. "Vanya, don't leave me. I need you. Stay. Stay."

"Andrei, I'll think about you."

The door opened and Svetlana rushed in looking flustered. She was carrying a sheaf of papers as she always did. Vanya noticed she was wearing her outdoor clothes. She picked Vanya up. "We must hurry. The car is waiting."

"Where are we going, Svetlana?" Vanya asked her as she carried him downstairs.

"How do you know my name?" she asked in surprise.

"I heard them call you that."

"Oh yes, you're the one who remembers everything. But now your papers have arrived, and you are being sent to the internat." She let out a sigh.

There was that word again. But what did it mean? Kiril had gone to an internat and he had never come back.

Now they were outside. The cold air hit Vanya like a slap in the face and made him gasp as he breathed it in. How different the yard looked from when Vika had taken him out. The ground was covered in something dirty white. This must be snow, he thought. Vika had told him she couldn't take him outside because it was cold and there was snow on the ground. Now he knew what she meant: snow.

The Volga was waiting by the entrance. Svetlana carried him around to the back and laid him on a stretcher. "Can I sit on your lap, Svetlana?" Vanya begged.

"No. That's not allowed," said the driver. He slammed the door. The car drove off. It kept stopping and starting. Vanya heard other engines on the road. He had only ever traveled in this makeshift ambulance and didn't know about cars. He thought to himself, they must be other ambulances taking children to the hospital. In his mind, the road was full of children on the move.

He wished he could sit up and look out of the windows. He really wanted to see the other ambulances and catch a glimpse of the other children. But even if he could sit up, there was nothing to see. The Volga had strange windows you couldn't see through. He tried to make sense of the world with his ears. He could hear Svetlana and the driver chatting in the front. He could hear the note of the engine rising and falling as the ambulance started and stopped. Then he could feel he was going faster and the stops became less frequent. Then suddenly the ambulance jerked and he was thrown against the side. Now he was being bumped up and down and shaken about. It really hurt. And then the Volga came to a halt. Then there was silence. No other cars could be heard, just a dog barking.

"What a dump." The driver sounded angry. "So where is this place, then?"

Svetlana sounded like she was afraid of him. "I don't know. I've never been there. The ministry has never assigned any children to this place before."

He heard papers shuffling. Her voice was even quieter as she came out with a string of words he did not understand. "Moscow province, Lenin district, village of Filimonki, Psycho-Neurological Internat No. 5. That's all it says."

"Well that's helpful . . ." Now the driver sounded even more angry. The ambulance set off again with a jolt. Then he heard Svetlana's voice, louder now. "Look there's a sign—INTERNAT." There was more bumping and then they stopped. He heard doors opening, and a moment later the driver released the rear door and Svetlana pulled Vanya out and into her arms. It was getting dark. He looked up and saw a tall building that seemed to reach up to the sky. It stretched away as far as he could see.

Svetlana caught sight of two women by a doorway, and with Vanya in her arms she hurried toward them. "Excuse me, do you work here?"

"No, I'm just visiting," said one. "Visiting my sister." She nodded toward the woman whose hand she was holding. The woman grinned and Vanya noticed the she had no teeth.

"Maybe you know were the children's wing is?"

"What children's wing? I've never seen a child, and I'm here every week."

Just then a woman in a white coat came out, carrying a big bunch of keys in her hand.

"Who are you?" she asked. She reminded Vanya of Tanya, with her bright red lipstick, except that this woman had a gold tooth at the front of her mouth. She was not happy to see them.

"We're from Baby House 10."

"What? I hadn't heard about a delivery today. Anyway, the director's gone home. I'm the deputy."

"I'm so sorry we're late. We got lost," said Svetlana. "But I have this boy for you, Pastukhov, age six. Look, I have all his papers with me."

At the sight of the documents, the woman gave in. "Okay, follow me."

Vanya began to feel alarmed. It obviously wasn't a hospital they had brought him to. The journey had been far too long. And there were no other ambulances outside. If only Auntie Valentina were here to explain things to him. Svetlana was not telling him anything.

Now they were inside the building. It was darker than the baby house. They walked up one flight of concrete stairs and then another. They came to a long corridor. There was a nasty smell. He could make out shapes of people through the dimness. They were swaying from side to side, like the children in Group 2, but these were adults. A man came out of a doorway. Vanya was shocked to see he had no clothes on.

The deputy director stopped before a locked door and fumbled noisily with her keys. She hustled Svetlana through the door and locked it. This time they turned right into another corridor. Vanya caught sight of a small figure. Was that a child, someone like him? As they moved nearer, he was disappointed to see the small person had an old face. It was a woman, wearing a gray shift, her limbs ghostly white and covered in bruises. Her head was shaved. She said nothing as they passed.

At the end of that corridor, they came to another flight of stairs, even darker than the last because there were no windows. The deputy slowed down. Svetlana started to breathe heavily, as these stairs were steeper. The weight of Vanya was beginning to tell on her.

"Here we are—children's wing," muttered the deputy, once more getting out her bunch of keys. She turned two locks, and the door swung open. She seemed to be in a hurry as she opened yet another door into a large room.

Already traumatized by his journey through the asylum, Vanya stared in horror at the scene before him. The room was crammed full of cribs. Not wooden ones like in the baby house, but bigger ones with high metal bars, like cages. In each crib was a bare mattress. There were no sheets or blankets. On each mattress lay a child. Some were naked. Some were wearing only a dirty undershirt. They were lying in puddles of their own urine. One was lying on his feces. Another child was banging his head violently against the bars of his crib. They were moaning and crying.

Before he could say anything, the deputy had taken Vanya from Svetlana and torn off his coat and boots and dumped him in an empty crib. As Vanya struggled to pull himself up, he noticed the boy in the crib next to him was tied up in an old sheet so that he could not move his arms. He was rocking from side to side.

Vanya grabbed hold of the bars of the crib and looked around frantically for Svetlana. She was by the door, not looking at him.

"Svetlana, Svetlana. Why am I here?" he shouted, breaking the silence. "Why has she put me in this crib?"

"Oh, he can talk can he?" said the deputy director, surprised. "You've brought us a talker—a troublemaker? As though we haven't got enough problems already."

Suddenly the terrible truth hit Vanya like a punch in the stomach. "You're not leaving me here, are you?" Svetlana was still not looking at him.

The deputy director went over to Svetlana. "Are you sure you've brought the right one?"

"Oh yes. The commission examined him just two months ago. He's been assigned here. I've got the letter from the ministry." Svetlana found the document.

From across the room, Vanya yelled, "Don't leave me here, Svetlana. Auntie Valentina wouldn't want it. I'm her little major." But Svetlana was still not looking at him. He searched his mind for reasons to persuade her to take him back to the baby house. "Adela will be bored without me. She likes the funny stories I tell."

Svetlana never turned around. The deputy ushered her out, shutting the door behind them. Vanya hurled his body against the bars of the crib and screamed as loud as he could. "Don't leave me here, Svetlana." He heard the key turn in the lock.

It was the middle of the night. He had been thinking of ways to escape. He tried to undo the side of the crib, but it was fixed tight. Then he grabbed the metal bars and tried to pull them apart with all the strength of his puny body. Finally, he collapsed exhausted on the bare mattress. It dawned on him that even if he did manage to escape from the crib, he had the problem of how to unlock the door. His brain hurt from so much thinking. Then he became aware how cold it was. They had taken away his clothes and he had no blanket. He started to sob, but there was no one to console him. He longed for Vika to come and pick him up and hold him and take him away. What was it she had told him to do? She had taken him to the window and told him to look toward Heaven and pray to God.

He grabbed the bars and looked around for a window. But he was not near one, so he couldn't see Heaven from his crib. And anyway, it was dark. And there were bars on the window. What had she said? Pray to God and your guardian angel will come. But how could the angel get through the bars on the window? He decided to pray anyway, kneeling on the plastic mattress and gripping the bars of the crib and staring fixedly at the pitch-black window. "Please, God, send me my guardian angel." He said it again, and again, until he fell asleep, his hands still holding the bars and his head resting against the cold metal.

The guardian angel did not appear that night, or the next day, or in a week's time. It seemed as if Vanya had slipped beyond the reach of angels, into a lower circle of hell, where his humanity was slowly stripped away. First his hair was brutally shaved off, so he looked like a prisoner. Next, with no one to talk to, his fluent speech deteriorated and his voice was reduced to a whisper. Then, as he was living amid the most distressing scenes of abuse and neglect, he lost his poise and confidence. Finally, his hands began to shake uncontrollably from the drugs he was given to sedate him. He was in free fall toward the lower depths, where a person stops being a member of the human race and reaches a point where he cannot be dragged back.

5

A Superhuman Feat

March–June 1996

It took three weeks for Sarah to find out that Vanya had been sent to a mental asylum. "That was unforgivable," says Sarah, trying to make sense of her actions over a decade ago.

"I wish I had been more vigilant, but there were so many things going on in my life at the time. I was struggling to understand this hidden world of neglected children that I had stumbled across. As I visited more and more baby houses, I tried to make sense of these institutions, where the staff appeared to be blind to the suffering of the small children in their care. I had no medical training, but I felt that the baby houses were creating disabilities. Any child born with a handicap, however slight, or even late in developing, was sucked into a downward spiral and given the label 'invalid' or 'sick.' It seemed to me that the system was sick, not the children."

A series of minor events clarified things. "Over Christmas, Stephanie

Wood, wife of the British ambassador, rang me up to say there was a cake left over from the embassy children's party, and would I take it to a baby house. I dutifully took it round to Baby House 10, where the staff gathered to admire it. As I left, I knew for sure that Stephanie's idea of hungry children tucking into a delicious cake and smiling through chocolaty mouths was being betrayed. The cake would end up as a treat for the staff during their long breaks over nap time. When I got home, I could not raise any indignation from Alan about the fate of the cake. He said the staff were barely paid enough to travel to work, so they deserved a treat as much as anybody.

"I fired back, 'But that's not the point. However little they are paid, they should put the children first.'"

At the same time, the welfare group was discovering Russian grass-roots organizations that believed institutional care was wrong and families should be encouraged to look after their children at home. Selfless and farsighted people were setting up day-care centers, on a shoestring budget and in the most appalling premises, to look after children who had disabilities or were seriously disturbed, so that their parents could keep them at home. These wonderful people needed support. They certainly got nothing from the state.

"One day I was standing chatting to my neighbor's Russian nanny while our children skated on the ice in Gorky Park," says Sarah. "I had grown to respect her intelligence and insight. At that time, everyone in Russia—from the president down—was in the wrong job. Such was the chaos that people everywhere fell into jobs quite by accident. She was a nanny, but she could have been a TV presenter. She had been rejected at the final interview because of her crooked teeth, and she could not afford to get them fixed. Like other talented women, who had trained as scientists or engineers and could find no work in their field, she had ended up working as a nanny in a foreign family, where the pay was good. She had obviously been building up to this conversation and saw it as her duty to set me right. She asked me why I was giving donations to baby houses. It was well known that people worked in baby houses not because they cared about the children, but only for what they could steal.

If meat was delivered, it would be pilfered and the children given bread and potatoes. The same went for bed linen. It would disappear out the back door. The whole system was corrupt, and I was making it worse by supporting it.

"Her words made sense of everything I had witnessed. I saw with growing clarity that the future of child care lay with the Russian grass-roots organizations, not the state."

Other members of the group were thinking along the same lines. As the welfare group changed, it aroused suspicions among its patrons in the International Women's Club. This was a diplomatic organization and demanded first of all that the ambassadorial hierarchy be respected. The welfare group had become too "professional"—a curse in the IWC lexicon.

"I can see now that we did not pay sufficient respect to the diplomatic hierarchy or its rather old-fashioned social mores. One of the leaders of our group, a gifted twenty-four-year-old psychologist, was shockingly not married to her partner. I can just imagine what they thought of that. For their part, the IWC failed to appreciate the work being done in their name.

"I freely admit that I felt much more at ease with the Russian enthusiasts working with autistic children in damp basements than with the leading ladies of the IWC. Weeks of ugly gossip and name blackening concluded with a disciplinary meeting at which we were branded—in a rare departure from diplomatic waffle—a 'cancerous cyst that had to be cut out' and expelled from the IWC. Luckily, none of this mattered. We established and registered a charity to continue the same work, unhindered by the dainty concerns of the IWC. But it did take over my life for several weeks."

Sarah returned to Baby House 10 at the end of March for what should have been a happy occasion—the delivery of a wheelchair for Anna, the vibrant, intelligent girl who had charmed the visiting American pediatrician. It had taken nine months, but at last she would be mobile. Anna gazed in wonder as doctors from a British charity assembled it, fitted the cushions around the seat, and finally placed her in it.

Within seconds, she had learned how to control it. She moved forward and backward and left and right, throwing her head back and laughing with delight. The caregivers gathered around, clasping their hands together in wonder. The little girl who had spent her days sitting in a plastic seat or propped up in the corner of a playpen had suddenly, before the eyes of everyone assembled, become a real child.

Without warning, Anna made a bid for freedom. She steered herself out of the room where she spent twenty-four hours a day and set off down the corridor, picking up speed as she moved from the carpeted floor to the bare linoleum. Sarah watched as a group of laughing admirers pursued her around the baby house. Thanks to the wheelchair, as the weather got warmer, she would be allowed outside with the children who could walk, not left on her own inside. As Sarah watched, though, she did not know that a wheelchair was not enough to save Anna from the miserable fate that awaited her. It would have had to sprout wings and fly her to a country where her potential would be recognized.

Seeing the delight on Anna's face pricked Sarah's conscience. This was her second visit with the wheelchair charity, and each time it had been too late for her to go upstairs to Group 2 and see Vanya.

As always when foreign specialists were about, Adela was nowhere to be seen. Sarah ran up the stairs two at a time and gently opened the door to Group 2. She could tell immediately something was wrong. The room seemed empty and lifeless. There was Andrei sitting in his usual seat, but he was rocking backward and forward, a look of misery on his face. The chair beside him was empty.

"Where's Vanya?" Sarah asked Andrei.

At the mention of his friend's name, Andrei's head jerked up. Seeing no sign of him, he sank back into his gloom.

It was lunchtime, and the caregiver was ladling slop into bowls.

"Where is he?" The caregiver was taken aback by this brusque interrogation.

"Where's who?"

"Vanya."

"Oh, him. He got his papers." She spoke as if he was a character from long ago, not someone whose bright personality had until recently lit up the room. "He's gone to the internat."

"Which one?"

"How would I know?"

The caregiver turned away to fetch a bottle for Masha. Since her horse chair had got broken, she was confined to her tethered baby walker whenever she was not in bed.

Sarah knelt down beside Andrei, and he turned a languid gaze toward her. She stroked his arm. "How you must miss Vanya."

"Vanya," he repeated, barely audibly. The cruel system had separated two little boys who were like brothers.

"Will Andrei go to the same place as Vanya?" Sarah asked. Now it was Masha's turn for lunch. It was as though the caregiver was feeding an animal. She was leaning over Masha, giving her a bottle from an outstretched hand, with less tenderness than a farmer would display when feeding a calf or a lamb. She did not look her in the eyes or address a word to her. She turned to face Sarah.

"I don't know. It depends on where there's a spare place."

"But Andrei's lost without him."

"That's got nothing to do with it."

With that, she signaled the end of the conversation. The corridors were deserted as Sarah walked down the stairs and toward the main door. She heard the clatter of crockery and the sound of chatter from inside the offices of the defectologists, the speech therapists, and the masseurs, and she grew angrier and angrier that they were not working with the children. In each group, there was one elderly caregiver in charge of changing and feeding twelve children. She thought "Why weren't these lazy women helping out at lunchtime? And where was Adela on this red-letter day?" There were other children who needed wheelchairs, but none of the staff had given the charity a list. This was a unique opportunity to improve the life of children in the baby house, but no one was bothering to seize it. An elderly woman in Wales had baked dozens of cakes and emptied her attic to raise money for that wheelchair. All these women here had done was accept passively what was offered.

Sarah pushed open the padded outside door. There was a spring chill outside. The snow was almost gone and there were pools of slush in the yard. The twigs of the linden trees were tipped with tiny shoots of green that would soon turn into leaves. After the long months of winter, nature was renewing itself, and soon it would be summer. But inside the baby house, nature stood still. It would always be winter for these children.

Sarah was almost at the gate when she heard the sloshing sound of someone rushing through the puddles behind her. She was astonished to see Adela, her Soviet doctor's hat slipped down over one ear and her indoor shoes soaked in the slush.

"Sarah, Sarah. I need to talk to you. Please come back inside."

How bizarre, Sarah thought, Adela asking me in. She must have been spying on me through her office window and seen me walking away. What could she want?

Adela ushered Sarah back inside and into her office and locked the door. There was a pile of old clothes in the corner—no more than rags. Adela said: "They're clothes for the internat. The children have no clothes, you see. It's where Vanya is. It's a terrible place."

Adela was becoming incoherent, but the story gradually emerged. Vanya was in Filimonki, an adult mental asylum. After hearing Svetlana's account of leaving him there, Adela felt ashamed at what she had allowed to happen and had sent her daughter to investigate. The daughter had returned with a shocking story. Vanya was kept naked. He was in distress and begged her to take him back to the baby house. And there was worse.

"My daughter met a girl there. She told her that men came in a bus. They paid money . . . The little girl was . . ." She could not bring herself to say it, but there was no mistaking her gesture.

"You mean the men paid to have sex with the girl?" Adela nodded. She seized a pen and a scrap of paper and began writing. She pressed the paper into Sarah's hand.

"Here's the address. This is what you must do."

Sarah nodded dumbly as Adela unlocked the door and let her out.

Out on the street, she unfolded Adela's scrap of paper. On it was written "Pastukhov I. A. 15/3/90. Psycho-Neurological Internat No. 5, Filimonki. Bus no. 611 from metro Yugo-Zapadnaya, then village bus no. 15."

So this was where Vanya had been sent. To a mental asylum several bus rides away. At the bottom, Adela had written: "Return him to Baby House 10." So those were her orders—not just visit with some clothes but to rescue him from an adult mental asylum. How was she, an ignorant foreigner, supposed to do that? What special powers did Adela think she had?

"If Adela had just asked me to visit Vanya," Sarah recalls, "I could have leaped into action. But springing him from this faraway institution was beyond me. I could organize medical visits, get funding for operations, and put Russian grassroots organizations in touch with western specialists, but doing battle with the bureaucracy was too much to ask. I didn't know where to start. I felt I was a character in a fairy tale, commanded by a witch disguised as a kindly old lady to carry out some superhuman feat.

"And so the bit of paper with the scrawled instructions lay on my desk, and was soon covered with papers with more realistic requests.

"Much pain and suffering could have been avoided if Adela had mobilized the virtual family which Vanya had gathered around him— Vika, me, and Valentina—and led us into battle against the bureaucracy. But that did not happen. She was a Soviet functionary, used to taking orders from her bosses and not challenging the hierarchy, even when she knew they were fatally wrong.

"I realized that Adela grew up under Stalin, when original thoughts had to be kept private. On that day, I still did not know about Vika's existence and she did not know about mine."

While Sarah was paralyzed by the enormity of what she had been asked to do, unbeknown to her, Adela had given Vika the same task and she had already embarked on it with all the fervor of her young soul.

6
Nobody Cares

May 1996

Just as Sarah was initially unable to embark on the task Adela had set her, it took Vika some time to find the strength to go and visit Vanya.

"I had gone to the baby house at the beginning of March," Vika recalls. "Adela and her deputy were in a state of great agitation. They told me that Vanya had been delivered the day before to an internat, according to the instructions from the ministry. Svetlana had been in shock when she came back. It was even worse than the other places she had taken children to. Vanya had become hysterical and hurled himself against the bars of the crib, begging Svetlana not to leave him there.

"I blurted out, 'Maybe I should go and visit him.' Adela took my hand and looked me in the eye and urged me to go. She grabbed a pen and wrote out directions on a scrap of paper and pressed it into my palm, saying again, 'Go, go to him.'

"Weeks passed. It weighed on my conscience. I made excuses: I needed a whole day to get there and back. Looking back, I was full of doubt about my ability to do anything for Vanya. Who was I, a young girl, to barge my way into an adult internat? I put it off and put it off.

"But one day I woke up and realized I could not delay any longer. The thought of Vanya as Adela had described him, naked behind high bars, drove me to take action. I rang my boss to call in sick. It had taken me a long time to find this job and I really needed the money. My new boss sounded displeased."

Vika took the metro to the end of the line and rooted around in her bag for the directions that Adela had given her. The scrap of paper said to look for bus number 611. She forced her way through the crowds onto the bus. The route took her past ranks of identical fourteen-story apartment blocks. They went on for miles, until suddenly they gave way to fields and forest. The bus stopped in the middle of nowhere. Vika followed a line of passengers and climbed up two flights of steps to a walkway over the highway. At the other side of the road, there was still no sign of life.

She wondered where on earth she was, but she just kept following. She climbed down into a ditch and over a grassy hump, and along a winding path that led to a concrete settlement. In the main square, three village buses were lined up. They were ancient vehicles with their engines permanently exposed so the driver could jump out and repair them whenever they broke down. Vika found the number 15 bus and sat down and waited for it to move off.

The old bus was filling up with passengers. A man carrying nothing but a bottle of Head & Shoulders shampoo got on. Vika wondered whether he was going to the asylum. It was an adult institution. Maybe he was going to bathe a relative. A woman carrying a string bag full of bananas sat down. Maybe, thought Vika, she was bringing a treat to her son. Soon the bus was full.

She looked out the window of the bus. She was traveling through open countryside now and the fields were lush with spring grass, a sight that lifted her spirits. The windows of the bus were so scratched and grimy that it seemed as though she was wearing a dirty pair of someone else's glasses.

The bus came to a village and stopped in front of a decrepit wooden house, tilted at a crazy angle as it sank into the ground. The yard in front was piled with scrap iron, and a tethered dog started barking at the bus.

"Is this Filimonki?" she asked the woman with the bananas. "No. The next stop."

The bus left the village and the road wound through fields overgrown with tall weeds. It rounded a bend in the road, and on the other side of a valley, plunked in the middle of the fields, was a monstrous blot on the landscape, a giant complex of six-story buildings like an army barracks. Vika knew that those forbidding buildings had to be the internat, and she wondered how she was going to find Vanya. Then she noticed a solitary brick tower poking up behind the blocks. It was a church steeple. If there was a church there, she thought to herself, maybe it was not such a bad place after all.

The bus stopped and she clambered down, followed by the man with the shampoo.

"Are you going to the internat too?" she asked.

"No. But I can tell you how to get there. Across the road, through the field, and then you'll see a sign." He turned in the opposite direction. The bus drove off and Vika was left alone to find her way along a winding path across a field. She set off with confident steps, enjoying the feel of the grass brushing her legs. She imagined taking Vanya out for a picnic. She'd brought with her a couple of buns and some apples and cucumbers.

The path took Vika into a grove of birch trees, and through their slim silver trunks she could see that the six-story buildings were connected by elevated walkways. Vika's pace slowed as she approached the gates. Now she could see more clearly the outline of the enormous redbrick church in the middle of the complex. Her heart sank when she realized the church and its steeple were crumbling and in terrible disrepair, with no roof and no glass in the windows, and its bricks blackened by decades of rain and frost. Branches grew out of the top of the steeple. It was being reclaimed by nature. To her surprise, the gate into the asylum grounds was open, and she just walked in.

She stood for a minute wondering which direction to turn. There was no obvious main entrance. She didn't know what to expect—probably something more like the baby house, where all the children were under control and locked away. But here these adult inmates seemed to have been left to fend for themselves. A woman with a shaved head, wearing only a simple shift, was struggling to support a man who could not walk unaided. His limbs were bent, and he was moving his head from side to side and dragging a brightly colored piece of plastic behind him on a piece of string. He slumped to the ground, and the woman bent down to try to get him up again. She scolded him, and looked around for help, staring imploringly at Vika. Vika was rooted to the spot. Three women were coming toward her, all with shaved heads. They were adults but the size of twelve-year-olds. One was wearing a buttoned-up cardigan, but one of the buttons was missing, revealing she had no underwear. They came up to her with outstretched hands and started feeling her hair and clothes, all the while muttering indecipherably. Their teeth were rotten and they had gaps in their mouths.

In the background, standing against a wall, was the tallest man Vika had ever seen. His lips were moving and he was burbling and shaking his hands in front of him. He was wearing a pajama top, and his trousers were held up by a piece of cloth tied around his waist. More of these strange people were crowding around her. She started to panic. One woman put her arms around her and tried to reach up to give her a kiss.

Just when Vika felt she had to turn around and run away, a male voice cried out, "Leave her alone." The women melted away, and a teenager in ill-fitting dirty clothes stepped forward. "Are you looking for someone?"

"I've come to visit Vanya, Vanya Pastukhov."

The young man looked puzzled. She continued: "He's six years old. He came here two months ago."

The young man thought for a moment. "Do you mean the one who can talk?"

"Yes, yes. How is he?"

"I'll take you to the children's wing."

The women made as if to follow, but the teenager motioned them to stay behind. He led her along a corridor, up a staircase and across a walkway, and up another set of steps until she had no idea where she was. They climbed another staircase and reached a locked door. The young man knocked and waited for a response.

While they stood in the enclosed stairwell, she asked what his name was.

"Ilya."

"Is Vanya really behind that door?"

The teenager said nothing but banged on the door again, this time more forcefully.

A hostile-looking woman in a white coat opened the door a crack. Vika smiled at her and said, "I've come to visit Vanya." There was no smile in return, but the woman grudgingly let her pass, motioning to Ilya to show her the way, and disappeared down the corridor. Ilya led her to a closed door. Nothing could have prepared her for what she saw when the door opened.

"First it was the smell that hit me. It was like a stable, and it nearly knocked me over. It was a bare room full of cribs. I suppose I had expected to hear 'Vika, Vika,' Vanya's glad cry of welcome. But as I scanned the cribs I could see no sign of a boy with curly hair and a happy smile. All I could see was children in torment—rows and rows of them. Some were lying down immobile, and others were rocking from side to side. Some were banging their heads against the sides of their cribs, and others were tied up in straitjackets with their naked bottoms in the air."

In shock, Vika looked around for a caregiver or even a cleaner to point Vanya out. There was no adult in the room. Ilya indicated the far corner of the room. She forced her way between the cribs, all her senses alert for signs of the boy she had known. Then, on a bare mattress, with a pool of urine at one end, she saw a boy kneeling and swaying quietly backward and forward. His head was shaved and he was wearing only a T-shirt. He slowly lifted his head to look at her and his vacant features broke into a feeble smile of recognition.

"Vanya, what have they done to you?" she gasped. She picked him up and hugged him close. She couldn't stop her tears. He opened his mouth and, as if he had lost the habit of using his vocal chords, whispered a single word: "Vika."

"Find some clothes for him please, Ilya," she asked. "I have to get him out of this room." She carried Vanya out into the corridor, where the stench of urine and feces was not so overpowering.

Ilya led her to a small white-tiled room, like a morgue. It had two little tables, some steel chairs, and a scrap of worn carpet on the floor. "This is where you can sit," Ilya said. "I have to give the children their bottles now."

She settled Vanya down on one of the chairs, and as she stood up, she banged her head on a ventilation pipe that hung uselessly from the ceiling. The pain, though, could not compare with the shock of seeing the state Vanya was in.

Vanya was chewing feebly on a cucumber but was barely strong enough to sit on the chair without toppling sideways. It was like death was taking him by degrees. Vika had entered the underworld, where children were dead even though their hearts continued to beat and their bodies continued to move. She remembered how close she and Vanya used to be. But now there was a barrier—a tombstone—between them. In the baby house, he had been so confident. He knew he was different from the other "incurables" and deserved a better fate. Now he had become a nobody, like all the others.

She was racked with guilt for having delayed her visit so long. If only she was a stronger person, she thought, not so immature and fearful, she could have stopped all this from happening.

She got a picture book out of her bag—the story of the three little pigs, Vanya's favorite.

"What sound does a pig make?" she asked. "You remember, we used to do it together."

Vanya thought and seemed about to say something, but nothing came out of his mouth. She read on, pronouncing the words automatically as her mind reeled from the shock of seeing Vanya locked in that terrible room. She shuddered as she recalled how she had told an American couple about this bright boy who would bring joy to their home. What would they say when they met this silent ghost of a child with a shaved head? How disappointed they would be.

She continued to read. "The wolf said, 'I'll blow your house down.'" Vika thought, If only a wolf could come and blow the whole internat down and she could rescue Vanya from the rubble and take him away.

Then the caregiver, who seemed to be the sole member of staff on duty, came in, carrying a bottle of gray liquid. She handed it to Vika, who understood it was Vanya's lunch.

"Excuse me. Can he have a bowl and a spoon today? I'll help him."

The woman scowled and returned with the same gray liquid in a bowl and an aluminium serving spoon that was farcically too big for his little hands and mouth. He grasped the spoon, and Vika was shocked to see his hands were trembling so much that he could not get the liquid from the bowl to his mouth without spilling it down his front. What had happened to him to make his hands tremble so badly?

When the caregiver came back, she noticed the mess. "As I thought, he can't feed himself. Now those clothes will have to be washed." Vika felt terrible. She had just ruined his chances of ever being allowed to feed himself again. And all the while, she was dreading the moment she would have to take Vanya back to his urine-puddled mattress.

Her thoughts were interrupted by Ilya, who had returned with a couple of bored teenage friends eager to investigate the visitor. They had intelligent faces, but they looked rougher than Ilya. One had no socks and was wearing trousers that were too short, revealing an expanse of skinny ankle. He had a dirty face. The other seemed to be the leader and walked with a swagger. He was wearing cut-off jeans that he had fashioned himself.

"Got any cigarettes?" the more confident one asked, without bothering with an introduction.

She said she hadn't any. She hunted in her bag and fished out two apples, which she offered to them. They took an apple each and put them in their pockets. The sockless one was holding a hand-made cigarette—a pinch of tobacco rolled up in a scrap of paper.

"Are you his mother?" asked the boy in the cutoffs.

"No. I'm not." She thought how to explain her relationship to Vanya. "I'm his godmother." While they talked, Vika was feeding bits of apple into Vanya's mouth, which he chewed thoughtfully. Chewing was another skill that he seemed to be in danger of losing.

She asked the three boys why they were in the asylum. The most confident one said he had run away from a children's home and been put here as punishment. He was going to run away from the asylum soon. "How will you survive?" Vika asked.

"I know how to get my hands on money," he boasted.

Ilya told her he too had run away from a children's home, and had sought refuge with a priest, but he was caught and sent here. That was two years ago, and now he believed he would never leave. From under his T-shirt he pulled out a cross attached to a bootlace. He said he went to all the services in the crypt of the ruined church and dreamed of being a priest.

Everyone in the asylum was labeled ineducable. But Ilya had learned to write before he was sent here. He took a pen and a piece of paper from Vika. While the others talked, he wrote out a note to the priest begging him to visit him. He handed it to Vika and asked her to deliver it. It was written all in capitals, without spaces between the words.

He was desperate to show Vika he could read. He picked up *The Three Little Pigs* and read aloud, struggling over the longer words, as if the letters were a code.

The caregiver put her head around the door and said it was quiet time, and Vanya should be taken back to his crib.

"I'll bring him," Ilya promised, and the caregiver seemed to trust him. Ilya explained that the staff put the teenagers to work, looking after the bedridden children and doing all the dirtiest jobs.

As he leaned over to pick Vanya up, Vika put a hand on Ilya's arm and asked, "Could you take Vanya outside sometimes? It would be good for him to get some fresh air."

"We're not allowed to take them outside."

"Could you let him crawl about? He really needs to exercise his legs."

"They're not allowed out of their cribs."

"But you could talk to him."

"Yes, I could talk to him."

Seizing on this promise, she kissed Vanya on the forehead and said she would come again soon.

As she made for the door, she heard a soft voice, almost a whisper: "Vika." Vanya wanted to tell her something. She was afraid he was going to ask her to take him with her.

"Say hello from me to Auntie Valentina and Adela."

Monday, May 20, 1996

Vika got back to her grandmother's flat in the evening, exhausted by the journey and haunted by what she had seen. She couldn't sleep that night. Every time she shut her eyes, she saw an image of a child in that room where a normal person could not stand to be for more than a minute. As dawn broke, she gave up on sleep and set off to church to catch the early morning service. As she entered the dimness of the church, she put a few rubles in the donation box and took a long thin wax candle, lit it, and placed it in the tray of sand in front of the icon of the Madonna and Child. "This is for Vanya," she whispered, and said a prayer.

As she listened to the familiar chant of the choir, with the voices of different pitches soaring above the harmony and then joining together again, she realized she had made a big mistake. She had tried to do everything on her own. How arrogant she had been. Her arrogance had stopped her from asking anyone else for help.

After the service, Vika confided in the priest and the other members of the parish. Elena, a woman she had barely noticed before, spoke up to say there was a place outside Moscow, Children's Home No. 19, in a town called Dmitrov, where they took children with cerebral palsy and gave them an education. Vika asked what she needed to do to get Vanya there. The first step was to petition the director of the children's wing of the asylum for a copy of Vanya's diagnosis and take it to Dmitrov.

The next day, Vika phoned in sick again and set out on the long journey to Filimonki, this time to talk to the director. Sitting outside his office, she was feeling faint from lack of sleep and wished she had had some breakfast. The secretary sitting across the room was taking loud slurps of tea from her cup. Vika was dressed in her work suit and had tied her hair back, in an attempt to look older than her twenty-four years.

"Vassily Ivanovich will see you now." The secretary pulled open the door to the director's office, to reveal a second door, thickly padded and covered with black leather. Vika opened the black door and stepped in.

The director was sitting behind a vast desk. To his left were three telephones in various tones of beige and gray and, next to him, a red one. At right angles to the desk, down the center of the room, stretched a table with chairs on either side, but he did not invite her to sit down, absorbed as he was by the pile of papers in front of him. He glanced up at her for a brief moment. His face was fleshy. His corpulent body was stuffed into a gray suit. He returned to his papers, and started to sign them, with great flourishes, one by one. Finally he picked up the red phone and barked orders to his secretary in the next room, telling her to be sure to tell the driver to deliver the papers to the department within the hour. He put the phone down and turned to Vika.

"Now, young lady. What brings you here?" His tone was patronizing. She was still standing in front of his desk, waiting to be asked to sit down. She took a deep breath and told him she had come to talk to him about a boy in his care, a boy in the children's wing on the fifth floor.

He picked up on the children's wing, and told Vika what trouble he had had setting it up. It was all because the children's asylums were full. The department had come to him and begged him to make some space available. It had been a huge inconvenience—he had had to get new staff at short notice—but he had managed it.

Vika did not know how to respond to this, so she just launched into what she had to say. "The boy's called Vanya, Vanya Pastukhov. He's with the children who are in bed all day. But it's a terrible mistake. He shouldn't be there. He's intelligent, he speaks, he needs education and help learning to walk."

"Nonsense," he said. "All the children sent here have been diagnosed as ineducable by the commission. In other words, they're incurable oligophrenics—they only need care. And we give them the care they need. We feed them and we keep them clean, I assure you."

His words hit her like a blow to the head. She summoned up all her strength to carry on.

"But I think you'll find, Vassily Ivanovich, that the commission made a mistake with Vanya. And I've come here to ask you for his medical record so that he can be transferred to Children's Home Number 19 in Dmitrov, where he'll get an education."

He saw that Vika was not just going to go away, and asked his secretary to bring Vanya's file. While they waited, he told Vika he had never heard of the Dmitrov children's home and had certainly never transferred anyone there.

He flicked through the file and then announced in a triumphant tone. "Look," he said, "here's the diagnosis and it's quite recent too. Oligophrenic at the stage of pronounced cretinism. Practically an imbecile. Just as I said." He gave a condescending look. "In layman's terms, young lady, that means he's incapable of learning."

Without waiting any longer for an invitation, Vika pulled out a chair and sat down. She had to make one last attempt to get through to this man. "I know Vanya. I visited him in the baby house every week for two years. He learns quickly. He knows songs and nursery rhymes. It is just that he was kept in a silent room where none of the other children could speak."

"So you think you know better than our medical specialists?"

She ploughed on. "He mustn't be kept in a crib twenty-four hours a day. He needs stimulation. He needs to live."

The man in the gray suit was clearly irritated. He pushed back his chair and said, "I'll go and look at the boy myself and see if I agree with *your* diagnosis."

He returned after ten minutes, sat down behind his desk, and took out his pen. He had regained his calm. "I've seen him now. I'll write you your note," he said.

"Oh, thank you, thank you, Vassily Ivanovich." He started to write. "And you will change his diagnosis, make it better so that he can go to school, won't you? They won't take him if you write imbecile on his diagnosis."

The director stopped writing and fixed Vika with a hostile stare. "I certainly will not change his diagnosis. He is not only an imbecile but he is dirty and incapable of looking after himself. His nose is running and he's not potty trained."

As he started writing again, all Vika could do was look at the floor and pray for the director, that he would cease to be blind about the children in his care and start seeing them as people, not hopeless cases. Suddenly the scratching stopped and she heard the director say, "Of course, if you and I were forced to live in such conditions, God knows what we'd turn into."

Vika looked up in astonishment. She could not believe her ears. She stared at the director, looking for signs that he had softened his attitude. Had she really heard those words? It was something she was to puzzle over for years to come. But he continued to write his malevolent indictment of Vanya, as though the words he had just uttered were not from his lips.

He stopped writing. Something had occurred to him. "But who are you anyway? Are you a relative?"

She had to think quickly. Should she lie and claim to be Vanya's aunt? She said, "I'm his godmother."

"Then you're nobody. And I don't have to give you anything."

He picked up the paper and tore it in half. "I've had enough of you. If you ask for anything else, I'll give you a bad diagnosis too. Now get out." His face was bright red and contorted as he stood up and fired off a parting shot. "We've got people just like you here. In fact, there's a place for you in this internat."

Outside the office, Vika felt humiliated, like a schoolgirl who has been reprimanded. She started to go up the stairs to the fifth floor and then stopped. How could she face Vanya now? She felt she had failed him. All her efforts had come to nothing. She walked as fast as she could to the exit and into the fresh air. She turned left into the birch grove and sat down on the grass, leaning her back against a tree trunk and staring out over the green fields.

Elena had given her a rescue plan, and she had just ruined it. No one was watching her, and she let the tears roll down her cheeks. Why hadn't she said she was an aunt? And why had she antagonized the director by asking him to change the diagnosis?

The pain of that confrontation has not left her to this day. "Because of what I had said, I felt Vanya would be stuck there for the rest of his life. Soon he would not be able to speak. He would stop moving about and his limbs would grow stiff, as I had seen happen with others. I thought it would be better for God to take him soon. I pictured him in Heaven running through a sunny meadow."

The original plan had been to take the director's letter to Children's Home No. 19 and beg them to take Vanya. But Vika had no letter, she had not managed to change his diagnosis, and there was no chance of any help from the director. She pulled up a clump of grass. She had spent the past five years getting a degree in physics, but what good was that in the world where you needed to flatter these bureaucrats before they would lift a finger to help? What was the lesson her physics professor had taught her? Even if you suspect you know the answer, you still have to ask the question in order to rule out all the possibilities. A negative result does not mean the experiment has failed. She realized there was only one course of action. She had to go to the children's home and ask the question.

She stood up, brushed the grass from her skirt, and headed for the bus stop.

By the time Vika arrived at Children's Home No. 19, her confidence had ebbed away. She was empty-handed. All that she could give them was her word that Vanya was capable of being educated. The only thing that kept her from giving up hope was the words of her new friend at church, who had assured her the staff at the children's home were good people and would listen to her.

The first thing they asked was what was Vanya's diagnosis? Vika could not lie. The director said straightaway, "We cannot take him with such a diagnosis. Our children here go to school."

She told him, that was exactly what Vanya needed—an education. But he would not be swayed.

Afterward she sat on a bench outside. She couldn't stop crying and must have been sitting there for quite a while. The director came out with an assistant. Vika tried to conceal that she'd been crying, but of course they noticed.

"Obviously you think a lot of this boy," the director said. He said they would go to see Vanya if Vika could find them a car to take them and bring them back.

Vika did not have a car, but she managed to arrange for a car to pick them up two days later, while she traveled by bus and met them at the asylum. Vanya was brought in to them. He was in a terrible condition, worse than when Vika had seen him two weeks before. He was traumatized. He barely recognized Vika and was scared of the strangers.

They asked him to identify squares and triangles and fit them together. Vika prayed as she watched him. He did manage to do a little of what they asked of him, but then the test got harder. They gave him a pencil and piece of paper, and asked him to draw a circle. His hands were shaking. He tried so hard to draw that circle, but he just couldn't. Vika could see by the expressions on the men's faces that they had already made up their minds. She tried to explain that he'd deteriorated since he'd been in the internat. The Dmitrov director said, "Maybe he has potential, but in his current state he really isn't suitable." He was sorry, but he could not take the boy. There was nothing Vika could do to persuade him.

"I blamed myself," she says. "If I had asked for help from the congregation earlier, Vanya would never have gone to the internat and ended up in such a state. It was my pride that had made me think I could do things on my own."

Vika finally realized she was wasting her time trying to find somewhere in Russia where Vanya could get an education and fulfill his promise. Russia, she realized, had rejected this exceptional boy, this gift from God. So she set out on another journey to find possibly the only person in Russia who might be able to help Vanya, his mother.

7

The Mother's Tale

June 1996

"It took us ages to find 2nd Myakininsky Street," Vika says, recalling that terrible June day. "Once again I had to put Vanya before my work. I had promised my boss I was only going to take the morning off, but when it got to midday and I still had not found the address I was looking for, it was clear I wasn't going to get in to work that day. The village of Mya-kinino was small, but we had still managed to get lost, and everyone I spoke to said no such street existed. There were no street names in the village, only wooden houses scattered haphazardly among the trees. As the time passed, I worried that the kind man who had offered to drive me on this complicated mission would lose patience and go back to Mos-cow. And I had not even started what I had set out to do."

The driver parked the car, for the third time, on the village's main street. A woman was walking by and they stopped to ask for directions.

"It's not in the village down here," she said. "You want the new settlement on top of the hill. Turn left and go up the steep road and you'll find it. It's the only three-story building."

She was clearly someone who made it her business to know all the goings-on in the village. "Who are you looking for up there?"

Vika said, "Natasha Pastukhova." The woman's eyes widened.

"Natasha Pastukhova—I don't think you'll find her in the flat. She lets the place out. I haven't seen her for months."

Vika and her driver set off again along the bumpy main street of the village and turned up the steep road. At the top of the hill they came to a cluster of four small apartment blocks made of white bricks. As she got out of the car, the driver said, "I'm here if you need me."

Only one of the blocks was three stories high, and Vika set off through the birch trees and past a children's playground toward the entrance. The man with the beard who was driving Vika worked for an American adoption agency. He had told Vika that one person held the key to rescuing Vanya from the asylum, and that was his birth mother. Thanks to his position at the agency, the man had found out her address, and when Vika had told him she had no one to accompany her, had agreed to drive her. Now it was up to Vika to persuade Natasha to do a terrible thing for the sake of her son.

She stood in front of the door to Natasha's flat and pushed the doorbell. The bell rang uncertainly inside, and she put her ear to the door. There was nothing but silence. She rang the bell again. This time she heard a rustling inside and a woman's voice called through the door, "Who is it?"

"My name is Vika. Are you Natasha, Natasha Pastukhova?"

There was a pause. The voice behind the door said, "Yes, that's me. What do you want?"

"I've come about Vanya, your son."

The lock turned, and the door opened to reveal a slight woman with wavy brown hair. She was wearing a faded cotton housecoat and slippers. She gestured to Vika to follow her into the sitting room. The room was almost bare apart from a sofa peppered with cigarette burns, with a pillow and a folded blanket at one end. A broken armchair, a coffee table stained with ring marks, and a television balanced on a kitchen stool completed the furnishings.

Natasha sat on the edge of the armchair, and Vika sat on the sofa. She had the same curly brown hair and mouth as Vanya. The flat was clean but had an unlived-in feel.

"Is Vanya all right? He's not dead is he?" Natasha asked softly.

"No, but he needs your help."

Vika explained how she had started visiting Vanya in the baby house, where he had charmed the staff and taught another little boy to speak. But despite his obvious intelligence, he had been diagnosed as ineducable and sent to an internat. He was now going backward, and was confined to a crib all day. Natasha did not speak, but she hung on Vika's every word.

Vika told her how she had been introduced to a representative of an American adoption agency. "He seems kind. He says he'll put Vanya in a clinic to have his legs operated on and change his diagnosis. Then he'll be able to find some foreign couple to adopt him. I think this is Vanya's only hope."

Vika looked Natasha in the eye and said, "But it's not possible to do any of this unless you give up your parental rights. Will you do this for Vanya?"

At first Natasha was silent, lost in painful memories. Vika kept going. "Will you do this for your son? Will you give up your parental rights for the sake of your son?"

"Will it really help him?"

"Yes. It's the only way."

"Okay. I'll do it for Vanya's sake."

Vika still looks back on this conversation with incredulity. "I was not aware at the time of the absurdity of this conversation. I was focused totally on getting Natasha to agree to give up her parental rights. But now when I look back, I see how cruel the system was. At the time of Vanya's greatest need, the only role for his birth mother was to sign him away."

This was the monstrous logic of the Soviet state childcare system. The Communists had downgraded the family, decreeing that the state should take over the care of children who were destined never to grow into able-bodied workers, which in reality meant hiding them away and depriving them of contact with their families, education, and medical treatment.

The advent of capitalism had bolted a first-class departure lounge onto the children's gulag, allowing a privileged few to escape abroad. If there was the chance of a child being exported, and if a foreign adoption agency could turn a profit on him, he could be treated in hospitals that were otherwise closed to him. Then Russian doctors would do their best to transform damaged goods into export-quality material. A mother's love was nowhere involved. Her role was merely to sign away her rights and let the cogs of the system grind into action.

Natasha understood the warped logic of the situation. There was no help available for parents of disabled children who chose to keep them at home. Vanya's future had to be abroad. And it was her duty to help him. This she accepted. But she was not prepared for the next demand that Vika placed on her, one that would bring to the fore all the guilt she felt about her son.

"I'll do it for Vanya's sake," she repeated. "I'll write a letter to the authorities now." She looked around the bare flat. "But I don't have any nice paper to write on."

"You don't understand. You have to come with us to the asylum and write out the declaration in front of the director."

"Can't I just write it out here and give it to you?"

"No. It's got to be done officially. You'll need to bring your ID."

"I can't do it today."

"But I've got a car waiting for you. I've only got it today, and it's difficult to get there by public transport."

"And there's another problem. I haven't got my ID with me. I gave it to my friend to look after."

"Well, let's go and find your friend."

Natasha realized that it was useless to argue, and she disappeared into the bedroom to get changed. Although she appeared to have given in and agreed to go to Filimonki, Vika was still worried that she would change her mind.

Natasha emerged with her hair brushed and wearing a once expensive but now tatty leather jacket and a black skirt. They got in the car and set off down the hill into the next village, and stopped in front of a small block of flats. This was where her friend, Mama Vina, lived. Vika wondered who this woman could be—clearly a pillar of society if she was worthy of looking after an ID.

A couple of grannies sitting on a bench outside her entrance recognized Natasha. "Mama Vina's not at home. She left for the grocery store an hour ago."

Without saying anything, Natasha climbed back into the car. The grocery store was two minutes' drive away. Natasha did not go inside the shop, but instead she headed for a patch of grass on the other side of the road. Vika followed close behind her. She was shocked to see Natasha get down on her knees and crawl into the bushes. From the undergrowth, Natasha hauled out a tipsy woman, who struggled to stand up. This was Mama Vina. As she swayed unsteadily, a derelict man in the final stages of alcoholism crawled out after her.

Vika laughs as she recalls how shocked she was. "For a second I saw myself through my grandmother's eyes—an innocent girl seeking out the company of down-and-outs who spent their days drinking in the park."

Natasha somehow herded the two drunks into the back of the car, and they returned to Mama Vina's home. There, in a drawer, was Natasha's ID. Standing next to the car, Natasha held out the ID to Vika. "Here—take it. Go without me."

Once again Vika had to remind her that this was Vanya's only chance, and she had no choice but to come with her.

As soon as she got into the car, Natasha started to cry. She told her everything. "It was as if she was repenting," Vika says. Before she got pregnant with Vanya, she already had two children. The first, Vadim, was born when she was only eighteen and married to her first husband. But she was not ready to be a mother and her mother had looked after the boy. Then four years later, after she had met her second husband, Anatoly, she gave birth to a daughter, Olga. She was a much better mother to her. But then a terrible thing happened. First her father died and then her mother died of cancer, in the course of a month. Thus she lost all her support. Her ex-husband took Vadim to live with him, and Olga was taken off to a children's home.

Then Natasha found out she was pregnant again. She moved back into her parents' place with Anatoly. They both gave up drinking and were determined to make a new start. She persuaded the authorities to give Olga back. But it was so difficult without her mother. She missed her mother so very much.

She did not look after herself properly during her pregnancy. She said it was her fault that Vanya was born premature. He was born at six months and weighed a little over two pounds. It was a miracle he survived. At the maternity home, they told her that premature babies always developed cerebral palsy and he would be a great burden on her and her family. They put pressure on her to renounce her parental rights and give him up to the state, and even started dictating the letter she had to write. But she had refused to give her baby up.

It had not been easy, though. From birth, he was in and out of the hospital. He got pneumonia and it was touch and go. She had visited him as often as she could. But Olga wasn't allowed in the hospital, and her husband was working. The neighbors got fed up with being asked to look after Olga. It would have been so different if her mother had been alive.

The doctors said her baby would never walk or talk. But he did make progress; only the doctors refused to see it. She had worked with him and got him to stand up. But the doctors still advised her to give him up.

"He was handsome and he had curly hair. I used to take him for massage every week. The masseur said one kind thing: 'Look at his broad shoulders. He's a real man.' That remark kept me going for months. But then I took him to a hospital and the orderly said to me, 'You've given birth to God knows what and now you've brought him to us to cure. Why are you bringing him here?'"

She spoke with such pain that, even six years later, those hurtful words were like an unhealed wound in her heart.

"That experience threw me into a terrible depression. And the neighbors weren't any help either. They said I should give him up to a baby house. If only I hadn't been so weak. I started drinking again. It's all my fault, what's happened to him. He has a lazy eye. I'm to blame for that too. I gave him the bottle in the wrong way."

Vika said that was not what causes a lazy eye and Natasha shouldn't blame herself. But she did not hear her and continued her confession. All the bad memories that she had tried to blot out with alcohol came tumbling out. She told Vika she had once left Olga in charge of him, and he had fallen off the bed.

Vika said all children fall off beds, but she ignored her and insisted it was her fault and Olga had been too little to be left alone with him.

She sobbed silently for a few minutes and turned to Vika and asked, "Vika, will someone really want him? Will someone take him and give him a good life? That's what I want more than anything in the world."

An hour later they were in the director's office—the same place where only two weeks ago Vika had been so humiliated. To Vika's surprise, the same man whose face had turned purple with rage at her insolence now greeted her with a smile of recognition. She soon understood why his mood toward her had changed—an even softer target for his bullying had appeared.

He turned on Natasha. "So what are you doing here in my office?"

"I'm here to help my son," Natasha replied, her voice barely audible.

"It's a bit late for that now," snorted the director.

"Please, I want him to get the treatment he needs and to be adopted." She shot an anxious glance at Vika.

"Well have you seen him? Do you know the state he's in?"

"N-n-o." She turned very pale.

"Let's have a look at him then." He picked up the red phone and barked, "Bring Pastukhov in."

A few minutes later a woman in a white coat entered, carrying Vanya, who was as pale as a ghost, his eyes darting around at the strange surroundings and unknown people. He was so frightened he did not even recognize Vika. The caregiver moved to the center of the room and stood, holding him by his upper arms.

"Turn him around," the director ordered. The caregiver turned Vanya around, like a farmer showing off an animal at a market, except in this case, the caregiver was being instructed to show him at his worst. "Take a good look at your son. This is what he's like."

"Natasha was as traumatized as her son," Vika remembers. "She was just sitting and staring. The man from the adoption agency sat between us, looking in turn at me and Natasha. I had to put a stop to Vanya's humiliation. I went up to him and tried to put him at his ease and encourage him to speak, but no words came. However hard I tried, he did not answer a single one of the director's questions. The system had reduced Vanya to the state the doctors had predicted for him six years before."

Nobody thought to tell Vanya that his mother was present and that she, for all her faults, still cared about him and thought about him every day. As for Natasha, by now she was too crushed to assert herself.

Vanya was taken back up to the fifth floor, to his crib in the children's wing. Natasha wrote her letter in the presence of the director, in long hand, as the law required. Taking dictation from the director she wrote the very same words—"I, Natalya Ivanovna Pastukhova, renounce parental rights to my son"—that she had so bravely refused to write six years ago in the maternity hospital.

Looking back, it is clear to Vika that the mother-son bond, so little prized by the Communists, was broken long before Natasha had written her letter signing away her parental rights. This degrading ordeal for mother and son was the last occasion they would ever see each other.

Back in the car, the man from the adoption agency announced he could not drive Natasha home but would drop her at the metro station at the end of the line. As she got out of the car, her ID slipped through the ripped lining of her leather jacket and fell into the gutter. Vika saw it, and gave it back to her. Natasha put it back into the same pocket, and disappeared down the steps into the metro, a fragile and lonely figure amid the swirling crowds.

8
The Rat

April–June 1996

Vanya was lying in his iron-barred crib, drowsy after being given a strong sedative. He had got used to feeling like this after many visits to the room with the brown tiles. The first time he had been taken there was after the caregiver on duty had tried to stick a bottle in his mouth. He had jerked his head away and declared, "I'm too old for a bottle. I eat at a table." Seconds later, he had been snatched from his crib, taken to another room, and laid facedown on a bench. He then felt a stabbing pain in his bottom. Back in the children's room, he was not offered anything to eat—not even a bottle—just thrown back in the crib.

Today as he lay there, he was too drowsy even to ask to use the pot. They always ignored his request, but he never stopped asking. He hated to pee on his plastic mattress as the other children did, but he had no choice. First it was warm, as the liquid made a comforting bath on the mattress, but then it got cold and he longed for someone to come and wipe it dry, which could take half the day. He felt shame as he remembered Auntie Valentina and how she had taught him to use the pot and deprived him of kisses if he had an accident.

In his drugged state, he heard a scratching. It sounded like the rats that scrabbled around the edges of the room at night. With all his strength, he lifted his head. There, at the end of the mattress, was an enormous rodent with huge eyes, staring at him. He wanted to sit up and scream, but the drugs had taken the strength from his body and tied his tongue. He tried to kick it, but his legs would not respond. The rat sat at the end of the mattress as if it were its own bed, mocking Vanya's inability to move. Emboldened, it leaned forward onto all four paws and scurried along the edge of the mattress toward his head. Vanya was terrified. The rat was coming for his face. It was going to bite him, and he could not move. Vanya shut his eyes tight and waited. He felt it dash past him, running down the leg of the crib and onto the floor.

He succumbed again to the drugs. All he wanted was to lie still. He no longer tried to move his legs and arms. His eyes were shut. Time passed, but he did not know how long. Suddenly a heavy weight had landed on his chest and was forcing the breath out of him. He opened his eyes and saw that Slava, the boy from the next crib who was usually tied up, was on top of him. Slava had somehow freed himself from his cloth bindings, escaped from his crib, and climbed into Vanya's. He had landed on Vanya's chest and was bouncing up and down. Vanya had no strength in his legs to tip the boy off, but he gathered all the force of his puny body into his arms and tried to push him off his chest. Slava grabbed one of Vanya's arms and bit it with all his force. Vanya cried out. Encouraged, Slava moved his jaws toward Vanya's head and clamped his teeth around one of his ears. Vanya used both his arms to push his tormentor off, all the while enduring the pain shooting from his wounded ear and arm.

Slava was using the force of all the demons spinning around his head. Vanya was struggling to breathe, but still they grappled. Just when Vanya felt he could not resist for a moment longer, the crushing weight was lifted from his chest. Now he could draw breath. Then his ear was released from Slava's jaws. He heard a male voice saying, "Enough. Let go." And strong fingers pried Slava's grip from Vanya's arm. His head flopped back onto the hard plastic mattress. He saw Slava being carried away, arms and legs flailing, and placed back in his crib. The person who broke up the fight returned to Vanya and examined his chewed ear and bitten arm.

"We'd better go and clean you up," said the person, picking him up. Vanya found himself staring into the face of a young man with unkempt reddish blond hair and freckles. There was a cross hanging around his neck on a bootlace. Vanya had never met a teenager before and he could not take his eyes off his rescuer, who appeared part boy, part man.

Vanya relaxed into the young man's arms as he strode down the corridor. He was thinking, could this be his angel? Is this what an angel looked like?

Now they were in a room that Vanya had never seen before. This room had white tiles and faucets. The teenager looked around for somewhere to put Vanya, and placed him in a basin. "I'll be back in a minute. Don't bleed all over the place." He grinned and Vanya saw one of his side teeth was missing.

As he sat in the basin, with his feet dangling over the side and blood dripping from his ear, Vanya ignored the throbbing pain. The discomfort was canceled out by the joy of having made his first human contact. After so long in the asylum, someone had smiled at him.

The teenager returned, holding a big brown bottle and a wad of cotton. He tipped out some of the liquid, which stained the cotton wool a shocking shade of green. He dabbed at Vanya's wounds, turning his whole forearm green. Vanya winced at each dab as the liquid stung his wounds.

"Don't cry, little one. It'll heal by your wedding day."

"It'll heal by my wedding day," echoed Vanya. "That's what Auntie Valentina says when I hurt myself."

"You speak, do you? Do you have a name?"

"Vanya. What's your name?"

"Ilya."

"Are you my guardian angel?"

Ilya looked astonished. "What do you mean?"

"Vika said if I was in trouble, I just had to call for my guardian angel and he would come. Slava was biting me and you rescued me. You must be my guardian angel."

"Do I have wings and a halo?" He smiled. It was the funniest thing he had heard for a long time.

"So you're not my guardian angel." Vanya was unable to hide his disappointment. He thought a moment. He'd never come across a male caregiver before. "Is it your shift today?"

"Sort of. They often make me clean up after you guys."

Ilya put down the bottle and bent down to pick Vanya up. Vanya was seized with panic that he was about to be put back in his crib among the moaning, rocking children. "Ilya, can you take me outside?" In desperation, he begged, "Just for a short while."

"I'm not allowed to take you outside."

Vanya was puzzled. "But you work here."

"Vanya. You don't understand. I live here, just like you." Ilya's voice trailed off. Seeing the look on Vanya's face, Ilya made a suggestion.

"I'll take the bottle back and then let's go and watch TV. It's time for my favorite program. I'm in charge of you today, so no one will notice you're not in your crib."

Ilya carried him down the corridor, which widened into a gloomy sitting area. They sat down on a thinly upholstered bench, in front of an old television set with a sickly plant in a white plastic pot on the top. Vanya was delighted not to have been put back to bed. Ilya switched the television on, and suddenly the dim corridor was transformed by a blast of rousing music.

Vanya's eyes grew wide. In quick succession the television was showing strong young men enjoying the sun, beautiful houses with lush gardens, and a sparkling sea with strange-shaped trees growing in the sand.

"This is Santa Barbara, in America," said Ilya. "The sun shines every day. There's no rain and no snow. Everyone is rich."

On the screen was a boy of about Vanya's age. His hair was well brushed, just as his had been when Auntie Valentina dressed him up as a major. There were two women, but neither of them looked like anyone he had ever seen. They were not wearing white coats, so they were more like Vika and Sarah than the caregivers. But unlike Vika and Sarah, their clothes were brightly colored and sparkling.

One was blond and the other dark-haired. They were shouting over the boy. Vanya was used to being shouted at by the caregivers. But these two women were shouting at each other, and the boy did not seem frightened. He was like Andrei when he had on his blank face.

The dark woman was shrieking, "He's my son. Stay away from him." And the blond was shouting back: "He's always been mine. You stole him! I'm his real mother." She had her hand on the boy's shoulder. She was protecting him. The dark woman looked very sad and left the room.

Vanya saw that Ilya was deeply affected by what was happening on the screen. He was shaking and could not talk. Vanya returned his gaze to the screen and tried to follow the story.

Now the boy with the brushed hair was being introduced to a girl slightly older than he was. "Brandon, this is your sister," said the new mother. The boy said, "I always wanted a sister." The mother, the boy, and the girl all hugged each other. "We will never be parted again," they said.

It was the end of the program, and Ilya switched the television off. Vanya could see he was crying but trying to hide it. When he had calmed down, he turned to Vanya and said, "That's America. Mothers don't give up their children in America. They fight to look after their children. What a country."

Vanya did not understand what he was saying. What was America? he wondered.

In Vanya's room, the children were unusually lively. He did not know it, but there was a simple reason: The supply of tranquilizing drugs had run out. Those children who could sit or kneel were rocking or banging their heads against the iron bars of their cribs. Those who were lying down just mewed pitifully. One harassed caregiver was in charge of all the children. The windows were tightly shuttered, but the sunlight outside still managed to poke through, painting bright bars on the floor. Flies buzzed around, feasting off the excrement on the children's mattresses and alighting on their bottoms and on their eyes.

Vanya had tried many times to make a connection with the children in the cribs on either side of him. The little blond girl they called Ivanova never tried to sit up, and the only part of her body she moved was her head, which she rolled from side to side to provide some slight diversion. Her body was stiff and her muscles were so tight that her legs were permanently bent at the knee. Her face was turned away from him, and Vanya could see the bald patch on the back of her head, where it had been rubbed smooth by contact with the mattress. She never spoke a word, and Vanya had noticed that over the past few days she had even stopped moaning and had become totally silent. Now there was no chance of even getting a smile from her. The caregivers still gave her a bottle three times a day, but she seemed to have lost the will to suck. Vanya noticed that the caregivers spent less and less time trying to get her to feed.

On the other side was Slava. His powerful arms were bound to his body by a coarse cloth, which was tied behind his back and then to one of the iron bars of his crib. Unable to move around even inside his crib, he rocked violently backward and forward. Vanya tried calling his name, but without much hope of getting a response. Vanya tried smiling, even though Slava had never smiled back. Unlike Vanya, he did not yearn for human contact. In fact, he did not show any sign of recognizing his neighbor, even after all this time.

In the center of Slava's forehead was a bruise, which was turning from red to violet. He must have got it from hurling himself at the bars. Vanya had never seen anything so big, and he stared at it in fascination. He thought of the time Slava had bitten him on the arm and ear, and he remembered with happiness the young man who had tended his wounds and put that stinging green stuff on them. He wondered whether Ilya would be working today. If he did come, he would call out to him and ask him to put the green stuff on Slava. And then Vanya and Ilya could have a conversation and talk about other things, because Slava never said anything, so Ilya was bound to want someone to chat to.

He could barely contain his excitement at the thought that this might happen. He listened out for the sound of rattling bottles that would signal that it was time for the midday feed. That was when Ilya would come. He turned to face the door in anticipation, already convinced that his friend was about to open it.

Crouched on all fours, facing the door, his concentration was intense, so intense that when the door finally opened he wondered if he had slipped into one of the daydreams that came upon him after his visits to the room with the brown tiles. It was not Ilya who came through the door, but a tall man with long, sticking-out black hair streaked with gray. He had hair growing around his mouth. Everything was enormous about him—his nose, his hands, his height. From the breast pocket of his shirt he pulled a plastic pipe and put it in his mouth, his long fingers finding their places over the little holes. The pipe looked so silly in his hands: it was so small and his hands were so big. He began to blow, and a tune emerged from the pipe. As he played, he jigged clumsily from foot to foot, like a dancing bear, squeezing between the cribs, bending over the iron bars and playing to each child. Vanya saw that every face in the room was turned toward the dancing piper. Even Slava had stopped rocking and was listening to the music.

While the other children watched silently, Vanya bounced up and down in his crib, desperate that the man should not pass him by. He mustn't go away without saying hello. It was so important. It was the most important thing ever—that the piper come to his crib and he could talk to him.

Luckily the piper was coming in his direction. He jigged his way to Vanya's crib and leaned over. Vanya stopped bouncing and sat up, gazing into the face of this musical giant. As he played, his eyelids dropped as if he had to blot out the world in order to concentrate on his fingers dancing over the holes in the pipe. Then he looked up, moved the pipe in a great arc through the air, and resumed his studious concentration. Then he took the pipe out of his mouth, and stroked Vanya on the head.

"Hello, young man. I think you like my music."

"Oh, yes. I do very much."

"You speak! What's your name?"

"Vanya. And I know who you are. You're my guardian angel, aren't you?"

The piper laughed. "Actually I'm a pianist. But I'd certainly like to be your guardian angel."

"Vika told me you'd come if I looked up to Heaven and prayed. But I can't see Heaven because there are shutters over the windows."

"I know Vika. She told me how to get here."

"And do you know Sarah too?"

"Of course."

"Say hello to her from me. Tell her I think about her."

"I will. And now I'll play another tune, specially for you."

Once again the room filled with the piper's jolly tunes. Vanya was so happy that he had attracted the attention of this kind-faced man. While he listened to the music, he racked his brains for other things to say to him.

Nobody heard the door open, but suddenly the music was interrupted by a scolding voice. "Who are you? What are you doing here?"

"I'm a musician. I've come to play to the children."

"You shouldn't be here. Outsiders are not allowed."

"But there's nobody looking after these children."

Vanya recognized the woman as the one with the jangling keys who had put him in his crib on the day he arrived.

"I've brought some fruit for the children." The musician indicated a plastic bag that he had left by the door.

"They have everything they need. They are fed three times a day. They don't need fresh fruit. And honestly, they don't know the difference."

"And I've brought some coloring books too."

"Look around you. Are they capable of coloring? As I said, they have everything they need."

"How can you say that?" Vanya watched the visitor getting more and more agitated. He started to shout, but it was not the sort of shouting that made Vanya frightened, like when the caregivers got angry with the children. The man was shouting, "You give them nothing here. They need love, stimulation, education. They're human beings."

"This is not an educational institution. And besides we don't have the staff. Today there's only me and two orderlies to look after sixty children."

"Then you should welcome help from outsiders."

"As I said, this is a closed institution."

"Well I want you to know, it's criminal what's going on here. In Finland, children like these would be going to school."

Now that the music had stopped, the children had started to cry out with renewed intensity.

"Look what you've done. You've stirred them up. How are we going to calm them down again? They're never going to sleep this afternoon. Now you must go."

With a sigh, the piper bent down to pick up his bags of presents. As he stood up, his eyes met Vanya's. His looked seemed to say, I won't forget you. Then he turned and left the room.

9
Message from the Gulag

June 1996

Friday evening was movie night in Sarah's apartment. Her children's friends used to gather to watch a video, while the mothers chatted in the kitchen over a bottle of wine. That evening, the conversation turned to Vanya's friend Andrei and his miraculous good fortune. Sarah was still taking volunteers into Baby House 10, and one of them had become attached to Andrei. When she heard that he, like Vanya, was about to be moved on to a mental asylum, she rang her sister in the U.S. with an urgent request to find him adoptive parents before it was too late.

Amazingly, it took her just a couple of phone calls to find a family in Florida who were looking to adopt. They had not thought of Russia, but after receiving the phone call, they concluded that God had guided them to Andrei.

There was no such quick fix for Vanya. Sarah's friend Viv made her feel uncomfortable by asking about Vanya and why she had not been to see him in the asylum. "Don't you think you should go? At least go and see him. I could drive you," she suggested.

"I was still hesitant," Sarah recalls. "I felt there was nothing I could do for Vanya. Russia had sentenced him to a slow death, and children were not adopted from asylums, so there was no chance of him going abroad. As for Adela's request for me to bring him back to the baby house, if she could not do it—and she a head doctor—how on earth could I? By visiting him, I would just give him false hope." But Vanya did not allow her to get off so easily.

A couple of weeks later, the phone rang at Sarah's home just before midnight. Only one person could be calling at that hour: Sergei, the concert pianist turned children's rights activist. He was the most inspirational—and the most exasperating—person on the planet. After his second child was born with Down syndrome, he made it his business to find out what happened to children with disabilities in Russia. He was so shocked at what he found that he had set up the Moscow Down Syndrome Association. With no money or political support, he was battling single-handedly to waken Russia's conscience to the plight of tens of thousands of children locked away in asylums. He accepted no limits to his activism: every ruble he possessed, every hour of the day and night, every friend and acquaintance, all were mobilized for his cause. He accepted nothing less than 100 percent commitment, which meant he was never satisfied, whatever help anyone offered. Sarah braced herself for an impossible request.

"I've got a message for you." His voice was soft, and he had a slight stutter, which only made what he had to say more urgent. "I visited another asylum today, way outside Moscow, a terrible place. I was playing music to the children, and I met a boy who said he knew Sarah. I assumed it must be you. He said to say hello, and he hasn't stopped thinking about you."

"That sounds like Vanya. I used to visit him in the baby house. He really is on my conscience. I know I should visit him. I'll try to go this weekend. It's good you rang."

"You must visit him. He's asking for you."

"I will. I promise."

The next day she rang Viv to take her up on the offer of a car and moral support.

Sarah and Viv did not have much in the way of instructions from Adela to get to the mental asylum—a metro stop, and two bus routes. After asking the way often, in the middle of nowhere, they came to a bus stop marked INTERNAT. They followed a dirt road to the left and came to a sign, with INTERNAT in big letters, with an arrow pointing to the right. Someone had crashed into the sign, bending one of its support pillars, so the arrow now pointed to the ground.

Unlike Baby House 10, which was hidden away in the heart of the city, the asylum was a landmark in the endless expanse of the Russian countryside. Only the most conscientious of relatives would traipse out to this forgotten spot.

They parked by the sign and approached the asylum on foot. There was no gate and no security guard. In fact, as Vika had found out, the place was so isolated it did not need a gate. Sarah and Viv entered the nearest door and were standing wondering what to do when they were approached by a teenager wearing dirty, ill-fitting clothes and smoking a roll-up. He agreed to take them to the children's wing, and he led them through a maze of corridors and staircases until they came to a metal door at the top of a windowless flight of steps. The teenager battered the door until a caregiver opened it a fraction. Sarah played the dumb foreigner. She told the caregiver, without pausing for breath, that she had come to visit a boy she'd known in Baby House 10 and brought a present and please could they come in, if only for a minute. She kept repeating it so the caregiver did not have a chance to slam the door in her face. The caregiver insisted they get permission from the duty doctor and summoned an orderly to take them downstairs to the office.

The duty doctor was in a cozy room with carpets and plants, sitting at her desk watching a big color TV.

"She was very hostile," Sarah says. "I was aware she would need a lot of convincing to let us in. She asked us why we'd come. Once again I kept talking and talking. I said I knew Vanya and used to visit him in his baby house and we had become good friends. She said, 'That's one place and this is another.' I told her, the head of the baby house told me to come. I told her I'd brought Vanya a present. That created a reaction. She wanted to know what I had brought him.

"She said we could not visit because there was a quarantine. It was obvious from the look she gave the orderly that this was a lie. I persisted, and eventually she gave in. She told the orderly, 'Don't take them into the children's room. And there must be someone watching them at all times.'"

Back upstairs, the orderly unlocked the metal door. Sarah and Viv followed her across the corridor to another door, which she opened. Like Vika before them, they froze in horror at the sight before their eyes—children naked on plastic mattresses behind high bars, like animals in cages. They were lying in pools of urine and their own feces. Some were tied up in makeshift straitjackets.

Sarah remembers, "I gasped as I recognized some of the children from baby houses I had visited. In a crib by the door, there was Dima from Baby House 17 lying in a river of urine. He recognized me too and he sloshed toward me. And the normal-looking toddler jumping up and down in the crib in the corner looked familiar too. It was Alyosha from Baby House 4."

Sarah scanned the cribs for Vanya; but before she could spot him, the orderly shoved her out of the room and closed the door.

As they were being ushered into a small visitors room, Viv whispered, "They know it's wrong and they don't want us to see."

Vanya was brought in by another teenage boy, who had hastily dressed him in a motley collection of clothes sewn from odd bits of once brightly colored but now faded material. He was wearing a green-and-black checked shirt made from coarse cloth, a pair of baggy pajama bottoms, and finally a garish purple-and-red cardigan.

As usual, the first thing he said was the most important thing he had to communicate. "I'm so sleepy," he said in a barely audible voice. They could see he was forcing himself to stay alert, fighting the effect of powerful sedatives. He could no longer sit up, but slumped back in a chair like an old man.

Sarah showed him a picture of Andrei and asked him who it was. At first he said it was himself, but eventually he said, "Andrei."

They had not been with Vanya for three minutes when the caregiver came in to check on them. Sarah asked her if the children had any toys to play with. She said, yes, there was a playroom with toys. Hearing this, Vanya turned his head and gave her a look that was more eloquent than words. It said, You liar. The caregiver gave them another five minutes.

The caregiver's interruptions to check up on the visitors became ever more frequent, making the atmosphere uncomfortable. "We were determined to have one last look at the room where we now realized Vanya spent twenty-four hours a day. As we entered, Dima once again sloshed toward me. I held out my hand toward him but was rudely told to go. As I handed Vanya over to the caregiver, he said softly, 'I'll be thinking of you.'"

The teenagers wanted to escort Sarah and Viv out of the building, but the caregiver refused to let them go. She just pointed the foreigners to the stairs, pulled the teenagers back inside, and locked the door.

When Sarah and Viv found their way outside, they were surprised to hear voices above them. It was the teenagers calling. Their faces were not visible, just their hands waving through the bars on the fifth floor. The teenagers followed them around the building on the top floor. They called, "Please come again, come back tomorrow. It'll be better tomorrow. Please come back."

Back in the car, both women were in a state of shock.

Viv struggled to make sense of what they had witnessed. "In the baby house, the staff are like zookeepers," she said. "In the asylum, the staff are more like jailers. They kicked us out so quickly. It was like we were visiting a prisoner."

"An especially dangerous prisoner, a murderer." As they drove through the fields, Sarah added, "The worst part is that the asylums are hidden away, out of sight from ordinary Russians, just like the Nazi concentration camps were. It's easy for people to say they don't know what's going on."

"The world's got to know about this, Sarah."

"Yes. But how do we start?"

"Your husband's a journalist. Get him to write about it."

"God, how I've tried. I have suggested it so many times, but he keeps telling me it's not news. All the paper wants from him are articles about the Communists coming back."

"But tell him what we've seen today. Maybe he should go out there himself."

Sarah and Viv reached the city center. Posters on every corner promised people a glittering future if they voted to reelect Yeltsin, the drunkard. Millions of dollars were being spent on advertising to convince Russian voters that life was getting better. In reality, nothing had changed for the poor and weak, while the powerful just got richer and richer. This presidential election meant little to Sarah. For her there was only one issue: How could a society call itself free when it locked up thousands of its children for no good reason?

Sarah had one more task to do that day. She asked Viv to drop her off near Baby House 10. For the first time, she was not worried about being turned away; she had been sent on an errand by Adela and had come to report back. To her surprise, under the linden trees she saw two playpens full of so-called incurable children being allowed out for a rare dose of fresh air. They were all lying down, in exactly the same way as they spent their days inside; but now they were blinking in the dappled sunshine, their faces ghostly pale, like nocturnal creatures suddenly dragged into the light. Three toddlers sat in baby walkers, not tethered to the playpens as they were inside, but still immobile as the wheels were stuck among the coarse grass and clumps of weeds.

Adela was fussing over one of the playpens. One of the sides had come loose and she was binding the corner with some old string. She looked up as Sarah approached.

"I've just been to see Vanya," Sarah blurted out without any formalities.

"Thank you, thank you. How is he?" Adela clasped her hands together, grateful for a wish fulfilled.

"You're right, Adela. It's an appalling place. It's worse than that. I can't understand why Vanya is there."

A couple of staff appeared from nowhere to listen in.

"It's a concentration camp. There's no other word for it." The staff gasped at Sarah's bold use of a taboo word. Adela shut her eyes as if to block out what she was saying.

"I don't understand," Sarah said, for once not watching her words. "Why do you send your children to those places?"

Adela had lost her tongue. One of the caregivers stepped in. "It's not we who send them. We come under the Ministry of Health. Those places come under another ministry, the Ministry of Social Welfare. They decide where the children go."

"But you do know about the conditions in the internats?"

"No. We've never been. When the children leave the baby house, we don't see them again."

Adela mumbled something unintelligible and went inside. The caregivers melted away. Sarah was left alone. This brief exchange of words had clarified in a flash what she had been puzzling over for months. She had never understood why the baby-house staff were so uninterested in the children's fates. Why were Dr. Swanger's prescriptions not acted on? Why weren't the staff teaching the children to speak and to walk? Why weren't they arranging simple operations? Why hadn't Vanya's lazy eye ever been corrected?

"It was all clear to me at that moment. The staff had no duty of continuing care. The baby house was just a way station through which the children passed on to an unknown destination—one they suspected was terrible but did not want to inquire about too closely. They could not get emotionally involved with any child, for reasons of self-preservation. Why establish bonds of affection if you are never going to see a child again? The baby house was just a warehouse where the children were stored for a while until a document arrived, and then the staff dispatched them to the indicated address.

"But one child, an extraordinary boy who refused to be crushed by this appalling system, had smashed a hole in the wall surrounding the asylums and was sending back messages from the other side. This weak little boy, starved and drugged, with no family, was fighting from within. But even he was having the fight crushed out of him by the system."

Adela had returned and was waving a single sheet of paper in front of her. The paper had eight handwritten lines in English on it. Sarah read them with increasing surprise. "I'm Victoria Kitaeva. I take care about boy (6 years) Vanya Pastukhov, who is in very bad conditions now, but he is very clever and good boy. Could you call me to work or to home before 8 or after 22."

"Adela, who's this person?"

"It's Vika. She became very close to Vanya when he was here."

"Is she on the staff?"

"No, she's a volunteer like you. She's a young girl, a churchgoer. She just used to come and visit."

"But how come I never met her? Why didn't you tell me about her before?"

Adela did not have an answer to that. "Vika's been going to visit him in the internat. She's been trying to help him. Now she needs you to contact her. I can't read English, but aren't those her telephone numbers?"

"I will call her. But I still don't understand why you didn't mention her before."

Adela mumbled something about the kitchen and escaped back inside.

Sarah stood holding the piece of paper, stunned. She'd always dreamed of meeting a Russian who saw the potential of the children who had been consigned to the trash. But how was she going to meet her? In two days' time, Sarah was leaving Moscow for the summer with her children. Months had been wasted because of Adela's passivity. "At least I can make contact with her before I leave," she thought.

10
The Sour Grape

July–October 1996

When the alarm went off at 7:30 on Saturday morning, all Vika wanted to do was to roll over and shut her eyes again. It had been so hot in the night that she had hardly slept. Her grandmother's apartment was under the roof, and it was unbearable in summer. But then she remembered Sarah's husband was coming around at eight. He had phoned a few nights ago and asked her to take him to Filimonki to meet Vanya. Vika really did not want to go back there. She was still recovering from the ordeal of taking Natasha to sign away her rights. And then the man from the adoption agency had said it would take another six months to complete the legal process, so Vanya would not be eligible for adoption until the end of the year. She did not think he could last that long. She was at a loss what to do next.

When Alan rang, Vika's first impulse was to say no, go on your own. But he was so polite and humble she could not refuse. Vika thought journalists were rough and bullying, but they have many techniques of getting their own way. She said, "If you pick me up at my granny's flat, I'll come." He said he would come at eight. That was in half an hour, and she was not even dressed.

Luckily, Vika's grandmother was already in the kitchen making tea. Vika hurriedly folded up the sofa bed they shared and hid the bedding. Vika shouted to her grandmother to find an extra cup and something to eat. The only food on the table was a bowl of sugar lumps, a plate of spring onions, and a dusty package of wafer biscuits.

Vika found a backpack and started looking for the little pair of boots a member of her church had given her for Vanya. There was no food for a picnic, so she would have to ask Alan to make a stop on the way to buy things. When the intercom rang, Vika buzzed him in. As Alan mounted the stairs, the dogs on each floor announced his arrival.

She opened the door, and her first thought was, how could she pass off this tall and lanky man in a checked shirt as her cousin? He just looked so English. He was not wearing a short-sleeved shirt as a Russian man would on a summer Saturday, but had his long sleeves rolled up halfway along his forearms.

"Are you ready?" he asked.

"Not quite. Come and sit down and have some tea and meet my grandmother."

Vika sat Alan down at the tea table and saw him scrutinizing her cramped living conditions. She thought maybe he had grown up in a castle. He sounded like it, with his aristocratic Russian accent, and then there were his highly polished brown shoes with holes punched in the leather. He said nothing to put her at her ease. As she poured some tea, she missed the cup and slopped water all over the table. The charm she had felt on the phone seemed to have evaporated, and all she could sense was his impatience to leave.

He stood up to go. "I've brought a carton of orange juice and some supermarket grapes. We can buy some other stuff on the road," he said. Vika thrust a few more things into her backpack and said a hurried good-bye to her grandmother, reminding her to study her Bible.

As she got into the car, Vika saw a big black camera, of the type used by professional photographers, on the backseat. "You can't take that into the asylum. If they know you're a journalist, they'll kick you out. And they'll never let me back in again."

"But I have to have a picture. No picture, no story."

Vika saw this was not going to be easy. She tried to explain that he couldn't just go blundering in. She told him the staff were suspicious of everyone after the visit of Sergei, the concert pianist. His secret video of the asylum had just been shown on Russian TV. The director had been furious and cut the staff's wages in half as punishment. It was Vika who had shown Sergei how to get there, but luckily the staff didn't know that. She knew it was vital that they not do anything to make the staff connect her with Sergei.

They drove on in an uncomfortable silence. The road was choked with cars escaping the city for the weekend.

Vika pointed out a market by the side of the road where they could buy some food. She led Alan past a line of kiosks selling bottles of vodka, cans of gin and tonic, cigarettes, and Snickers bars, and made for a cluster of traders who had set up tables selling produce from their gardens.

She stopped at a peasant woman selling little piles of cucumbers, spring onions, and beets. There was a solitary plastic cup full of black currants. They were plump and ripe, just what Vanya needed, she thought. Alan said he would pay for them, and, after a halfhearted attempt at bargaining, he handed the peasant woman a wad of rubles, a sum that would have fed Vika's grandmother for a week.

Alan asked Vika if she wanted a bun. Without thinking, she pointed to a pile of spicy meat pasties being hawked by a Georgian man with a Roman nose and bristling moustache. "I'd rather have one of those." Vika immediately felt ashamed for being so forward and greedy. The vendor winked and smiled lasciviously at her, revealing a mouth full of gold teeth and making her blush even more deeply.

As they took the purchases—a sweet bun, two meat pasties, a bunch of grapes, and the precious black currants—back to the car, they saw a notice saying FAST FOOD. Vika had never come across this English expression before. Without thinking, she asked, "Does that mean food you can eat when you are fasting?" Alan smiled kindly. "Now that would be a money-spinner, with all the fasting days in the Orthodox Church calendar."

The shopping trip had lightened the atmosphere. Alan asked what she did, and she explained that she was working as a secretary in a Finnish construction firm, but her real interest was studying the New Testament in the evenings. The classes sometimes went on until midnight. What with taking days off to visit Vanya and studying at night, she had no energy for work. Her boss was losing patience.

"So why are you still visiting Vanya?" Alan asked.

She said only, "No one has ever asked me that before," and no more. "Your article will help him, won't it? What are you going to write?"

"I don't know until I get there. I don't normally do weepy stuff. The principle of the British press is not helping people but causing trouble. I'll just run the story up the flagpole and see who salutes."

"What is flagpole?"

"I mean, we'll see if anyone responds."

The traffic eased once they were outside the urban sprawl of Moscow and started driving through open fields. They could take Vanya outside for a picnic, Vika thought. That would make him happy.

As they got out of the car, it seemed as if nature was holding its breath. The sun had gone in, and the landscape had suddenly gone quiet as the birds and insects waited for rain. The gates of the asylum were still open despite the security alert prompted by Sergei. But Vika's feeling of relief came too soon, as once inside they were confronted by two new security guards wearing mirror sunglasses, like tough guys from a Hollywood movie. Vika wondered how she was going to get past them with this foreigner in tow. But she kept walking, telling the guards casually they had come to see the chief doctor, whose name she remembered. Alan kept silent, and the guards let them pass.

There was more evidence that security was now a top priority. The single glass pane in the door to the children's wing had now been boarded up with a piece of wood, completing the children's isolation from the outside world. Vika banged on the door and shouted. After some minutes a caregiver opened it.

"You can't come in without permission."

"But I've been here many times before to visit Vanya," she insisted. "The director knows me."

"We have new regulations."

"But I've been calling all week to get permission. It's not my fault that the phone's broken."

The caregiver's resistance dissolved. "You can stay for fifteen minutes."

The stench of urine and feces was even more overpowering in the hot weather. Vika showed Alan to the room with white tiles and told him to wait for her there.

"But can't I see the room where the children are kept in cages? I need to see these things."

"No. That would make them suspicious. You have to do as I say or we'll be thrown out."

Vika went to fetch Vanya and brought him to the visitors room. The caregiver was following her. Vika asked her if she could take him outside. "He needs fresh air and sunlight."

But the caregiver was resolute. "It's about to rain. The children are exhausted by the heat and we cannot risk them getting wet."

She left the room, and Alan remarked, "How could a spot of summer rain harm the children? Surely what harmed them was being kept inside twenty-four hours a day?"

Vika placed Vanya kneeling on a chair against the window and sat beside him so that he could look down into the concrete courtyard of the asylum. Nothing was moving except a pack of stray dogs. The first spots of rain fell and Vika stuck her hand outside through the bars, and drew it back to show Vanya. "Rain. You remember rain," she said. But Vanya was more interested in the cup of black currants. Although it was difficult for him, he picked the berries up one by one and popped them in his mouth, enjoying the strong, sweet taste.

Outside, the rain became a torrent, falling so fast that it overwhelmed the drain pipes and overflowed the gutters in great sheets.

Vanya turned from the window and looked at Vika. He was finding his voice again. "How's Andrei?"

"He's fine, but he misses you a lot."

"Tell him I think about him. When will they bring him?"

"I don't know, Vanya. I don't know when you'll see Andrei again." She could not bring herself to tell him the truth, that Andrei would never be joining him. She turned to Alan and said in English: "You know Andrei's going to America, don't you?"

"Yes I know. To a family in Florida."

"He would have come here too, but he wouldn't have survived very long." She told Alan that Vanya had taught Andrei everything he knew. Without Vanya he would never have learned to speak.

Vika laid out a line of black currants on the table and asked Vanya to share them out. He was slowly coming back to life, like a parched flower when it is watered. He had regained his poise enough to hand out the berries, and was now saying please and thank you in all the right places.

"You see he's an intelligent boy."

"Yes. No different from my son."

The caregiver came in with a bowl with some very thin vegetable soup and a crust of bread, and set it down in front of Vanya. "You feed him since you're here, and then you really must go."

Vika asked if they could feed the little girl in the crib next to Vanya's and went to fetch her. "This is Sveta," she said, placing her on Alan's lap. "We must get some food down her. They say she never wants to eat."

She inserted a spoonful of soup into Sveta's mouth. But the girl winced in pain and drew her head back.

"It must be too hot," said Alan. "Speaking as a dad, I know you have to blow on food to cool it down."

"Speaking as a physics graduate, I don't need the principle explained to me."

With the attention of a father and a physics major, Sveta found her appetite.

Alan told Vika he had an idea for the article. "Two little boys in a baby house become like brothers. But their fates diverge dramatically:

One is cruelly incarcerated in an insane asylum in the Russian country-side and the other heads for a life of freedom in Florida. A tale of two boys—that's the way to do it. Even the most granite-hearted news editor couldn't turn that one down. But I need a picture, Vika. Without the right shot, I can't do the story."

He made a move to get up, but seemed surprised to find he was still cradling Sveta. The movement made him aware that she was all wet and his lap was now soaked.

"Vika I absolutely have to get my camera," he said. "I need a photo of Vanya."

"No. That would cause too many problems," Vika said firmly.

"Vika, Vika," Vanya piped up, but was ignored.

"You don't understand the press. Without the right picture, I can't get Vanya in the paper."

"But you don't understand how difficult it is to get into this place." Vika waved the spoon to emphasize her point propelling some of the soup across the room onto the floor. "They could shut the door in my face at any moment."

"Well, I came here to do something for him, not just to sit in a pool of piss." They glared at each other over the top of Sveta's head.

"Vika, Vika. Uncle Alan!" This time Vanya got their attention. They both turned to look at Vanya, astonished that he had remembered the English name. He smiled and pointed to the window. "The rain has stopped. Will you take me outside now?"

Despite the staff's having hectored them to leave throughout the visit, there was no one about when they picked up Vanya and carried him down the corridor. Having fed the children, the staff were taking their break. The only person around was Ilya, the teenage boy with the cross on a bootlace around his neck.

"Ilya, I was hoping to see you today. We're taking Vanya outside."

"I'll come with you."

Outside, the rain had washed the world clean again. Grateful to be freed of the farmyard stench, they breathed deeply of the fresh air. They walked by the ruins of the enormous red-brick church. Luxuriant weeds were sprouting up around its base and tall unpruned trees encircled the building, as if trying to hide it from view. Only the pink finger of the steeple and the empty windows of the clerestory rose defiantly above the foliage.

Beyond the church was an orchard of straggling apple trees and un-mown grass. Ilya wiped dry a bench for Vanya to sit on. While Vanya blinked in the bright light, Vika took the boots from her backpack and struggled to get them on his feet.

"Don't they have any boots for him here?" asked Alan.

"He's in permanent bed regime. None of those children have shoes. They don't have clothes. They only dress them when someone comes to visit."

Vika picked Vanya up, held him under one shoulder, and got Ilya to hold him on the other side. They tried to encourage him to walk along the sandy path. She knew this exercise was fruitless. He needed encour-agement and practice every day, not occasional help from well-meaning amateurs.

Alan's eye was caught by what looked like a trim little hut attached to the base of the church, which, in contrast to the rest of the structure, was in good repair. It was painted yellow, with a smart tiled roof, and a steel door with two brand-new padlocks. A single word was written above the door. It said MORGUE.

"Is that really a morgue?" Alan asked Ilya.

"Yes. And it's one of my duties to take the dead bodies there."

"Does that happen often?"

"Oh yes. Several every week. Including from the children's wing." He enjoyed shocking the visitors with the grim truth of life in the asylum. "What a set-up," said Alan, breaking into English so the boys could not understand. "All that's guaranteed to these children is a place in this morgue, and they're reminded of it every time they're allowed outside."

Alan said he was going to the car to get the camera. Ilya's eyes lit up. "You've got a car! Can I come with you?" When Alan returned, Vanya had regained some of his old spirit thanks to all the attention he had been getting. But the journalist was not happy.

February 15, 1996: Sarah, with Vanya and Andrei in Baby House 10, taken a few days before Vanya was transferred to Filimonki asylum. *(Photo courtesy of Sarah Philps)*

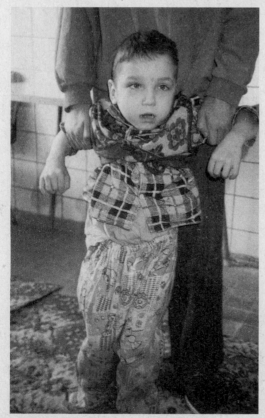

June 8, 1996: Vanya, hastily dressed, is presented to Sarah and Viv in the visitor's room of the children's wing of the Filimonki asylum. He is being held up by one of the teenage inmates. *(Photo courtesy of Sarah Philps)*

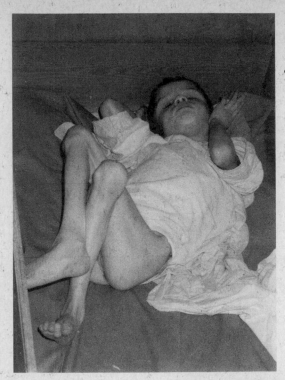

January 1996: Unnamed boy in permanent bed regime in Internat 30, Moscow. *(Photo courtesy of Alan Philps)*

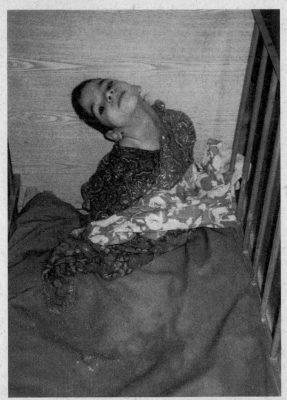

January 1996: Unnamed child in permanent bed regime in Internat 30, Moscow. *(Photo courtesy of Alan Philps)*

March 1996: Portrait of Adela, head doctor of Baby House 10. *(Photo © Dmitry Feklisov)*

March 1996: Anna, the girl who got the wheelchair, in Group 6 with Adela in the background. *(Photo © Dmitry Feklisov)*

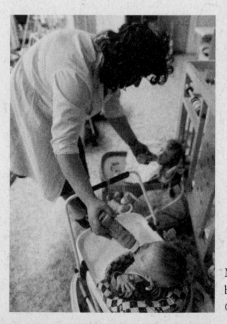

March 1996: A caregiver feeds children in baby walkers tethered to a playpen. *(Photo © Dmitry Feklisov)*

July 13, 1996: Vanya, with a Red Sox cap hiding his shaven head, is held by Vika in the grounds of the Filimonki mental asylum. *(Photo courtesy of Alan Philps)*

July 13, 1996: Vanya makes a pained face as he chews on a sour grape, in the grounds of the Filimonki asylum. *(Photo courtesy of Alan Philps)*

December 20, 1996: Vanya, with Andrei posing with an accordion in Baby House 10. *(Photo courtesy of Sarah Philps)*

March 1997: Vanya, on Vika's lap, celebrates his birthday for the first time. *(Photo courtesy of Sarah Philps)*

April 15, 1997: Vanya with Auntie Valentina in Sanatorium No. 26 in Moscow. *(Photo courtesy of Sarah Philps)*

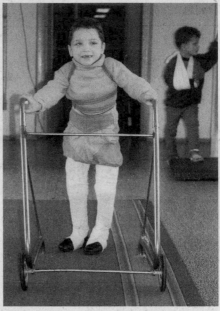

September 23, 1997: Vanya learns to walk after being operated on in Hospital 58. *(Photo courtesy of Sarah Philps)*

July 1998: Vanya on a bench outside Baby House 10, on the day Sarah said good-bye to him. *(Photo courtesy of Sarah Philps)*

August 31, 2008: John shows Alan around his neighborhood in Bethlehem, Pennsylvania. *(Photo courtesy of Sarah Philps)*

September 1, 2008: John on the porch of his home in Bethlehem, Pennsylvania. *(Photo courtesy of Alan Philps)*

June 2009: John and Paula outside their home in Bethlehem, Pennsylvania. *(Photo courtesy of Margaret Sanders)*

"Come on, Vanya," said Alan looking at him through the viewfinder. "No more smiling. I need a sad face. We need to stir the emotions of *Daily Telegraph* readers. I can't do that with a picture of a smiling boy."

Vika laughed. "He's smiling because he's happy to be with us," she said.

"Can't you get him to look sad?"

"Well, he's not suffering at the moment."

"Vika, you've got a lot to learn about the media," said Alan. "Give me a grape."

"But they're not very ripe. They'll give him a tummy upset."

"Perfect. Vanya, have a grape."

Vanya took the grape and put it in his mouth and bit it with enthusiasm. As the sour juice spurted around his mouth, he made a pained face. The shutter clicked.

"Great. I knew you could do it. You can spit it out now."

Turning to Vika, Alan said, "That'll tug a few heartstrings. I think we're done here. We can go."

Half an hour later, they were back in the car. Vika suddenly felt very hungry and suggested they eat their pasties immediately. But Alan was determined to put some distance between them and the asylum. He parked next to a birch grove. Under the trees there was a profusion of pretty yellow legume-like flowers with lilac-colored leaves at the top. The ground was still soaked, so they sat with the car doors open, sharing the orange juice and eating the pasties.

He offered Vika a cigarette, which she willingly accepted. "You're corrupting me," she said.

"No. You're the one who's corrupting me. I shouldn't be involved in this kind of thing. My job is to reinforce my readers' prejudices about Russia. I should stand back and not get involved in charity cases."

"Then why are you doing it?"

"When I asked you that question this morning, you wouldn't give me a proper answer. So I won't either."

"But you will write something about Vanya? It's his only hope."

"I'll do my best. But I can't write anything about Vanya while the elections are on and all these buses are being blown up in Moscow. He'll have to wait." Alan switched the car radio on, to catch the news bulletin.

Once again Vika felt her hopes being crushed. Did this journalist not realize all the emotional effort she had to expend every time she went to Filimonki? If only she had the bus fare, she would make her own way home.

They threw their cigarettes into the soggy grass and, both wrapped in their own thoughts, the noncommittal journalist and the young girl turned passionate crusader drove off back to Moscow.

Twenty-four hours later, Vika was still feeling let down by the journalist's indifference to Vanya's fate, and she needed to know whether he was going to write that article. Although it was nearly midnight, she decided to phone Alan. He was once again the charming Englishman. He said he could not forget Vanya because the smell of the asylum had impregnated his notebook. He had spoken to his editor, who was worried that the story would get the readers in England hot and bothered and they would all be phoning the newspaper to offer help.

"But surely that's a good thing?" she asked. "Maybe one of them will want to adopt Vanya."

Alan said the paper did not want to get involved and did not have the staff to respond to all the readers' calls. Anyway, he had persuaded the editor to find a space in August, when the paper would be short of news.

Vika put the phone down. She couldn't believe that Alan had failed to understand the urgency of the situation. Each day Vanya spent in that place sucked a bit more of the life out of him. She felt she was the only person who understood.

But Alan did write the article and showed it to Vika before publication. She could not accept one thing. He wrote that boys like Ilya were destined for early death, prison, or life in a mental institution. "This is wrong. You should write that Ilya's belief in God gives grounds to hope that he will be spared the fate of the others," she said.

Alan's article finally came out in mid-August, under the headline THE ORPHANS WHOM MOTHER RUSSIA FORGOT. There were a couple of distressing pictures of a boy in a straitjacket and several children with Down syndrome herded in a communal playpen with no toys. These pictures were taken in Internat 30, a grim asylum on the outskirts of Moscow where hundreds of children were kept in conditions no better than Filimonki. There was a single-column picture of Andrei, smiling jauntily with the sun dappling his blond hair. With a plastic telephone to his ear, he seemed to be chatting to his future family in Florida. This was in sharp contrast to the picture beside him of Vanya, shaven-headed, looking directly at the camera with furrowed brow as if asking, "Why am I here? Why do I deserve this fate?" Only the most eagle-eyed reader would notice the small bulge in his cheek where a sour grape was nestling.

There was a big response from the British public. One woman expressed her determination to adopt Vanya, but international adoption to Britain was very difficult, and particularly from Russia, as there was no agreement between the two countries. So the chances of her succeeding seemed virtually nil. Vanya was still waiting for his guardian angel.

By October, Vika had lost her job. She turned over in her mind everything she had tried to do for Vanya. All of it had come to naught. She kept asking herself, what more she could have done? She had tried to get him into a children's home where he would get an education, but they had rejected him. She had used all her powers of persuasion to get Natasha to relinquish her parental rights so that he could be adopted, only to be told that this was just the beginning of a long legal process. She had taken journalists to see for themselves the conditions the children were in, and nothing had changed. Vanya was still enduring a slow death.

Vika had no more strength to continue the fight. When she prayed for guidance, it suddenly came to her that she was not to blame for Vanya's fate. It wasn't she who had given birth to him. She hadn't given him up to the care of the state. She hadn't sent him to the asylum. She felt she could do nothing for him. "I had hit rock bottom. I realized I was nothing. I washed my hands of it all."

All that remained for Vika was to break the news to the baby house that she had failed in all her attempts to help Vanya. She felt she owed it to them, as she believed they too were suffering. Vika forced herself out of bed and poured herself a strong cup of tea with three spoonfuls of sugar. She took it to the phone and dialed the number of the baby house. The phone rang unanswered for a long time. When someone picked up, it was a timid voice almost totally obscured by crackling.

"Adela, is that you?"

There was an indistinct response, but she shouted, "Adela. I need to talk to you about Vanya."

"Yes it's wonderful, isn't it?" said the voice.

Vika frowned at the phone. What was Adela talking about?

"But Adela I haven't been able to do anything. I've failed. I'm so sorry."

The crackling on the line intensified. She could only make out a few words. But she thought she heard Adela saying, "He's here. He's back."

"Who? Back where?" She sank down onto the floor.

"Vanya's here, back in the baby house. They brought him back this morning." Adela continued, "He's just arrived. Come and see for yourself."

It took Vika less than an hour to reach Baby House 10. When she arrived, there was no one around. But there was a loud screaming echoing down the corridor, and she set off in the direction of the screaming. The voice sounded familiar, but surely it couldn't be Vanya? Why would he be screaming hysterically on this day of all days? A woman in a white coat was approaching from the opposite direction.

She gave Vika an accusing look. "Oh, it's you. Perhaps you can explain. He says he wants to go back to the asylum. But you told us it was a terrible place."

Now she could indeed make out Vanya's voice shouting, "I want to go home!"

"Where is he?"

"They've put him in Group 6. Adela's gone upstairs to fetch Valentina to see if she can get any sense out of him."

Vika rushed into Group 6. Red-faced and with tears streaming down his cheeks, Vanya was writhing in the arms of an unknown caregiver. He kept pointing to the ceiling and screaming, "home, home, home." Vika had never seen him in such a state. He was too upset to notice she had come into the room. The baby-house staff were gathered around, their faces frozen in mute incomprehension. Such a display of willfulness had never been witnessed in the baby house before.

They did not have to wait long for Vanya's meaning to become clear. Valentina appeared at the door, followed by Adela, who was trembling at the responsibility of resolving this crisis. As soon as Vanya saw his favorite caregiver, he all but leaped into her arms and sank into her ample bosom. Calm was restored. Like a stately ocean liner, Valentina bore him off in her arms back to the room upstairs that was the only home he had known. All the hurt of the past eight months exploded in that impassioned plea to go "home" to Valentina. For any other child, the silent room of the incurables was the last place on earth they would want to live. But for Vanya, coming from permanent bed regime in a mental asylum, Group 2 was home.

What Vika had exhausted herself striving for had suddenly and totally unexpectedly come to pass, but how? She really needed an explanation. Adela was too overcome with emotion to make any sense. Vika went around to all the staff asking how it was that Vanya had returned to the baby house, something that everyone had said was unthinkable.

Adela's deputy said, "A new law has been passed."

Her colleague nodded. "It allows him to return to the baby house for further treatment and review of his diagnosis."

Vika asked, "What about the other children in the asylum? Have they gone back to their baby houses?

"No. It only applies to Vanya. They've all gone to Internat Number 30."

The children's wing at Filimonki had been evacuated and closed down. They needed more room to house down-and-outs.

Vika tried to make sense of these confused bits of information. It was clear that the exposure of the abuse at the Filimonki asylum after Vanya's arrival had prompted the authorities to close down the children's wing. All the children were transferred to Internat 30, on the outskirts of Moscow.

But one question remained unanswered. How did Vanya escape this fate? Everyone agreed that such a thing had never happened before. It was unheard of that a child could return to the baby house. Adela could only mutter, "It's a miracle."

On the metro ride home, Vika finally understood the nature of faith. "I learned a lesson during that fateful summer of 1996. Even when there is no hope, you must continue working. But it is only when you acknowledge you are powerless that God answers your prayers. Vanya's return was indeed a miracle."

11

A Narrow Escape

August–December 1996

Only one thing was wrong with the article on Vanya—the timing. It came out in August while Alan and Sarah were on vacation in Greece, staying in a remote villa belonging to an eccentric English professor, which had no electricity and no telephone. Alan had left as a contact number the telephone of a nearby beach taverna, where no one spoke much English.

The article came out on a Saturday, and throughout the weekend the dusty phone on the wall by the kebab grill rang incessantly. None of the callers got through the language barrier until Monday, when Sarah was having lunch there and was summoned to the phone. It was a woman from England with a kind voice who told her she had called the *Telegraph* in London and Moscow, and then the office of her charity, and then the taverna, several times. She came straight to the point. "I cannot spend the rest of my life enjoying all the things that I enjoy knowing that this little boy is in a hellhole." The woman told her the photo of Vanya in the paper showed an uncanny resemblance to her own son, Philip, now fourteen, who was diagnosed with cerebral palsy but had effectively overcome it. She herself was a physical therapist and knew exactly how to teach Vanya to walk.

Sarah told her that before she could do any of those things, she would have to overcome the obstacle of adoption from Russia to Britain. It would be costly and time-consuming; it might not even be possible to adopt a child who had been in an internat. Nothing she said could put this persistent caller off. The woman promised to start fund-raising and apply for a passport.

As Sarah put down the phone, she was of two minds. From the sound of her, there could not be a more perfect mother for Vanya. But Sarah had never intended to get involved in international adoption. She was still thinking there should be a place for this gifted and determined boy in Russia, though she had yet to find it. The phone call jolted her into realizing that she and Alan had been naive. They had made him into a poster boy to illustrate the misdiagnosis of abandoned children in Russia and the terrible fate they suffered. But they had not foreseen that this would inevitably lead to offers to adopt him. When she got to know Vika better, she saw that she was a step ahead. She had already tried all the Russian options and realized that adoption abroad was the only solution.

Over the months that followed, the woman, named Linda, remained in the background, raising money to fund a trip to Moscow to see Vanya.

As for Vanya himself, being sprung from the asylum did not signal the start of a new life. He was back in the room with the lying-down incurables. The only change was his physical condition. The asylum had reduced him to a skeleton; his hands shook and looked enormous compared to his sticklike limbs; and his face was deathly pale, with dark rings under his eyes. The good things were the same as before: the presence of his friend Andrei and the love of his caregiver Valentina once every four days. But the promised "further treatment"—the reason he had supposedly been sent back to the baby house—never materialized.

None of the defectologists, speech therapists, masseurs, or doctors on the baby-house payroll took it upon themselves to build up his skills, and Adela never ordered them to.

Around this time, Sarah took to the baby house the young wife of a diplomat who was a trained nursery teacher and was keen to practice her music-therapy skills. Normally, Adela would have fled and hidden in her office at the sight of a visiting foreigner. But today she came right up to the visitors. It was obvious she was in a nervous state and needed to unburden herself.

Without even saying hello, she blurted out, "Life is so difficult these days." Sarah put on a concerned face.

"Yesterday the woman who looks after Group 3 had a mad fit and she went around beating everyone and I couldn't stop her. She had been nagging me for a bonus. She said she couldn't cope, as she has two daughters to support. But I don't have any money to give her. And it didn't make sense. She had just won a million rubles on the cockroach races. But she said she still needs more. And the worst thing is, she might not come back to work."

Sarah could see her embassy friend looking puzzled. Her face was easy to read: Who is this deranged old woman? Sarah debated whether to translate Adela's human resources problems, but decided that the truth would have stopped her coming to the baby house.

As suddenly as Adela had poured out her heart, she clammed up and reluctantly agreed to a music-therapy class. As with all good things in Baby House 10, it did not last long. After three or four classes, she was banned. It was obvious that music classes stirred up the children too much.

Just as Sarah had lost all faith in the baby house, she was stunned to read a Russian newspaper article that portrayed Adela's kingdom as a "nest of angels," a lonely outpost of good in a wicked city, with a hardworking, loving, and attentive staff. Everything the journalist portrayed as positive, Sarah saw as harmful and restrictive. In her article, the journalist, a member of the Tuesday church group, praised the high fence for protecting the children from bums and alcoholics. "To me, the fence isolated the children from real life," Sarah says, looking at a faded copy of the article. "It created a hidden world, where all kinds of abuse were possible, and kept out relatives who wanted to visit. I couldn't believe it when she praised the 'monotony' of life in the baby house as a blessed relief from the hectic, depraved world outside. She even excused the staff for their neglect of the children: Since all the children were 'very sick' and therefore 'doomed' they didn't need medical care.

"It was when I read her account of Anna, the bright little girl who got a wheelchair from a British charity, that my blood boiled. The journalist condoned the staff's negligence in not fitting a corset to correct Anna's crooked spine as Dr. Swanger had urged. She accepted their excuse that there was no need to subject the girl to discomfort when she had no prospects anyway.

"Even more extraordinary, she mentioned that Anna, 'a bright and inquisitive girl,' had just been given the diagnosis of 'imbecile,' just like Vanya, which would condemn her to 'intellectual death.' But she did not attribute this sentence to Anna's being cruelly neglected and kept in a room of silent children. I could only conclude that for the Tuesday church group, Adela—simply because she was a believer—could do no wrong. How different from Vika, who despite her strong religious belief, instantly saw that far from treating disabilities, baby houses created them."

One day in December, Sarah and Vika took Vanya for an assessment at the Center for Curative Pedagogics, a pioneering independent daycare center. "It was not long after he returned to the baby house, and the contrast between the two institutions was mind-blowing. How could this center exist in the same city that nurtured Baby House 10? Here, for the first time, he was being treated as a person. No one was wearing a white coat. The director was wearing a T-shirt saying, 'No child is ineducable.' The staff asked if he was comfortable before inviting him to play with an abacus. They encouraged him to enjoy the feel of the wooden beads and praised him when he said clever things. For the first time in his life, he had a session with a physiotherapist who stretched him out over a huge rubber ball. At the end of the session, he was invited to sit with the staff and drink tea—from a china cup and saucer—

and encouraged to help himself to sugar. What a change from being fed slop in a bottle through the bars of a crib. We got a glimpse of what his life could be.

"As I watched this emaciated six-year-old with sticklike legs being assessed, I tried to imagine how an outsider with no knowledge of Russian state care would react to seeing him in this appalling condition. He or she would be surprised that none of the experts around the tea table was reaching for the phone to call the police and report a severe case of child abuse. But everyone in that room knew the way Vanya was treated was acceptable to the state and not against any law. In state institutions, it was always the child who was to blame for his own condition—he was sick, an imbecile. In the official view, the institutions were never wrong. But we around that tea table knew that it was the other way around. It was the system that had reduced a gifted child to a skeletal invalid."

Back in the baby house, the only people who took responsibility for Vanya's development were volunteers. Vika mobilized her friend Asya to come and teach him and Andrei twice a week. Vanya rapidly learned colors and seasons and Russian fairy tales. Within two months, Vanya had become a different child. Sarah sat in on one of the lessons given by Asya to Vanya and Andrei. It was the first education these two boys had received. That day, Asya had been allowed to use a room with climbing bars, a huge wall mirror, and child-height handrails. The carpet, which looked as if it had never been trod on, revealed the true purpose of this room: It was for show. Despite having spent their lives in the baby house, the boys had never been in this therapy room, and they treated it like an Aladdin's cave.

"I was astonished to see that, unlike other institutionalized children, Vanya knew his own mind," Sarah recalls. "He chose which of the activities to join in. If he was not interested, he would go and pull himself up over a rail, launch himself over the other side, and somersault onto his back. He was always testing himself to the limits. When Asya called him over, he would say, 'Just a moment,' and finish what he was doing before joining her."

As the two boys explored the room and put things in boxes, it was clear they were rapidly catching up on stages of development they had not been allowed to go through. They were taking delight in doing things that a two-year-old would enjoy—being bounced on a knee, or putting things in boxes and taking them out.

Vanya was fascinated by a disconnected telephone on a small table. Sarah pretended she was talking to Vika and encouraged him to join in. But he dismissed the game. "Sarah, this phone is broken," he said. "How can I talk to Vika on it?"

When Asya started to sing one particular song, he stopped his exploration of the room and crawled over to her as fast as he could. He loved to bellow out the refrain: *"I've woken up."*

While Vanya was developing at such a rapid rate, the baby house was unchanging. No one was going to arrange any medical treatment for him, so thanks to another Russian grassroots organization set up by the mother of a disabled child, Sarah got Vanya an appointment with the head doctor of Hospital No. 58 for children with cerebral palsy.

While Vanya was doing his somersaults and listening with half an ear to one of Asya's fairy tales, Svetlana—the woman who had taken him to the asylum—came into the room and sat down at the table in the corner. Sarah reminded her that she was taking Vanya to the hospital in two days. She seemed pleased, and told her where to pick up the results of his blood tests. Sarah pointed to Andrei. "Isn't it good he's going to Florida? Wouldn't it be good for Vanya to go abroad too?"

"Oh yes. Especially now the papers have come for him to go to Internat 30 next month."

"Internat 30—that's a terrible place." Sarah was aghast. "It would be like sending him back to the place he was before."

Svetlana looked embarrassed. "But that's where he's been assigned."

Vanya was listening intently to the conversation. He had stopped doing somersaults when he realized the conversation concerned him. The boy who a minute ago had been happily absorbed in toddler-like activities was transformed into a miniadult who had only himself to rely on.

Back at home, Sarah could not believe that Svetlana had so casually delivered her bombshell. He had barely recovered from eight months' incarceration in one asylum, and now they were ready to send him to another one—a great warehouse for written-off children. This was even more astounding given that Svetlana had been genuinely traumatized by the experience of taking Vanya to the first mental asylum. She clearly cared for him and in her heart wanted the best for him. Yet the idea that she might change his fate seemed impossible to her. What a narrow escape: Vanya would be safe in Hospital No. 58 when the next batch of children were being cleared out of the baby house and distributed among the asylums.

Two days later, Vanya was having his limbs pulled and prodded by the hospital's head doctor, an impressive figure with a bouffant mane of white hair. By all accounts, this hospital was the best in the former Soviet Union for rehabilitating children with cerebral palsy. Sarah thought it would be jam-packed, with children arriving in wheelchairs and walking out the door a few weeks later. It was certainly huge, but there seemed to be nothing much going on and very few people around. There were endless empty corridors and whole wards with no patients in them. Despite the vast size of the hospital, the head doctor examined Vanya in a corridor. He was confident in the way of surgeons all over the world and said he could operate on Vanya. "Why wasn't this child brought to me before?" he asked sternly.

The young therapist from the baby house who had been delegated to accompany Vanya to the hospital looked utterly indifferent at this reprimand. She did not see Vanya's physical condition as her responsibility.

In fact, this was not Vanya's first visit to Hospital No. 58. Vanya's birth mother had brought him here as a baby, pinning all her hopes on the powers of the doctors, only to have them dashed. It was here that she had been so wounded by an orderly who uttered the spiteful words, "You've given birth to God knows what and now you've brought him to us to cure."

The surgeon carried out the first operation on Vanya's legs within days. One would think that he was assured of first-class care in this prestigious institution. Sarah certainly did, perhaps naively, and she did not rush to visit him, not being sure whether she would be welcomed. But a

friend who had a son with cerebral palsy and knew the hospital reprimanded her for leaving Vanya all alone while racked with pain in his
postoperative state.

Sarah called Vika, and they agreed to visit him the next day. On the
way to the hospital, they stopped at the baby house to pick up Valentina,
who had just finished her shift and had put on a smart blue wool coat
and matching hat. Sarah fetched a giant physiotherapy ball, which she
had bought for the baby-house staff to use with Vanya but which was
lying unused in the special room. This huge ball was going to be the
charm that would get the women, the three musketeers whom Vanya
had recruited to change his destiny, into the hospital.

In the car, Valentina unwrapped a gift she had made for Vanya, an
orangey-brown sweater she had knitted out of leftover wool. She had em-
broidered on the front "V Pastukhov" so that it would not disappear in
the hospital. Out of her meager wages, about $40 a month, she had bought
him apples, biscuits, and a plastic toy.

When they arrived, the three of them with their huge ball attracted
the attention of the security guards, who stopped them from going to the
ward. Vika had to call the ward and plead to be allowed in, saying she
was part of a Western delegation bringing important medical equipment.
As they approached, they ran into the head of department, a weasel-faced
little man. He greeted them politely enough. Sarah presented him with
the physiotherapy ball. He disappeared with the ball; and when he returned a couples of minutes later, the polite Dr. Jekyll had transformed
into Mr. Hyde. Barring entry to the ward, he screamed at Vika, "Who
gave you permission to visit this boy? Why do you think he needs visitors? You are not his mother. He has had an operation. No one is permitted to visit except mothers."

As he ranted like a madman, Sarah butted in. "But he has no mother,"
she said. "Vika is the person he loves most in the world."

While the argument raged, out of the corner of her eye Sarah could
see Valentina taking off her boots and putting on her white coat and
hat—her baby house uniform. Thus disguised, she slipped behind the
ranting doctor to go and find Vanya in the ward.

Eventually it was agreed that Vanya's bed would be wheeled out into the corridor where the "nonmothers" could be with him. Sarah asked a passing nurse, "Why is the doctor behaving so oddly?"

"Oh, him. He's always in a state," she shrugged. "We call him psycho-doctor."

From their place of banishment in the corridor, the three visitors could see the ward was full of mothers tending to their children, feeding them food brought from home, and reading them stories. Vanya was deprived of all of this. He was the center of no one's universe.

Vanya was clearly delighted to see them, but all he could do was smile weakly through the pain in his legs. They became more and more gloomy as they began to understand what a lonely place the hospital was for a child without a mother. As they stood beside him, a nurse came to check the cotton between his toes but did not address a word to him.

"As I got to know the hospital over time," says Sarah, "I realized that the whole system depended on a child's having his mother with him. The children who had mothers were given sessions in the swimming pool and taken for postoperative exercises. Vanya was left on his own. Once again, it was up to me and Vika to mobilize people to visit him. Vika organized a roster of people from her church and I found two willing English students who were taking a year off after high school."

But Vanya also took his fate into his own hands. He found himself a new best friend—Elvira, a raven-haired beauty of his own age who was the brightest of the orphanage children in the ward. He charmed the mother of one of the children and got her to read him stories and bring him food from home. But his greatest achievement was to convince the hospital's head doctor to look beyond his diagnosis and declare that he was a "perfectly normal little boy." Unfortunately, for a child in the care of the state, with no parent to fight for him, this assessment could not change his fate.

12

Babes in the Wood

March 1997

Vanya squealed with delight as he watched Sarah and Vika transforming the hospital ward that he shared with Elvira. They pushed all the small tables together to form one long one. He started to feel uneasy when he saw they were dragging chairs in from outside and putting them around the table. He felt he should warn them.

"Sarah, Vika. It's not allowed to move the chairs around. They'll scold you."

Vika rumpled his hair. "Don't worry, Vanya. Today's a special day. It's allowed." He thought to himself, Why is today special?

Vika put the biggest chair, the one with arms, at the end of the table. It towered above the other small plastic chairs. "This is your seat, Vanya," she said, helping him into it.

Sarah placed a shopping bag in front of Vanya. "Now, Vanya, I want you to find the tablecloth and napkins." He started rummaging in the bag, which was full of exciting things he had never seen before. He took out a bag full of floppy colored things and started to examine them through the plastic. "What are these?" he asked.

"Thank you, Vanya, you've found the balloons. We'll blow them up in a moment." Then he pulled out an interesting looking tin. He prised open the lid and was delighted to see it was full of chocolate cookies. Without hesitating, he put his hand in, pulled one out, and took a great bite out of it. He looked up guiltily, and saw Sarah and Vika laughing. "Don't worry, Vanya. You can have one. It's your birthday."

He took another bite and tried to remember where he had heard the word "birthday." It was in the baby house. He had overheard the caregivers talking about drinking tea and eating cake. But birthdays were only for the staff. Could children have birthdays too? he wondered.

While he was munching away, Sarah found the paper tablecloth. It was blue and decorated with cars. There were matching napkins and plates.

Now Vika wanted to show him something. She also had a tin and was taking the lid off. "Look what I've made for you Vanya. It's a cake. I've never made a cake before. It's a birthday cake for you."

The table was ready now. In addition to the cookies and cake, there were apples cut into pieces and bananas and cartons of juice.

Vanya noticed two of the nurses standing in the doorway and eyeing the preparations with disapproval. He started to feel anxious again. "We're not allowed to have food in the room we sleep in. It's forbidden to eat here," he said.

"Don't worry. We're having a party." Sarah followed his glance and reassured the nurses. "We'll clear up everything afterward. There won't be any mess."

"Don't forget to put all that furniture back in place," said one of them.

Vika had started blowing up the balloons. Vanya laughed to see her puffed cheeks and red face. She paused for breath. "You are seven years old today. You've never had a birthday party. This party is going to make up for all the ones you've missed." She finished blowing up the balloon and tied it to the end of his crib. "I've invited all your friends—everyone who visits you."

A familiar face appeared in the doorway. It was Vika's friend Olya, who came every week and read him stories. "Olya," shrieked Vanya. "It's my birthday today."

"Happy Birthday," said Olya, as she stooped to kiss him and asked him to sit still while she tied a little wooden cross around his neck. She presented him with a big bag of candies and told him to share them with all his guests.

Close behind were two other friends of Vika's. The first gave Vanya a marshmallow cake. "Vanya you lucky boy—bird's milk cake!" exclaimed Vika. "It was my favorite cake when I was your age."

But Vanya's gaze had moved on to the next guest, who was reaching into the depths of a woven bag. He could barely contain his excitement as he waited. Out came a wooden toy rocking horse, delicately carved and decorated with wood burning. He would have preferred a car, but he kept on smiling, delighting in all the attention he was receiving.

Suddenly two young English voices reverberated through the ward. "Hey, birthday boy. It's us."

"Barnik! Emilia!" Vanya whooped with delight at the sight of Barney and Emily, the two English students. Barney took a little plastic bag out of his backpack and handed it to Vanya. Vanya pulled a baseball cap from the bag, examined it, and handed back to the young Englishman. "Barnik. It's your cap."

"It's yours now, Vanya. You love it so much I've decided to give it to you." He stuck it on Vanya's head.

Meanwhile, Emily was carefully guiding into the room a beautiful dark-haired girl whose legs were in plaster up to the thigh.

"Elvira come and sit next to me!" said Vanya to his new best friend.

With a determined look on her face, Elvira moved her stiff legs forward one by one like a robot, with Emily standing behind her, holding her hands to keep her balanced and directing her steps toward Vanya. As she approached the birthday boy, Vika stepped forward to put a bunch of carnations in her hand. With great poise, despite the pain of her legs encased in plaster, Elvira presented Vanya with the flowers.

As if by magic, about a dozen children dressed in tights and cast-off clothing appeared. Word had spread around the nurses that there was entertainment being provided for the orphanage children, who had no mothers to look after them. The staff sent all the members of this abandoned tribe to join in the party.

Sarah looked around in panic. "We've got food but not enough chairs." She sent Barney to scour all the wards for more chairs for the beggar's banquet.

Before the children could stuff themselves with chocolate cookies, Vika clapped her hands and shouted. "Stop. Don't start eating yet. We must sing 'Karavai'!"

She and her friends arranged the children in a circle around Vanya, who was standing in the middle, supported by a walking frame. The adults started to sing a traditional song that tells the story of baking an enormous loaf of bread for a birthday party.

"It's this high!" sang Vika, raising both her hands to the ceiling, and the children stretched to their full heights as best they could.

"And it's this low," sang Vika, sinking to the ground, the others following suit.

"And it's this wide," and the circle expanded. At that moment, another abandoned child who had timidly entered the room was welcomed into the circle.

"And this narrow," and the whole circle clustered around Vanya. They all addressed Vanya: *"Loaf, dear loaf, choose the one you love!"*

Prompted by Vika, Vanya said, "I love you all, but most of all I love . . ." There was a pause while he looked around the circle. The children held their breath in anticipation.

"Elvira."

The two of them exchanged grins and changed places. Elvira was now in the middle, still propped up by Emily. And so the game went on until every child had occupied the middle spot and played the role of the loaf. As the circle expanded, more children standing in the doorway were invited in.

By the time the game was over and the foreigners had learned at least some of the words, Vika's thoughts had moved on to cake and candles.

The children were sat down again, seven candles were placed on the irregular circle of Vika's cake, and Vika told Vanya to blow the candles out.

She did not tell him he had to blow them out in one go, and he had never been to a birthday party before. With great deliberation he blew them out one by one. Vika hastily relit the candles, and this time Vanya extinguished them all with one big puff. He was so proud, he wanted to do it again. Vika distracted him by telling him to make a wish and explained that a wish was something you really wanted to happen. She cut up the cake into tiny bits to feed the growing number of guests.

When every crumb had been devoured, Sarah got out a bag of presents, all individually wrapped. She handed Vanya the biggest one, and his eyes lit up as he ripped off the wrapping paper to reveal a car, a green Jaguar, on which she had written his name in yellow paint, in an attempt to stop it from being stolen.

A little girl piped up and said, "Can I give him one too?" Sarah gave her a small package to give to Vanya. Now all the children, who had never possessed anything of their own, were clamoring to give Vanya a present. to join in giving him something, and he made sure to thank each one of them after they had tottered toward him on their unsteady legs, bearing their gifts.

Next everyone sang a cheery "Happy Birthday" in English. This was followed by a melancholic church hymn sung by one of Vika's friends in a deep voice, wishing Vanya a long life. And finally, at Vanya's request, Barney played a tape of African pop.

Vika's dream had come true. The party was declared to be an unalloyed success. By the time Barney and Emily visited two days later, all the presents had disappeared, but nobody could steal from Vanya the memory of the first time he had celebrated his birthday.

Vanya and Elvira were sitting in the hospital canteen at a table reserved for the orphanage children, waiting for their lunch. A nurse put a plate and an aluminium spoon in front of each of them. On each plate was a mound of congealed rice, some overcooked carrot, and a big piece of meat. They were not given knives and forks to cut the meat into pieces, and the nurses standing around with their arms folded did not offer to do it for them. Vanya whispered to Elvira, "See that meat on your plate. It looks like your brown boot." Elvira stifled a giggle.

As they sat over their uneaten food, Vanya and Elvira kept staring in fascination at the neighboring tables where children with mothers were being lovingly fed. The mothers had rejected the hospital fare and brought in home-made soup, meat pasties, and cream-cheese fritters. They had even been allowed to heat up the food in the canteen, and the smell was irresistible. One boy's mother was peeling an apple for him and lovingly popping pieces into his mouth. Vanya and Elvira pushed the food around on their plates and hoped that one of the mothers would take pity on them. There was one mother who was kind to them. She read them stories and even gave them treats from time to time, but she was not around today. After ten minutes, their plates of cold food were taken away and they where wheeled back to their ward and put in their cribs.

"Did you see what Sasha's mother brought him for lunch?" asked Vanya.

"Yes. It was chocolate!" said Elvira.

"Don't be stupid. Mummies don't give their children chocolate for lunch."

"But it was wrapped in silver paper. It must have been chocolate."

"But it was white. It looked like cheese to me."

"If I had a mother," Elvira said, "she'd give me chocolate for lunch. She'd give me anything I wanted."

"Well if I had a mother, she'd make me a pie," said Vanya. "Not a small one. A great big one. And it would be full of apples . . . and . . . salami."

"You can't put salami in a pie, stupid."

Vanya's face took on a mischievous look as he initiated one of their favorite hospital games. Still lying in his bed, he started moving his shoulders from side to side, mimicking the expansive gait of a grown man. Glancing through the bars of his crib he was happy to see that

Elvira was following his lead—they were two important doctors doing the rounds of the ward.

"Dr. Elvira, how is patient Slyozkin today?" Vanya asked, in his best attempt at an authoritative voice. Elvira let out a yelp of delight at hearing the name of their least favorite doctor.

"Very bad," she said in a deep voice, shaking her head and frowning. "He's making no progress at all."

"None at all? But yesterday we gave him two injections."

"Oh, but he's a very difficult case," said Elvira. "What should we do? Give him three injections?"

"That's not enough," pronounced Vanya. "I prescribe Slyozkin . . ." He paused for dramatic effect. ". . . five injections a day."

Elvira was the first to let out a giggle, and then they both dissolved into helpless laughter.

"Vanya, don't make me laugh any more. I need to pee. You know the nurse won't come for ages."

"I'll tell you what. I'm going to read you a story." Vanya grabbed the crib bars and pulled himself up into a sitting position, wincing at the pain from his bandaged legs. He stretched his hand through the bars and grabbed a battered old book from on top of the night table. As he sat up, he pretended to read from the dog-eared pages, as he had seen Olya and Vika do on many occasions.

"Once upon a time there lived a blacksmith and his wife and their beautiful daughter Vassilisa."

"And what did she look like?"

"Don't interrupt. I'm reading." He tried to sound like a stern adult.

He sneaked a look at Elvira. "She had beautiful long dark hair. But one day a terrible thing happened. Her mother died. And her father married an evil stepmother. And she was very cruel to Vassilisa. She preferred her own two daughters.

"The blacksmith had to go away to look for work. They were so poor they lived on the edge of a dark forest. As he left, he told his wife not to let the children go into the forest. That was where Baba Yaga, the evil witch, lived. And she liked to eat up children."

"What did Baba Yaga look like?"

"Her nose was so big it touched her chin. And she had iron teeth that gave off sparks. And her house stood on chicken's legs," said Vanya, repeating the words he had learned by heart.

"So what happened next?"

Vanya looked at the page, as if trying to find his place in the story. "The stepmother told Vassilisa to go into the forest to pick berries. And she got lost."

"Oh no. Baba Yaga's in the forest. She'll eat her up!"

"Yes. There's Baba Yaga's house in front of her and the trees have closed behind her. And Baba Yaga sticks her head out of the window . . ."

"Don't tell me any more," pleaded Elvira. "I know the ending. She escapes. And she marries the prince. And she wears a silver dress."

"How do you know it was silver? It doesn't say that in the book."

"I know because it's my favorite color."

"Enough of that story. I'll read you another one. You don't know this one. It's called *The Golden Fish*.

"Once upon a time there was a poor fisherman who lived by the sea. One day in his net he caught a tiny fish. It was gold and sparkly. The little fish spoke to the man. 'I'm too small to make you a supper. Put me back in the water and you can make a wish.'

"And the fisherman said, 'But I have everything I need.'

"And he put the fish back in the water. But when he got home, his wife told him he was really stupid not to have asked for anything. She said, 'Go back to the fish and ask for a big palace filled with gold.'"

Elvira was bored with the story. "Oh, Vanya. Let's make our own wishes. I'd wish for as much chocolate as I could eat."

"I'd like a cake every day, like the one Vika made for my birthday."

"And I'd like a Walkman like Barney's and a purse with money in it."

"And I'd like to drive my own car."

"Vanya, what would you wish for most of all?"

"You say first."

"No, you."

"No, you."

The two children fell silent. There were some thoughts that were too painful to share. In the hospital they had seen that they were not like other children. They were different. Other children had one special person, a person who brought them food that tasted so good, a person who comforted them when they lay in pain after operations, a person who took them to pee whenever they needed to and kissed them good night.

13
Cognac and Chocolate

April–September 1997

Eight long months passed between Linda Fletcher's reading about Vanya in *The Daily Telegraph* and her arrival in Moscow. In that time, Vanya had moved from the asylum to the baby house, to the hospital, and finally to Children's Sanatorium No. 26, hidden away in a Moscow park. The whole system cruelly ignored all Vanya's friendships. No sooner had he forged a strong bond with Elvira than he was torn away from her and put in the sanatorium. No one told him whether he would ever see her again, or return to Hospital No. 58. The only permanent feature in his life was his support network, which followed him wherever he went. Sometimes it took a while for people to catch up with him, but they always found him in the end.

Linda had never before left the shores of Britain, but she took Moscow in stride. The city was looking its worst. The winter snow had turned to slush, but spring was still endlessly delayed. Sarah and Vika took Linda by train to the park and they found themselves in a forest of birch trees. Vika led the way across a rickety bridge, down a muddy track, to an old villa.

Sanatorium No. 26 had a less forbidding atmosphere than the baby house. In this place, Vanya was in Group 4. Through the door, they could see four children seated at a table eating soup from bowls. Vanya had his back to the door. Even though the little boy was utterly transformed from the grape-chewing, shaven-headed child who had caught her eye in the newspaper, Linda did not have to ask which one was Vanya. She went straight up to him. He turned to look over his shoulder and flashed a smile at Linda. It was as if he was saying, You've come for me at last.

From the first instant, there was no awkwardness between them. Minutes later, Linda was sitting on the carpeted floor, holding Vanya in her arms. He was leaning into her, totally at ease. As she chatted to Vika and Sarah, he absentmindedly grasped a lock of her hair. Vika looked on, delighted to see her protégé bonding so speedily with his future mother. Linda rummaged in her bag and pulled out a pair of sturdy sneakers with Velcro fasteners to replace the pink bootees he was wearing.

When Vika explained to the staff that this was Vanya's future mother, they grudgingly consented to his going out for a souvenir photo against a background of the silver birches. This photo was shortly to be pinned up in Baby House 10 as evidence of the happy conclusion of a shameful chapter in Vanya's life.

Linda's visit seemed to be divinely guided. By amazing good fortune, her brief trip to Moscow coincided with the arrival of a family from Florida, who had come to conclude the adoption process of Andrei. Tom was a hotel manager. His wife, Roz, homeschooled their two children, John David and Sarah. The fact that they felt they were doing God's work gave them confidence to take on the Russian bureaucracy. Although Russia was alien to them, they never complained.

It was the day Tom and Roz were going to collect Andrei from the baby house. Baby House 10 had never had so many visitors at one time. Sarah was first to arrive, bringing the American family. For once, Adela was on hand to greet her visitors. These foreigners were on official business, so no one was going to reprimand her for allowing them in. Then came Alan, who was planning to write a follow-up article on the two boys, bringing with him a professional photographer. Finally Vika arrived with Linda and Vanya, who had been granted special leave from the sanatorium to say good-bye to his friend.

There was an emotional reunion between the two boys, who had not seen each other for three months. When Vanya saw his old friend, he screeched in delight. "Andryusha, where have you been?"

Adela opened up yet another room kept for special occasions. One wall was covered by a giant photograph of a bright Mediterranean scene, with pine trees marching down the rocks toward a calm sea of irresistible blue. Against this backdrop, so at odds with the gloom outside, Adela had laid out a table to serve tea, Russian salads, and an assortment of shop-bought cakes. She bustled around giving everyone cups of tea.

Everything was as perfect as it could be—though not entirely without mishap, of course. Andrei's future sister could not stomach the stale, cabbage-laden air of the baby house and had to rush outside at regular intervals to gulp lungfuls of fresh air. Vanya's new shoes, which had been bought after much tracing of the outline of his feet and faxing the result to Linda in Manchester, had mysteriously disappeared and he was wearing his old pink bootees. And finally, Adela could not quite overcome her distrust of foreign adoption. She confided her doubts in an urgent series of whispers into Alan's ear.

"These Americans look like good people," she said, seeking Alan's reassurance. By now Alan understood that this meant she was thinking the opposite.

"Yes they are. Good Christian folk."

"They won't sell him for body parts, will they?"

"For God's sake, Adela. Why would they do such a thing?"

"That's what foreigners do. I've read it in the papers. They steal sick Russian children, cut them up, and sell their organs for transplant."

"Just look at them, Adela. They believe God has called them to give this child a good home." It was not the right occasion to point out that had they not come forward to take him to America, Andrei would have been sentenced to slow extinction in a Russian mental asylum.

The photographer hustled everyone into position for a group photograph—the two adoptive mothers in the center with the boys in their arms. Everyone was struck at the amazing physical similarities between the boys and the adoptive families: Andrei, with his blond hair and dark eyes, had the same coloring as his adoptive sister. Vanya had dark curly hair, like Linda.

Like many childhood celebrations, this one ended in tears when Vanya was told his friend was going to America with his new family. "I'll miss you, Andryusha," he cried, at the same time enjoying all the attention. The tears soon dried up. Though no one had told him that he too was going to be adopted, he sensed that the motherly woman holding him in her arms was going to play an important role in his life.

Tom and Roz insisted on Sarah's taking one last group photo inside Group 2. The photo shows Valentina holding Andrei, while Roz has her arm around Adela. Adela is smiling warmly, all her suspicions apparently allayed.

What sticks in Sarah's memory is what happened after the shutter clicked, as the Americans were carrying Andrei out of the room. "I heard a wail like a howl of pain. I turned and looked down. I saw it was Masha, confined as usual in a tethered baby walker. Tears were streaming down her face. There was no doubt she understood that Andrei had found himself a family, and with all her being she was trying to say, 'Take me too.' She understood she would never be the center of anyone's world."

In the next few days, everything fell into place for Andrei's adoption and seemed to augur well for Vanya and Linda too. In court, the Russian judge approved without hesitation the Americans' application to adopt, Andrei put up with a full medical examination as required by the U.S. government, the American embassy produced a U.S. visa at lightning speed, Andrei began effortlessly to use English words and developed a passion for Cheerios. His new brother and sister adored him.

Among all their appointments, they managed to video him discovering the city of Moscow so that he would know where he was from. They took him to Red Square and the Kremlin and on a boat trip down the Moscow River. It was a roots trip for a child with no roots. Ever since he had been born five and a half years before, he had known nothing except the four walls of Group 1 and then Group 2 of Baby House 10. He had never seen the city outside nor been told anything about it.

As they said good-bye to Linda, Tom and Roz urged her to use the same lawyer they had used, a young man called Grigory who had been recommended by the American embassy as a cut-price alternative to the big U.S. adoption agencies. Grigory had served on the committee of the Russian parliament that wrote the adoption law and was making a reputation for himself as a fighter against corruption in the adoption business. When Linda went to see him, in a tiny room leased from the ministry of foreign trade, he told her of the stupendous sums of money that went into greasing the wheels of international adoption in Moscow. A big U.S. adoption agency would charge $30,000 per child, some of which would find its way into the pockets of Russian bureaucrats. "Instead, if you allow me to represent you, I give you my word of honor that not a cent will be paid in bribes," Grigory assured her. When Linda reported back on her meeting, none of Vanya's support group realized that in a deeply corrupt system, ruling out paying bribes might be a recipe for trouble.

As Linda packed her suitcase to return home, she assured everyone that she was committed to adopting Vanya. She said she felt he was already a member of her family, and she was worried that he was not getting the daily physiotherapy he needed. She was psyching herself up to be vetted by her local authority as a suitable candidate to adopt, and was planning to involve her family in fund-raising the several thousand pounds she needed to proceed. She had no idea what a long and treacherous road lay ahead.

Ten days after Linda arrived back in Britain, Alan got an early call from the *Telegraph*'s foreign desk manager in London. "That boy of yours is on the front page. If it's anything like last time, we won't have a moment's peace for weeks."

"Don't worry," Alan reassured him. "That's the last time I write about him. He's on his way to England now. The home desk can deal with him then."

Half an hour later, Linda called. She was stunned. "The photo's huge. It shows Vanya and Andrei, with me and Vika in the background. Vanya looks angelic with all those curls." She could not believe that the Vanya story took pride of place on the front page, over Tony Blair's imminent move into No. 10 Downing Street and an intruder's almost getting into Buckingham Palace.

Inside were more photos, including the shaven-headed shot of Vanya frowning in the asylum. At the bottom of the article was a post office box number where readers could send donations.

Over the coming weeks, Linda received a steady stream of donations—five-pound notes from poor pensioners and checks from the more well-heeled readers. All of them wanted to help give Vanya a new life.

While Vanya was becoming famous in England, his medical treatment followed the prescribed timetable in Russia. Spring turned to summer, and he moved from Sanatorium No. 26 back to Hospital No. 58 for another operation. By September, it was time for Vanya to leave the hospital, where he had been, on and off, for the past nine months, and return to the baby house.

Sarah had been fretting for days how to thank the doctors and nurses for looking after him and, more importantly, to ensure they would welcome him back for further treatment. They had already received a physiotherapy ball, and some lucky doctor had got a television for his office. Vika suggested putting lots of $50 bills in plain brown envelopes and distributing them among the staff. The mother of a boy with cerebral palsy said cash was expected from children who lived at home with their parents, but not from children in state care, and tea and cakes would do.

So early in the morning, Alan and Sarah set off to the Prague Hotel, with its famous café and cake shop. This shop had been the height of

Soviet chic in the old days, with its chandeliers and marble floor. Now the floor was worn and grimy, and the inlaid tables were irreparably chipped. But progress was coming. A gleaming espresso machine had arrived and was dispensing shots of coffee into plastic cups. Strangely, the coffee tasted the same as it had in Soviet times, murky with grains in the bottom. Pooling all their cash, they bought the biggest chocolate cake, a "Prague," two huge boxes of chocolates from the newly privatized Red October factory, and some bars of chocolate for the children.

These presents would do for the nurses, but there was still the question of what to give to the surgeon. They were told that he was a man of irascible temper and expensive tastes—and too late, they found out he was a cigar lover. Clearly his present had to be special. Vodka had been downgraded to something you gave to a yard-sweeper. Alan dashed outside, raided a cash machine for a thick wad of rubles, and returned, this time to the alcohol counter to buy a bottle of Rémy Martin cognac. The surgeon would surely think fondly of Vanya after receiving that and welcome him back in the hospital for further treatment if necessary.

Feeling very pleased for having catered to all tastes, they set off to the hospital. The plan was to meet Vika outside, but as ever she was late.

On the third floor, Sarah and Alan walked past rooms of empty cribs. There seemed to be no one around. They decided to track down the neurologist before seeing Vanya. She was sitting in a spacious office dominated by a big TV with the volume down low. Calm pervaded the room, as if the hospital's work was done and every child in Russia with cerebral palsy had been attended to.

At the mention of Vanya, the neurologist actually said something encouraging—a first for a doctor in a state institution. She was impressed by the long sentences he used. She even went as far as to blame his condition on social and educational neglect.

"This is a positive thing," she said. "It means he can catch up quickly."

For the first time, a doctor was talking about him as a boy with a future. Outside the confines of the baby house and the asylum, the hospital doctors could allow themselves to see him as the intelligent child he was.

She revealed that she and her colleagues had got together to convince the chief psychiatrist of Vanya's abilities. "We have upgraded his diagnosis," she said proudly. "He's no longer an imbecile. His diagnosis is now cretin, and he can go to school next year."

Sarah said she would pass the good news on to the woman who was hoping to adopt him. She seized the opportunity to hand over a box of chocolates decorated in the Russian folk style with firebirds and troikas. But the meeting was to end on a strained note.

"We'll have him back in December," the neurologist continued. "Until then, the baby house will look after him and give him daily exercise with his splints on."

"I don't think they will," said Sarah. "He's never had any proper care from the baby house."

The neurologist looked pained. She had never allowed herself to acknowledge this truth about the idleness of the specialists in the baby houses.

Outside her office, at the end of a long corridor, was a small boy, his face lit up by a broad grin. "Sarah, Alan! Look at me," the boy shouted as he made his way with a walking frame toward them. The whole hospital seemed to echo to his triumphant cry. As he approached, he was standing tall, with his legs in plaster splints, his head held high. Gone was the child who used to crawl on the floor or had to be held in an adult's arms. His progress was slow and painful, but Vanya was determined to put on a show for his expanding audience. Looking behind him, to where Vika—an hour late as usual—was smiling beatifically, he shouted, "You can't catch me! You can't catch me!" Inside his head he was sprinting down the corridor. But in reality he was merely inching along, his face distorted with the effort of dragging his stiff legs along, one by one, and pushing the walker forward. No one could fail to be moved by the boy's determined spirit.

Later, exhausted by the exercise, Vanya stood by the window, looking out for the gray Volga that would soon take him back to the baby house. Alan and Sarah bade him and Vika good-bye, and as they pressed the button for the elevator, the door opened and out popped a confused looking old lady in a green doctor's bonnet. It was Adela, who surprisingly had come herself to pick Vanya up. She was in some confusion about being so late, and muttered about having come straight from a funeral.

The next day, over tea, Vika related the strange tale of Vanya's leaving the hospital and returning to the baby house. Adela looked on as the staff of Hospital No. 58 said a proper good-bye to Vanya, as to a real person worthy of respect. Suddenly the mother of one of the children on the ward—the one who had brought Vanya food from home—burst through the semicircle of white coats and hugged him good-bye, kissing him, with tears running down her cheeks. Adela was visibly moved. When she brought him back to the baby house, none of her colleagues greeted him. Indeed, no one said a word to him. Adela was shocked at the contrast, and, for once, found the courage to reprimand her staff. "In the hospital, they taught him to walk and everyone said good-bye to him. And you—you can't even say hello when he comes back." Vika witnessed this outburst openmouthed.

Despite Adela's newfound assertiveness and a $50 bill to ensure that one of the baby-house specialists did her job, Vanya's life was little different. For some reason he was put in Group 6, a room for two- and three-year-olds, on the ground floor. As ever, there was no one for him to talk to. None of the staff bothered to continue his therapy. Vanya's splints had arrived with him, but no one in the baby house knew how to tie them on or showed any interest in learning. Over the next few weeks Vanya's walking skills atrophied, and nobody gave a damn.

That evening, Alan phoned Linda in England to give her the news. Vanya had had two operations on his legs. In the hospital he had started to learn, with enormous pain, to walk; and now he was back in the baby house. The news from England was not promising. Linda had not foreseen the invasiveness and expense of a British home study, in which social workers conduct an exhaustive investigation of the family to determine if they are suitable to adopt. The social workers were not prepared to speed up the process because the child was in urgent need of rescue.

Linda complained that the English social workers seemed to be doing their best to sabotage Vanya's adoption. Her local council was going to charge £3,000 to do a home study, and it would take many months to complete. The social workers were heartless, obstructive, and shamelessly nosy: They had warned her they would be investigating the sex lives of all the members of her family.

"Have you thought of sorting things out in the Russian way?" Alan tried to lighten her mood.

"What's that? Nothing will melt the hearts of these gray clones."

"A bottle of cognac, some chocolates, and brown envelopes stuffed with dollars. That usually gets things moving."

14
Groundhog Day

October 1997

Vanya was nearly eight years old and still waiting for his life to begin. As ever, he spent his days sitting at a little wooden table, in a room full of children far younger than he was. But now he was in Group 6, not Group 2. There was only one child he could talk to—a girl called Julia, who shared his table, just as Andrei used to.

But Julia was more interesting to talk to than Andrei. She could not walk, but she knew lots of things and she did not mind answering all his questions. She used to live with her papa in an apartment. In the day-time, he took her out to an underpass to beg for money. Her papa made her sit still all day. But sometimes he would fall asleep and she would crawl around. One day he fell asleep and did not wake up, and then she was brought to the baby house.

Best of all he liked her to tell him about living in an apartment. She and her papa had a bathroom all to themselves. Her papa let her sit in the bath and splash and turn the faucet on whenever she wanted. By her bed, there was a light she could switch on and off all by herself. Vanya was fascinated by this. Barney and Emily had let him splash water in the sink in the hospital, but he was not allowed to play with water in the baby house. And he had never in his life turned a light on. When Julia heard this, she told him that if you lived in an apartment, you could even switch the television on and off whenever you wanted. Vanya's eyes grew big. And when you live in a flat, you are never hungry, she said. You can have as much bread as you like. You just crawl into the kitchen and get it off the table.

He and Julia had beds next to each other, and their whispered conversations would last long into the night. But when Julia finally went to sleep, he would think about everything she had told him and try to make sense of it. And when he had finished doing that, he would think about all the people he loved and what they might be doing. First there was Auntie Valentina. She was easy to imagine. She was upstairs in Group 2. Before starting her shift, she would pop her head around the door of Group 6 and tell him to practice his walking. She could never stay long, as she had to look after the children in Group 2.

He loved to remember all the exciting things he had done with Barney and Emily when they came to visit him in the hospital. He would tell Barney he needed to pee, and Barney had to take him to the washroom; and once they were in there, he let him switch on the tap and play with the running water and splash it all over his face and arms. Once, he got so wet Barney had to take him back to the ward and find him a dry shirt. The nurse had been really cross and shouted at Barney. But luckily, Barney did not understand what she was saying. Barney was from England, and so was Emily. The nurses used to shout at Emily too, especially when she wanted to take him outside. But she could not understand them either. She took him outside in a wheelchair. The best time was when Vanya shouted, "Faster, Emily." She started to run. He said, "Faster, faster, Emily," and she ran even faster. He screamed and she screamed too. She kept on running until she ran out of breath and collapsed in the snow beside the path and pretended she was too tired to move. How they had laughed. Now Barney and Emily had gone back to England. England was far away.

Andrei was far away too. He had gone to America. He had a mama, a papa, and a brother and a sister. He imagined Andrei in an apartment. He would have a bed that he shared with his brother and sister. But Andrei was the one who would switch the light off. And if he was hungry, he would crawl to the kitchen and help himself to a slice of bread.

He remembered the day Andrei had left the baby house. There was a woman called Linda who had hugged him and brought him new boots. He understood that she had come from far away especially to see him. She said she would come back. But where was she?

Then there was Elvira. She was far away too. She was back in her baby house. He remembered how they used to make each other scared. Vika and her friends came to visit him and teach him poems and read him stories. Sarah was always dropping by with different people, and they were all from far away too. He would lie awake thinking of all these people and all the things they had said. He practiced saying the funny names of the people from faraway. And then at last he would fall asleep.

One day Vanya was sitting at his table and hoping that Asya would come. She might bring him that little wooden ladder with the monkey, which if you fitted it properly at the top would climb down the bars one by one.

For the moment, however, he had nothing to focus on except what the staff were saying. Svetlana had come into the room and was chatting with the caregiver. She had just stopped in at the new cake shop that had opened across the street from the baby house, and she wanted to report back on what she had found.

"Can you imagine the prices?" she said. "More than my salary for one cake. Where will it end?"

The conversation turned to baby-house gossip, and Vanya's ears pricked up as he realized they were discussing a subject that concerned him. The two women were oblivious to his presence in the corner of the room.

"The Englishwoman, the one who said she was going to adopt him—what's happened to her?" the caregiver asked.

"It's at least six months since she was here," Svetlana replied. "That's usually plenty of time for an adoption to go through. We haven't heard anything official."

"And wasn't she over fifty and a grandmother?"

"Yes."

"So what's she doing adopting a child at that age? She didn't look rich either. Did you see her clothes?"

"You're right. I don't think we'll see her again."

"So will it be back to the internat for him? He's far too old to stay here."

"Yes. There's nowhere else for him."

The conversation moved on, leaving Vanya stunned. It was only now he realized how much he had been counting on Linda. She had come from faraway especially to see him, and she had promised to come back. Now the caregivers seemed to be saying she would never be back. He felt a huge knot in his stomach. Had they really said he would have to go back to the internat? It was too terrible to think about. He stared into space, seeing nothing and feeling nothing until suddenly arms lifted him from his seat. It was Adela, come to take him to the weekly service in the baby-house chapel.

15

The Blame Game

November 1997

Seven months had passed since Linda visited Moscow, and there was still no progress on Vanya's adoption. Sarah was at home one day when the doorbell rang. It was Vika, and she was angrily stamping the snow off her boots. Her cheeks were flushed.

"Vika, have you been running? I'm not sure it's a good idea for someone in your condition."

Vika brushed aside the reference to her pregnancy. "I've just come from the baby house. They've done it again." She pulled off her hat and shook her hair. "I'm sick and tired of all the surprises they spring on us."

Sarah steered her into the kitchen and made her some tea. Vika had just had a row with Adela. It started with Adela's mentioning that the medical commission from Hospital No. 6 was about to come to give the older children their diagnoses.

Before Adela had finished, Vika had butted in: "Adela, you're not thinking of letting Vanya go in front of the commission again, are you? You can't let them give him another bad diagnosis. They're likely to downgrade him to imbecile. And then he'll never be adopted."

Children with the diagnosis of imbecile were never put on the adoption register, so it was vital for Adela to hide him away from the commission. Vika then reminded her of her obligation to keep him safe until the adoption went through. But Adela refused to give her a straight answer. As ever, she seemed resigned to just letting events take their course. She complained that she had heard nothing about Vanya's adoption from the ministry. Without some paperwork, she could not do anything for him. As it was, Vanya was nearly eight, and she was in trouble for keeping him way beyond the time when he should have left.

Something inside Vika snapped and she challenged Adela: "So you're happy for him to go back to the internat? And lie in a crib twenty-four hours a day? Is that what you want for him?"

"Are you saying I don't love him too?" Adela retorted. "I'm in trouble because of everything I've done for him. They'll give my job to someone else."

Now, Sarah poured Vika some more tea and tried to comfort her. She reminded her that Adela was afraid of her own shadow. She suggested they let Adela calm down for a couple of days and then go and see her with a Prague cake.

"Sarah, you don't understand," Vika said. "She's banned me from the baby house. She said I can't visit Vanya anymore."

Vika then revealed something that had been happening to her that was even more shocking. She lowered her voice to a whisper. She had been getting obscene phone calls in the middle of the night. She had stopped picking up the phone and bought an answering machine, but it was still scary to be woken up at 2:00 A.M. and hear the ominous clicking and know that a stream of filth was being recorded. What made it more sinister was that she was still receiving these calls after moving in with her new husband and taking on his name.

They sat for a long time speculating who was behind the calls. What could Vika have done to provoke this campaign against her? They could not see exactly what the connection was, but both women were thinking it must be something to do with her struggle to save Vanya. What else had she done in her life to attract attention to herself?

Although nothing was ever said to her face, Sarah sensed the staff of Baby House 10 blamed her for the lack of progress in Vanya's adoption. They had believed that Vanya was going to England, and they had even stuck up the photo of Linda and Vanya in one of the doctors' offices. No one said, So what's happened to this adoptive family? But their manner betrayed what they were thinking. When a letter arrived from Linda for Adela, Sarah asked Alan to take it to her and translate it. Adela had always preferred to unburden herself to him.

When he arrived, he was met by a distinctly sour and aggressive Adela.

"Why do you bring so many people here?" she asked, no longer the scatterbrained old lady. "You torture me. You make me ill. My bosses say I'm a bad head doctor."

"But I don't bring anyone here," Alan said.

Adela wagged her finger. "You and Sarah and Vika—aren't you the sly ones?"

"Well, we do come to visit Vanya. He needs company."

At the mention of Vanya, her tone changed. "Oh, you should have seen him in chapel today. He was singing along to the psalms and crossing himself. He's an angel, that boy." Adela went misty-eyed at the memory.

Minutes later, she and Alan were drinking tea together like old friends. But the conversation took another bizarre turn. Anneke, a Dutch friend of Sarah's, had set her heart on adopting a little boy from the baby house. The boy had been born premature and was considered retarded.

"I'm to blame. I'm to blame for trying to get him adopted. I should never have put his name forward," Adela said, wringing her hands.

"What's wrong with that?" Alan asked. "He should be adopted. He needs a chance in life."

"But you don't understand. The mother's Dutch. In Holland they practice euthanasia. When he grows up, they'll see he's a retard and they'll kill him off. That's what they do in Holland."

She explained that she didn't mind sending children to "Orthodox" countries like America and England, but was determined that this boy would not go to Holland. "I don't like them," she muttered.

While Alan was digesting this bizarre logic that was going to deprive a child of a chance in life, he became aware that Adela was now talking about Vanya. "We can't keep him here forever. At his age, he should really be in Internat 30."

"Adela, you're not talking about Vanya, are you? I've brought you a letter from Linda. She says things are progressing, but it's really slow in England. They have to satisfy themselves that she is suitable to adopt."

Adela dismissed the letter. "It's not enough. I need something official." She said the commission was due to come around any day now, and she would surely get a reprimand if they found a seven-year-old still living in the baby house.

"But, Adela. Think what happened to him in Filimonki. You can't allow it to happen again."

When Alan was leaving, he felt Adela still had something she could not quite bring herself to say. Eventually she blurted out, "I asked the priest to bless you today."

"That's very thoughtful. I'm touched."

"I asked the priest to bless you so that you don't write bad things about us."

As he left the baby house, Alan wondered what Adela could have meant. He had never mentioned Adela or Baby House 10 in the articles he had written. He had only ever mentioned Vanya's incarceration in the asylum. Why after all these months, he wondered, was Adela getting anxious about what he might write?

As soon as he got back to the office, he called Grigory, the lawyer who had been hired by Linda after he had so ably managed Andrei's adoption to America. Grigory sounded stressed, no longer the confident young lawyer who had told the world he was going to clean up the adoption business. Alan asked him what the problem was with Vanya's adoption. If he did not get a move on, Vanya was going to be shunted off to another asylum.

Grigory snapped. "It's not my fault. I'm still waiting for the home study from England. How long have I been waiting for that? Eight months."

"Can't you at least produce something official for the baby house so they can show he's going to be adopted?"

"No. It doesn't work like that. I need proof from England that she's eligible to adopt, and then I can make a formal application."

That evening, Sarah phoned Linda in England to tell her that Adela had got her letter, but it was not enough. Time was running out for Vanya in the baby house, and Grigory needed documents to move the case on. Things had to be speeded up.

It was clear that Linda was concerned about the process. She explained that her local council had promised to complete the home study in six months—but that was already eight months ago. She suspected that British social workers were against international adoption. One social worker was due to come tomorrow, but she had just phoned to say someone had dented her car and it was in the garage so she could not come this week.

"Couldn't she come by public transport?" Sarah asked.

"These women will seize any excuse to take a week off work."

The social workers had been going round questioning Linda's family members. They seemed to be looking for reasons to turn her down. They had blown out of all proportion a misunderstanding she had had with her daughter two years ago. Everything was patched up now, but the social workers would not let it go. If there was any friction in the family, they insisted, the adopted child would be the scapegoat.

Sarah listened to all this with a growing sense of foreboding. When she put the phone down, she allowed herself to think a terrible thought: Vanya might not go to England after all.

16

Narrow Escape (Reprise)

December 1997

Vika managed to sneak into Baby House 10 one evening, avoiding Adela and the other senior staff. When she got to Group 6, Vanya had already had his supper. She took him to sit with her on a plastic sofa in a corner, hoping the caregiver would not tell anyone she was there. She was nervous after her last visit, when Adela had told her she was not welcome anymore.

She could tell Vanya sensed something was wrong, but she was not able to reveal to a child all her worries. Adela was not prepared to protect him any longer, she had started to doubt whether Linda was ever going to overcome the difficulties of the adoption process in England, and she had heard that Grigory the lawyer was in trouble with the authorities and this might cause problems for Vanya's adoption. Everything seemed to be going wrong. And to cap it all, last night she had received another obscene phone call at 2:00 A.M. Only the KGB would call at that time, or so everyone said. She knew she had to give Vanya a big piece of news.

"Vanya, I have something to tell you."

He fixed her with a serious gaze.

"You remember I told you I got married in June? Now I'm going to have a baby." Vanya looked blank.

"Can't you see my tummy's got bigger?" She put his hand on her stomach. Vanya looked politely puzzled. It dawned on her that he did not know where babies come from.

"The baby's in here." She laughed at Vanya's look of astonishment and hugged him. The moment was bittersweet. She knew her relationship with him was soon to change forever. He could no longer be the main focus of her concern. She would have her own baby to look after.

The next day, Sarah and Vika commandeered a desk and a computer in the *Telegraph* office. Linda had telephoned in a state of great excitement to say that the adoption panel was due to convene shortly to make a final decision on her suitability as an adoptive parent. It had taken nine months to reach this point.

She was still not convinced the social workers were on her side; she needed evidence to sway the panel in her favor. Vika sat at the computer and wrote down Vanya's life story. She described all the institutions he had lived in and all the ways his development had been held back. She wrote how, despite his fluent speech, he had been sent to the children's wing of an adult mental asylum, and of the 60 children there, he was the only one who could speak. When he was returned to the baby house, he had regressed to the level of a two-year-old. If he was not adopted, he would be sent to a similar asylum and suffer the same fate.

"I believe Vanya is an extraordinary person," Vika concluded. "He understands subtle things about people and how they interact. He will thrive in a family because he is caring, and capable of responding to love and of giving love."

Sarah had an idea. She got out faxes she had received from Tom and

Roz in Florida joyfully relating Andrei's extraordinary progress since they had adopted him.

"Let's include these—the story of Vanya's best friend, the boy he taught to speak." Tom and Roz described how he had grown four inches in the first five months. He was learning English very fast. In that short period, his developmental age had shot up from eighteen months to six and a half years, and now he was well on the way to learning to walk. Of his time in Baby House 10, Andrei recalled, "Eat, sleep, eat, sleep, that's what I did." More disturbing facts were emerging. When they collected Andrei, his parents noticed his bottom was covered in needle marks. Now they believed he had been regularly drugged at 11:30 in the morning so that he would sleep until 5:00 in the afternoon.

In America, Andrei had been seen by a whole range of specialists, who had ruled out the diagnoses on his Russian medical record of rickets and dislocated hips. As for cerebral palsy, the neurologist said it was so very mild that it should not stop him walking.

"Look what the Americans say about his inability to walk," shrieked Sarah, jabbing her finger at one fax. "Just like we always suspected. They say his condition is the result of shameful neglect. It could easily have been corrected at a young age."

Sarah became emotional. "It's criminal what happens in these baby houses. They get children who are born prematurely and they turn them into cripples. Instead of encouraging them to walk, they won't let them move about. They stick them in cribs or keep them in tethered baby walkers with their legs folded underneath them."

Vika felt Sarah was being too harsh. "Adela and her staff are not heartless, Sarah. It's just that they're overworked. They're rushed off their feet just cleaning and feeding them. They can't spend time with the children individually."

"But there are seventy staff on the payroll of that baby house and only sixty-two children there. What are they all doing? And anyway, if they taught the children to look after themselves—dress themselves and use a pot—they'd have less work. Look at Vanya, he's perfectly capable of using a pot and dressing himself, but he's not given the opportunity.

And what about all those specialists? They just sit in their offices all day, drinking tea and filling out the odd form. Why don't they get up and encourage the ones kept in baby walkers to use their legs? There's a room with wall bars and physiotherapy equipment, but it's never used."

"But they get so little pay . . ." Vika started to say.

"But that's not the point. I've heard that the more disabled the children, the more perks the staff get—like longer holidays. So there's no incentive for them to work with the children."

Vika tried to steer Sarah back to the business at hand. "We need some independent medical reports about Vanya."

"What about this one?" said Sarah, handing her a typed letter from a child psychologist from St. Petersburg who had trained at the Anna Freud Centre in London.

The psychologist had written, "Vanya will successfully develop his abilities only in a family environment, where he will receive love, care, and stimulation, which are not possible within the walls of the baby house."

They stuffed the letter into a big plastic courier's envelope addressed to Linda, along with the secretly filmed video taken by Sergei, the concert pianist, showing the horrific conditions in the internats, including a few seconds of Vanya in Filimonki.

"That should clinch it," said Sarah as they sat waiting for the courier to arrive to pick up the package.

They had done good work, but now they were faced with the next threat to Vanya's survival. The commission was due at the baby house any day. And once Vanya had been seen by the commission, it would put him back onto the conveyor belt to the internat. And Adela would be too weak to stop it. That night Vika prayed for a miracle.

It is only now, more than ten years later, after months of painstaking collection of evidence, that the truth has emerged about what happened on the day of the commission's visit.

While Sarah and Vika were preparing material for Linda to present to the adoption panel in England, Adela was standing in front of ten thick cardboard files and putting them in order. The files contained the medical records of the children who were to be shown to the commission the next day. The file of Vanya Pastukhov was exceptionally thick—he was older than the others—and some of the papers had come adrift from the binding. A slip of paper caught her eye. It was a reminder from Hospital No. 58 that he was due back for the third stage of his treatment on December 23. Adela gasped when she realized it was tomorrow's date, the day of the commission's visit, a coincidence that cast her into a tizzy. She sat down to think what to do. Should she show him to the commission and then send him straight off to hospital? For reasons she could not come to grips with, those two actions did not fit together. She saw herself showing him to the commission, and the letter arriving on her desk a few days later telling her which internat he had been assigned to; and then she saw herself saying good-bye to Vanya, knowing she had sent him to a place of suffering.

And then another image came into her mind. Vanya was in the hospital where the doctors had praised his abilities; she saw him learning to walk, and striding into the future. It was clear what she had to do. She reassured herself that the commission could not reprimand her for Vanya's absence because she could say in all honesty that he was in the hospital having treatment. All that remained to do was to make sure he set off before the commission arrived. She summoned up all her courage to ring the lazy driver and tell him it was vital he got to work on time the next day.

In the morning, the traffic was bad in Moscow. It was getting worse every week as more cars took to the roads. The commission from Psychiatric Hospital No. 6 was driving to its annual appointment at Baby House 10. They were late and bad-tempered, and as the car turned into the alley between two building sites, they saw an old gray Volga lumbering toward them through the snow.

The baby house gates were shut, so the Volga could not reverse. Swearing and crunching the gears, the commission's driver was forced to back into the heavy traffic on the main road to let the vehicle go by.

The commission did now know it, but inside the Volga was a small boy who was on their list to be assessed that morning. He was escaping their scrutiny, with just a minute to spare.

Vika had prayed for a miracle, and God had answered her prayers. Vika, of course, recoils from the suggestion that her prayers alone saved Vanya that day. She points out that at least 100 people from her congregation were praying for him. Vika thought that Sarah was secretly praying too, even though she hotly denied it.

17

The Empire Strikes Back

January–May 1998

The adoption panel met on January 9, but a week later Sarah still had not heard anything from Linda, and she jumped every time the phone rang. Then late one evening she picked up the phone and heard a voice obscured by sobbing.

"Linda, is that you? What's the matter?"

"Yes. It's me." The crying continued. She must have had bad news. It took Linda some time to pull herself together.

"I've been approved. The panel said yes."

"That's wonderful, but you don't sound very happy."

"I'm so relieved I can't stop crying. I know it's not the right way to behave."

Linda told Sarah she and her daughter were celebrating together and had opened a bottle of sherry, even though it was not yet 6:00, to toast the good news. Vanya would still have to wait a couple of months, she said, but now he was definitely on his way to England.

"Linda, I can't wait to ring everyone and tell them. Vika will be thrilled. She's been praying for you."

Sarah spent the next hour on the phone spreading the good news. Vika said she was going to visit Vanya the next day in Hospital No. 58, but both agreed she would not tell him he had a mother until the whole process was complete.

The only person who did not sound overjoyed was Grigory, the lawyer. He sounded depressed and snappy on the phone. "That's good news, but I'm having a terrible time. The bitches are out to get me. They want to destroy me."

Sarah could not make out what he was talking about, but she understood that this was not a subject to be discussed on the telephone, and told him she would come and see him the next day. "I have to admit I felt out of my depth when it came to the Russian end of the adoption process," Sarah concedes. "I did not understand the role of all the ministries and departments and databases and courts that Grigory was dealing with. And now it sounded like he was in trouble. I did what any girl would do in these circumstances and told Alan he had to come with me to talk to Grigory.

"We discovered that Grigory's office was hidden in the bowels of a Stalin-era ministry building. He was just starting out, so he did not actually have his own office. He was squatting in the anteroom of some bigwig until he got himself established. We were shocked to see that the confident young lawyer had had the stuffing knocked out of him. He was unshaven, with dark bags under his eyes, in clothes that looked like they had been slept in."

Grigory motioned for his visitors to sit at the other side of the desk.

"So what's going on?" asked Alan.

Grigory thrust a newspaper into his hand.

"They're trying to ruin me. They're planting stories against me in the press."

"Who's they?" Alan asked.

"Those women—those bitches in the ministry who are earning big bucks from the adoption agencies. They can't stand that I've tried to clean things up."

Sarah and Alan read the article in disbelief. It was an all-out attack on Grigory, falsely accusing him of profiteering from the adoption trade. Far from operating a charitable service for childless couples, he was described as taking tens of thousands of dollars from foreigners desperate to adopt. The article mentioned Vanya, so clearly the author had read the *Telegraph* coverage of his case. Alan felt uneasy because only three days before he had transferred to Grigory's account $1,000 from Linda as a down payment for his work.

"But, Grigory, is it true what the article says that you're charging thousands of dollars to Americans who want to adopt?" Alan asked. "If so, there's a contradiction here. You can't be a charity and a moneymaking business at the same time."

A secretary had emerged from the boss's office and was trying to squeeze past. They moved their chairs closer to the desk.

The lawyer said, "I've got to make some money from somewhere. I've got to pay the rent." He gestured to the chipped wood paneling and a dying plant on the edge of his desk. "I can't even afford a secretary. Besides, my fee is only a fraction of what the American agencies charge."

His show of indignation seemed to revive him, and he regained his lawyerly coherence. He explained that the article was part of a campaign against him inspired by the bureaucrats in charge of adoption. Every year, he said, these bureaucrats got big money in bribes from the foreign adoption agencies. This lucrative business was under threat from Grigory's cut-price freelancing, and they were determined to crush him. "You have to understand," he said. "This is not just about Vanya. I'm doing this for all the orphaned children of Russia and all the childless couples who cannot afford huge fees."

Sarah expressed admiration for his campaign, but there was a more pressing worry: Vanya's adoption. She asked him how he could proceed with Vanya's adoption when he was at war with the ministry.

Grigory dismissed the problem. There was a new law on adoption, and he knew it inside out. Indeed, he had helped to write it when he worked as a parliamentary aide. There was nothing the witches in the ministry could do to stop Vanya's adoption going through. He squared his shoulders and leaned back in his chair. All he needed was the paperwork from England.

Sarah reminded him that the home study was completed. Grigory made a dismissive gesture and said that was only the start. He opened a desk drawer and pulled out a closely typed sheet of paper, listing fifteen separate documents he needed from England. "If I had those, Vanya would be free now."

Over the coming weeks, the press campaign against Grigory gathered speed. He was accused of selling children for adoption abroad. He was said to have taken money from gullible Americans and given them nothing in return. One article concluded with the chilling words, "We are in possession of documents that prove . . ." suggesting it had received a whole file of allegedly incriminating material. Another article was headlined: "Russian mothers sell their babies for $10,000."

Every journalist in Moscow seemed to have become an expert on the cost of a Russian baby—and as luck would have it, just at this time a couple of incidents involving American adoptive parents fanned the campaign. One adoptive mother beat to death her two-year-old son; a couple lost control of their adopted Russian girls on the plane to New York and started slapping and abusing them, to the outrage of the passengers. An unwary reader of the Russian newspapers could have concluded that Grigory was somehow responsible for all this misery.

It took a couple of phone calls to find out why Grigory had acquired so many enemies. Back in February, at the time when Andrei's adoption was nearing completion, Grigory decided to flourish his credentials as a fighter against corruption. He called a press conference to denounce officials involved in foreign adoption for taking bribes, and accused them of keeping a "golden fund" of children for sale to the highest bidder. Grigory had presented himself as the champion of the common man, the childless Russian couple who wanted to adopt but were outbid by the Americans.

Grigory may have been right about illegal payments, but when he poked this sleeping bear he grossly misjudged the balance of power between lawyer and government. The angry and vengeful bureaucracy lost no time in pointing out that he himself was representing foreign adoptive parents—even though at a fraction of the price charged by U.S. agencies—and threw in a thousand other accusations for good measure.

With hindsight, at this point Vanya's adoption should have been taken out of Grigory's hands. But who would have taken Grigory's place, at a price that Linda could afford? Sarah and Alan did not know of anyone else.

It was not until March that a courier arrived at Sarah's flat bearing a package addressed to Grigory. It was reassuringly heavy. It was so precious, Sarah hardly dared remove the packaging. She sat down at the dining table, carefully pulled apart the plastic courier's envelope, and removed a thick bundle of documents bound in red ribbon, with a scarlet seal on each one. She had never seen anything like it. It was like something out of *Bleak House.* She gingerly turned over the eighty pages. On each page were signatures, and more stamps and, in pride of place, a document called an apostille (a legalization of a document for international use), which was stamped by the British Foreign Office with its lion and unicorn seal, at a cost of £62, to authenticate the whole thing. She wanted more than anything to take it to the baby house and thrust its stamps and seals under Adela's nose. Was this not the proof she was looking for that Vanya was going abroad? But of course it had to go immediately to the lawyer.

A week went by before anyone heard from Grigory. Sarah was so confident in the British legal system's providing what was necessary that she had not given the dossier another thought. Thus it came as a shock when Grigory phoned to say he had just been to the ministry and there was a problem. Sarah asked him to come by immediately.

The first thing Grigory asked for was a pair of scissors. She watched appalled as he put the blades to the red ribbon binding the dossier. "You can't do that, Grigory," she shrieked. "These are legal documents."

"It's got to be done," he said. There was a rasping sound as the blades closed on the ribbon and snipped it in two.

While he was butchering the dossier, Grigory explained that the women at the ministry had rejected it because all the documents were bound together as one. He had tried to argue, but they said they would not look at it until all the documents were separated and each one individually bound, notarized, and apostilled.

"But having that done will cost Linda half the money she's raised. Each one of those apostilles costs 62 pounds, you know." The red tape, which was supposed to be the Ariadne's thread to lead Vanya out of Russia, lay in snippets on the floor.

"But that's not all," the lawyer continued. "They say the documents are not bound properly. You must tell Linda to tell her notary that the ends of the ribbon have to be firmly stuck under the seals. It's not acceptable if the ends of the ribbons are loose."

"You've got to be joking, Grigory. Are you sure they're not playing with you?" Sarah recalled a home study done for an American friend. It was half a typed page, and clearly the result of one afternoon's work by a social worker. How could they accept that and reject this report that was the product of eight months of investigation?

These were not the only problems. Grigory sorted the documents into two piles and asked for a waste basket.

"These are not required. You can throw them away," he said, handing Sarah a substantial wad. Some of them had important-looking embossed stamps. "And what's more, they need four more documents." He handed over a list.

The first document on the new list was confirmation that the agency that carried out the home study was authorized to do so. "Of course it's authorized. The home study was commissioned by the local council. If the council asks this agency to do it, then by definition they're authorized to do it." Sarah looked at Grigory. "Are you sure these women aren't just trying to slow things down?" He did not reply.

Grigory left, and Sarah phoned Linda immediately to give her the shocking, bad news. The last time they had spoken, she had sounded elated at completing the legal formalities. And now Sarah had to tell her that the dossier she had so painstakingly assembled had been rejected by the ministry. She tried not to make it sound as if Linda was having to start all over again, but that must have been how it seemed. As she put the phone down, she thought there could only be two reasons why the women in the ministry were being so obstructive. It could be they were looking for a bribe; or—a dreadful thought came to her—they were so hard-hearted that they were sabotaging Vanya's adoption as part of their feud with Grigory.

The next morning, Sarah woke up with a feeling there was something urgent she had to do. The rejection of the dossier was going to delay things, and she had to keep in with the baby-house staff. Luckily, she had just received some photographs of Andrei in Florida, including one of him looking blissfully happy stroking animals in the zoo. She ripped a family photo out of a gold frame and replaced it with Andrei. A neighbor had dropped off a donation of children's clothes. She was just loading all this into the car when her new friend Rachel, another trailing spouse and a corporate lawyer by profession, appeared. She was eager to come and see what a baby house looked like.

Even though it was early April, the weather had suddenly got colder and there was fresh snow on the ground. They arrived to see the children from Vanya's group playing outside.

"I say playing, but they did not know how to play," says Sarah. "They were just wandering around, supervised by Dusya, an old caregiver who was often seen cadging cigarettes from the new security guards. Vanya cut a tragic figure, abandoned in a stroller, from which he was sliding out into the snow. As usual, the first thing he said was the most important. 'I'm frozen.' I got him out of the stroller and started walking with him to warm him up. Rachel approached the children, and Dusya very obviously shepherded the other children away from her, as though she were diseased. Vanya asked to sit in the car, and I left him teaching Rachel some Russian."

Sarah decided to butter up Dusya, as it looked like she was going to be in charge of Vanya for several months to come. Out of the blue, Dusya said, "He's just had his medical tests done. He's all set to go."

"It might take some time, you know," said Sarah.

"Oh, no. It'll be soon. He and the others have got their papers for Internat 30."

Sarah stared at her dumbstruck. "But he's going to be adopted. He's going to England."

"That's not what I've heard. He's going to Number 30 with the others."

Sarah rushed up the steps and inside to find Adela. She was taking her boots off when an officious security guard started shouting to the staff that they should not let outsiders in. "I understood he was referring to me, even though he had seen me several times before. He demanded I sign myself in."

Adela's deputy appeared and told Sarah that Adela had taken a month's vacation. She had left no instructions that Vanya should not be sent to the internat along with all the others.

"Why didn't you tell us the adoption was still on?" the deputy demanded accusingly.

It seemed Sarah was getting the blame again. She had assumed the lawyer had informed the baby house that Linda finally had been approved as an adoptive parent. But this was news to them. She told them the adoption dossier was almost complete. It just required a few small changes. Vanya would definitely be going to England.

As Sarah went back to the car, she was fuming. Adela had gone on vacation for a month and left no instructions about Vanya. It was clear what she was up to in her cowardly way. Without her having to take responsibility, the "Vanya problem" would be solved by his being carted off to Internat 30 during her absence. With Adela not there, all morning the staff had been referring to him as a difficult case and a great burden, ignoring all the progress he had made in Hospital No. 58. They could not wait to get rid of him.

Back at the car, she found Vanya had charmed Rachel into letting him sit behind the steering wheel. They walked him back through the snow, but he was clearly upset to be parted from the car. He complained petulantly that Sarah was hurting his hand: He had learned that he could freely express his feelings with people not working for the baby house.

Rachel taught him how to make and throw snowballs, a skill that no one in the baby house had thought he needed to learn. Suddenly he spotted Svetlana coming toward them and his mood changed. "Why did you say I was going to the internat when I'm not?" he demanded of her, as though he was talking to an equal.

Later he asked Sarah, "Am I going to England?"

"Yes."

"And I won't be coming back, will I?"

He did not know what England meant, but it had to be better than what he was living through.

The sacks of donations were lying in the snow. Vanya insisted on helping to carry them inside. He wanted to do everything to identify himself with the visitors.

Back in Vanya's room, Dusya left Sarah and Rachel alone with the children. As she closed the door behind her, all hell broke loose and the children ran around madly and took toys off the shelves. When they heard her coming back, they raced back to their chairs and sat up straight, obviously very scared of their caregiver. She brought in their lunch, a slice of gray eggy thing and peas. They each got a tiny square of bread. Vanya asked Sarah to take him to the toilet, and she was shocked to see how emaciated he was. He barely had any buttocks. He needed to be fed properly and grow. The boy whose adoption to Holland Adela had vetoed looked utterly forlorn. During the mayhem, the other boys had been bullying him.

"When I got home, I marveled at how strong Vanya's spirit was and how articulate he had become," Sarah recalls of that unpleasant day. "I would have loved to bring him home with me and give him a square meal."

Two weeks later, on April 20, something happened that confirmed Sarah's worst suspicions about Grigory's relationship with the bureaucrats. He called her to say he needed her help to resolve a problem with one of the

Russian documents. The ministry had to certify that Vanya had been on the adoption database for six months, to allow time for a Russian family to adopt him, before he was eligible to go abroad. This was a routine clerical matter.

"It normally takes two weeks for the ministry to respond to the inquiry," Grigory said. "Could you call them and ask them sweetly to speed things up? Otherwise the whole thing will get delayed until God knows when, by the May holidays."

"Can't you ask them yourself?"

"It's better coming from you," Grigory concluded. "Say you're a relative of Linda's—a cousin or something."

"A cousin who just happens to be in Moscow?"

The Fletchers were hoping to come to Moscow in May, bringing with them the new dossier, and if Grigory could get his hands on this document, there was a slight—infinitesimally slight—chance of the adoption being concluded during their visit.

When Sarah called the ministry, the voice on the end of the telephone seemed to be aware of Vanya's case. Perhaps these ministry officials did have a heart after all and were ready to help a disabled boy in danger of being put back in a mental asylum. But the voice remained steadfastly noncommittal as she found herself pleading. "I know the document should be ready by May first, but that's the start of the May holidays. So if you could speed things up a bit, it would be really helpful."

"That is out of the question," said the bureaucrat. "The document will not be ready until the end of the May holidays. May eleventh is the first date it could be dispatched."

"But the lawyer won't get it for another month. That'll be too late."

"In all probability, yes."

Feeling desperate, Sarah pressed on. "But it's only a confirmation that he's been on the database. Surely it's just a simple document? I kindly request you to do it this week. I'm happy to come and pick it up myself. I live in Moscow."

The voice became distinctly frosty. "That's not possible. Everything has to go through official channels."

Sarah was left puzzled and hurt. The thoughts she had been suppressing for weeks suddenly crowded into her mind. Why did that woman take such delight in being unhelpful? Why had Grigory asked her to make the call? Was it open war between Grigory and the women in the ministry? The phone call convinced her of one thing: Someone very high up was determined to sabotage Vanya's adoption.

A few days later Sarah and Rachel went to check up on Vanya again. Winter had disappeared, and it was sunny and warm. Vanya's group had been corralled into a tiny outdoor playpen, with the caregiver, Dusya, crammed inside it with the toddlers. She was slouched, exhausted, against the side of the pen.

While one depressed old woman looked after a dozen three-year-olds in one corner, the rest of the yard was full of adults enjoying the sunshine. Three security guards were sitting on the porch smoking, doing crosswords, and listening to the radio. Every month they had smarter and more elaborate uniforms. Today they were sporting a new type of cap—like a sailor's hat, with a ribbon coming down the back.

As Sarah and Rachel approached the playpen, the little children held out their arms toward the foreigners, saying, "Mama, Mama." Sarah picked up one little girl and gave her to Rachel. She herself took Anastasia, a little girl with Down syndrome who was teaching herself to speak. Dusya gave them a sour look as all the other children wailed to be picked up. With their help not wanted, they retreated inside the baby house.

It was Tuesday, and the baby house was bustling with church women carrying little babies to be blessed by the priest. They were coming out of every door. The baby house had just received a consignment of babies fresh from the hospitals where their mothers had given them up. These little ones were filling the places vacated by the older children who had just been dispatched to children's homes and asylums. This was the great transfer that Vanya should have been caught up in.

Sarah wanted to take Rachel upstairs to Group 2, where Vanya had spent his early years. For the first time, one of the old ladies barred her way. Sarah said she had brought some aloe vera for Tolya, a blind boy who had a serious skin complaint on his face. The old lady said the boy had been sent with the others to the internat.

By the main door, they bumped into Svetlana, who since Sarah's last visit had become a bundle of energy, commandeering the old Volga to drive her around Moscow to collect documents and signatures for Vanya's adoption. At last things were really moving.

"Rachel." They heard Vanya's voice booming from the end of the corridor. He had remembered her name after hearing it only once. He had just been blessed in the chapel, but unlike other children, who were given a single candy afterward, Vanya had two fistfuls.

Outside, Sarah asked the officious chief security guard if she could take Vanya to the car. He responded with a torrent of officialese—"It is forbidden to remove children from the territory of the baby house"—so that everyone should know he was doing his job. In a conspiratorial tone, he added, "They check up on us. We have an inspector. He even inspects our uniform." It was good to know that even if the children were being neglected, at least the security guards' dress code was strictly enforced.

At the end of the visit, as Sarah was surreptitiously stuffing apple into Vanya's mouth because Linda had asked her to get as many vitamins as she could inside him, she looked up and saw the church volunteers had assembled outside, behind a beautiful young priest, who looked like Leonardo DiCaprio with a beard. Holding aloft a pole with a banner of Jesus, he led a procession around the orphanage, with the religious members of staff falling in behind. Easter was coming up, and they were doing the traditional Easter Sunday church procession around the baby house. Of course, no children were included.

At the beginning of May, Sarah started getting anxious phone calls from Linda. She had been talking to a specialist in England who said Vanya's physical condition must be rapidly deteriorating, given that he had been out of the hospital for a month and no one in the baby house was bothering to do any exercises with him. Linda said that she was coming out to Moscow in the middle of May, bringing her husband and son, and they would stay for two and a half weeks and sort things out. This was the only time her husband could get off work, so she would make it their annual vacation.

So although these dates were very inconvenient for Sarah—it was school break for her son William, and her parents were coming out to stay—she agreed. She would arrange their visas, find a travel agent, sort out their accommodation, and be at their beck and call to translate and drive them around.

At the back of her mind Sarah felt uneasy about the family staying so long in a strange city. Was Moscow really a place for a family vacation? Even Muscovites fled the city to the countryside or the Black Sea in the summer.

With hindsight, mixing adoption business with a vacation was a recipe for stress and disappointment. But Sarah suppressed her doubts. "I would have done anything to get Vanya adopted, and time was running out," Sarah recalls. "The baby house was ready to move him on at the slightest excuse, and there was something else. Alan's newspaper was demanding he move to a new posting over the summer. In three months, we would be gone. I had never imagined that Vanya's fate would still be unresolved while we were preparing for our departure."

It was the day the Fletchers were arriving, and the weather had turned rainy and foul. Sarah went to the baby house to make sure that the officious security guards would let the Fletchers in when they appeared the next day and would allow them to take Vanya away from the territory—as they put it—of the baby house.

Sarah remembers that Adela was in her office with one of her deputies, who had just dyed her hair and was wearing a sexy split skirt under her white coat. "She looked me up and down, said I had put on weight, and told me I should not get so stressed. I was in such a state, she said, that steam was coming out of my bottom.

"I told them I was stressed because the adoption had to be completed while Linda was in Moscow, and the women at the ministry were dragging their feet. Adela said naively, 'Just tell them and they will do it.'

"I noticed that Adela was being treated by her deputy as if she was a bit daft. Every time I said something, the deputy repeated it as if to a demented person. But they both seemed happy that Linda and her family were coming the next day and promised to warn the security guards."

When Sarah entered Vanya's group, he gave out his usual shriek and was thrilled when she told him, "Your mummy's coming tomorrow." He wanted to shout the news from the rooftops. He grabbed hold of his walker and almost bounded out of his group to tell the hordes of people who worked in Baby House 10, "My mother is coming and my father and my brother." In his head, he was already free.

He wanted to tell the news to the caregivers in all the groups. What followed was a spontaneous valedictory tour of the baby house, something no child had ever done before because they were all confined in their groups behind locked doors. As he made his way down the corridor, he shouted to Adela, "Give me some sausage!" When he saw the woman in charge of the storeroom, he boldly demanded some chocolate from her. He was oblivious to her disapproving look.

Leading the way, he headed for the group on the ground floor where Anna, the girl who got the wheelchair, used to live. Now she was in an internat, and she and Vanya would never meet. The caregiver on duty was looking after 10 disabled children, including sad little Masha, who had moved down from Group 2. Her legs had become as stiff as boards as a result of total neglect. She too would soon be kicked out to an internat, where she would not last long.

Next, Vanya wanted to go upstairs to Group 2, his old home. The stairs were too narrow for the walker, but he insisted on trying, and succeeded. At the top, he was met by the chief caregiver. She said he could not go into Group 2 because the dayroom was being redecorated. Without missing a beat, he told her they were on their way to the sleeping room. She said that was forbidden too, but he ignored her and, following his lead, so did Sarah.

He pointed out the spot where he used to sit. The table was still there. Although it was not nap time, the children were imprisoned in their cribs and there was no sign of any caregiver.

He wanted to go to Group 3, next door, where he had never been. Sarah knocked on the door, but there was no reply. The chief caregiver told them, "She can't hear, she's deaf." Sarah pushed open the door to discover a frail old lady who looked at least eighty in charge of a dozen two-year-olds. They were all desperate for love and communication, and she could not hear them. They had obviously just finished their supper and were asking her for bread. She was trying to comfort them as best she could.

Sarah's heart went out to her. She looked like an intellectual who had fallen on hard times. She was so pleased to see Vanya. He was looking with compassion at the little ones, but at the same time was so glad to be leaving all this behind him.

"The old caregiver gave him a candy and me one too. She made me feel very young. Here was one frail old woman struggling on her own, while downstairs two security guards, three drivers, and a boiler man— not to mention numerous women in white coats—were chatting idly.

"I could not bear to be in that room any longer. I said, 'Let's go, Vanya.' He was determined to walk down the stairs. But I was afraid he would slip and crack his head open just before the family came to adopt him, so I carried him down."

From the moment Linda arrived with her husband, George, and their fifteen-year-old son, Philip, it was clear something had changed in her. Over supper on the first evening, she talked brightly and at length about her grandchildren. Halfway through the evening, her daughter telephoned to talk over a minor crisis with one of her children.

Since she had been in Moscow the last time, her daughter had produced a third child, and a fourth was on the way. It seemed Linda was seeing them daily. She asked if Asya, the special-needs teacher, would be willing to come out to England with Vanya and look after him while she was working as a physiotherapist. Asya could stay as long as she liked. It soon became clear that Vanya would have to fit in around the grandchildren. Sarah sensed he would not be the center of Linda's world.

The next morning, Sarah drove Linda and her family to Baby House

10 for the great reunion. Vanya had last seen Linda more than a year ago, and he shrieked with delight at seeing her again. But Linda held back, and it was George who picked him up and held him. Having been told his name by the baby-house staff, he had already made up an affectionate name for him, Papa Jora, and was an instant hit with George. The only sticky moment came when he greeted Philip with the words *"brat, brat"*—brother in Russian, but not what a teenager wants to be called. Adela was nowhere to be seen, but her deputy gave the Fletchers permission to take him off with them each day they were in Moscow.

With hindsight, this was a big mistake. No social worker would have recommended spending more than an hour together, given the strain of being in a foreign city with no language in common. But the baby house had no expertise in helping adoptive families. And Linda was completely unprepared for the challenge of expanding her family in a daunting foreign environment.

An hour later, Vanya was sitting contentedly on George's knee in Sarah and Alan's kitchen, eating potato croquettes and baked beans. For the first time in his life, he had a knife to cut up his potatoes, and he called on everyone to watch him. For almost eight years he had lived like Oliver Twist—not allowed to ask for any food, but forced to accept meekly only what was provided. But now he knew that a new chapter in his life was opening up. In an imperious tone, he demanded, "Give me some more bread." No punishment came, only a slice of bread and a firm suggestion that he say "please." Linda sat at the end of the table, sniffing and looking miserable. She could not decide whether it was a cold developing or an allergy.

A routine evolved in which Vanya would sit by the entrance to the baby house early every morning, dressed in his outdoor clothes and ready to go, waiting excitedly for his new family to pick him up.

His social skills improved by the hour. He lost no time in exploring his new environment and making sense of how a family lived. Why were there no beds in the sitting room? he asked. Having never been offered a choice in anything, he made up his mind quickly when offered orange juice or apple juice. He adapted to being with a dog, and was

fascinated to see that children of his age were not always perfectly behaved. When Sarah's nine-year-old daughter scribbled all over the menu
in a pizza restaurant, he exclaimed in delight: "Catherine's a hooligan.
I'd like to be a hooligan too."

Linda had studied Russian over the past year, but it is a complicated
language and all Vanya's conversation was beyond her comprehension.
Although everything was translated, it was obvious from Linda's glum
face that she felt left out.

The weather turned from winter to summer in two days. On the
fourth day of the Fletchers' visit, everyone went sightseeing and gathered
around the fountain in front of the Bolshoi Theatre. Vanya asked if he
could get out of his stroller and put his hand in the fountain. The simple
act of putting his hand in front of the cascading water caused him such
intense delight that it even inspired Linda to join him at the side of the
fountain.

The next day, Vanya discovered nature for the first time on a picnic
by the banks of the Moscow River. As the adults chatted away, Vanya
was silent for once, discovering the colors and feel of nature—the soft
grass and the spiky pine needles on the ground. When a walk was organized, Vanya somehow arranged to be carried on the shoulders of every
male member of the party. From his high vantage point, he sang softly to
himself, a look of utter contentment on his face.

There was panic when someone realized it was already five o'clock
and Vanya was expected back at the baby house in an hour. The atmosphere in the car was tense and silent as it got stuck in heavy traffic
heading back to Moscow. The only sound was Vanya's voice piping up at
regular intervals, "It's still a long way isn't it? It's still far?" He did not
want to be put back in his silent world. How different from every other
impatient child who says, Are we there yet? Are we there yet?

With hindsight, everyone should have realized that Vanya's late arrival would be a big issue for the baby house, but no one was expecting
to find the staff in full crisis mode. The deputy director had stayed late
to deal with a potential case of kidnap. Sarah apologized profusely, but
in her heart she felt anger that the same people who had put up no resis-

tance to his being sent to die in a mental asylum were terrified of getting into trouble for letting him go on a picnic.

The next day, Linda and George went with Grigory the lawyer and Nellie, the *Telegraph*'s translator, to find out what was holding up the adoption. They had a 2:00 appointment with Mrs. Morozova, who was in charge of all adoptions. Everyone was sure at that stage that the obstructive bureaucrats would soften when they met this good-hearted English family of modest means who only wanted to give a home to a disabled child. What's more, Linda had brought a new set of documents with her, bound and sealed according to their instructions.

Alan and Sarah stayed behind with Vanya. He had one of the most exciting afternoons in his life. Alan asked him to help him fix a new handle on the storeroom door. First he was allowed to choose a handle, and then the correct screws. He sighed with delight at being able to investigate the little cabinet containing drawers of screws and nails of all possible sizes. Then there was the pleasure of being helped up the step ladder to reach the lock. Lastly, there was the joy of being allowed to wield the screwdriver. When it was all done, he summoned Sarah. "Look what we've done for you. Now you can open the door." It was a perfect afternoon.

When Linda arrived back, she had a face like thunder. It seemed she could not even bring herself to say hello to Vanya and hear about his new expertise with a screwdriver. She said she had had a dreadful time with the bureaucrats. "You, Sarah, made things worse with your phone call. That's what they told us," was her parting shot as she went to lie down.

They had arrived on time but were motioned by a secretary to sit on hard chairs in the corridor outside Mrs. Morozova's office. As the minutes ticked by, Linda expressed her resentment at being kept waiting. She told Nellie about all the sacrifices they had had to make. They had scrimped and saved for almost two years, they had put up with the indignities of the home study, even answering the most intrusive questions about their personal lives, and cleared out some of their prized possessions—including George's collection of rugby videos—to make room for Vanya. She had brought her family to Moscow, using up her husband's precious vacation time and forcing her teenage son Philip to spend two weeks in a place where there was nothing for him to do. By coming to Moscow, she was letting down her elderly physiotherapy clients, and now there was a strong chance they might think she was unreliable and turn to someone else.

After thirty minutes of waiting, the door to the office opened and there emerged a regal figure. Mrs. Morozova was dressed in a navy blue suit, a starched white blouse, and had an Hermès scarf draped around her neck. Her fingers were weighed down with gold rings, and her sleek dark hair was immaculately coiffed.

She looked down the line of the petitioners, and an expression of distaste crossed her face when she spotted Grigory, who was looking very crumpled, his hair unwashed and his face tinged with a sickly pallor. Mrs. Morozova barked a sentence at Grigory, turned on her heels, and marched off down the corridor.

Nellie was embarrassed at having to translate Mrs. Morozova's words. She was going for her lunch and they would have to wait.

Linda was boiling with indignation. She asked Nellie why this woman felt she could treat them this way. Didn't she realize they had come all the way from England to adopt a child who would otherwise be abandoned in a mental asylum? What sort of heartless creature was she?

They had plenty of time to ponder these questions. It was over an hour before Mrs. Morozova returned. The sumptuous decor of the bureaucrat's office—the highly polished dark wood desk with matching glass-fronted cabinet, the giant television in one corner, and a glass dish of chocolates on a lace cloth—made a strong impression on Nellie. The contrast with her own miserable workstation in the *Telegraph* office could not be more complete.

Mrs. Morozova offered no apology for keeping them waiting for so long. Grigory asked if she had received the letter of confirmation that Sarah had tried to speed up more than a month before.

With malice in her eyes, she said she did not take kindly to interference by outsiders in official business. As a lesson to Grigory and his clients, she had delayed the process. What is more, the new dossier sent from England was still wholly inadequate. The British authorities did not know how to compile a dossier to an acceptable standard. In due course, she would advise them of the number of documents that needed to be resubmitted. With a wave of her glittering hand, she signaled that the meeting was at an end.

Grigory recalls his impression of that afternoon with clarity. "Mrs. Morozova wanted to crush Linda. She wanted to beat out of her any desire to adopt a Russian child."

They all left utterly deflated. Linda was angry at Grigory. Why had he not stood up to the bullying woman? How could it be that documents assembled with so much pain and expense were so woefully inadequate? Her frustration was intensified by having to talk to him through a translator. On the pavement outside the office building, they parted in silence, Grigory walking in one direction to the metro and the Fletchers and Nellie climbing into their car.

Despite her humiliation, two days later Linda pulled herself together and organized a birthday party for her husband. Everyone was invited— Alan, Sarah, and Catherine, Nellie from the *Telegraph* office, and even the dog. With Vanya on the sofa beside her, Linda smiled happily as she distributed pieces of gooey cake decorated with fluorescent green and orange flowers. She had allowed Vanya to make her a crown with some tinsel that he had come across in a box of Christmas decorations. "Vanya's holding a celebration for Daddy's birthday," she announced.

On that afternoon, it seemed Vanya had at last found his place in the world. Encircled by his new family and friends, he sat contentedly at the coffee table, eating his cake with a fork, sipping his tea, and joking with the adults. You would never have known he had lived in institutions since he was a baby. Suddenly, without a change of tone in his voice, he announced: "I cried, you know. My tears spurted out all over the floor. But do you know what I did?"

"What did you do, Vanya?" someone asked softly.

"I jumped, just like a cat. I jumped right out of my crib. Then I turned the tap on. I turned the water on full. And I put my bottom in the water and I cleaned myself."

The assembled adults tut-tutted and steered him away from lavatory talk. But with hindsight it is clear he was recalling his time in Filimonki when he was forced to lie for hours in his own filth. His keenest desire was to escape from his cot and wash himself.

The tea party ended with Nellie and Philip teaching Vanya to walk on the crutches that Linda had brought from England. When he was tired he begged to be allowed to operate the video so he could see his friend Andrei visiting a zoo in Florida. The adults checked their watches. There was still an hour to go before he had to be returned to Baby House 10.

After the party things took a turn for the worse. The next day, Linda complained that Vanya had turned aggressive and had lashed out at her son, Philip. Sarah summoned a friend, Ann, recently arrived in Moscow, who was an adoptive parent herself and ran a support group for adoptive parents back in Britain. Linda poured her heart out to Ann. Vanya was uncontrollable when he was with them. She was finding his tantrums impossible to deal with. She was worried about the effect his extreme behavior would have on her grandchildren. This was the first time that anyone had complained about Vanya. On the contrary, he had melted the heart of Nellie, who had inspired fear in generations of *Telegraph* correspondents. He sat on her knee for hours while she lovingly taught him how to work the mouse on her computer. To this day, Sarah's mother talks about how she taught him to use a vacuum cleaner and how quickly he had learned to say Hoover. In those two weeks he learned twenty-seven English words and phrases.

One morning, the office car and driver were ready as usual to take Linda to collect Vanya from the baby house. Nine o'clock passed, and at Sarah's house, there was still no sign of Linda. Ten o'clock passed. The thought of Vanya, sitting on his little chair by the entrance to the baby house, ready for the day's adventures, waiting for the couple who had told him to call them Mummy and Daddy, was unbearable. Sarah's children, William and Catherine, who had also grown very fond of Vanya, begged her to go and collect him; but Vanya was Linda's responsibility, and Sarah could not interfere.

Finally, at 11:00, Linda came in for her breakfast. She said she was exhausted, needed a break, and wanted to spend the day buying souvenirs. She did not mention Vanya.

The next day, Linda took Vanya to a shoe shop to buy him some sturdy boots. She was able to do practical tasks; but as the days passed, she grew more cold and critical of the boy and left him increasingly often with her hosts and the *Telegraph* staff, saying she was feeling unwell. George, who had so enjoyed being called Papa, took a cue from his wife and also withdrew the demonstration of his affection.

Vika pitched in and, despite having a baby at her breast, organized a tea party for Linda to meet all her friends who had been visiting Vanya. They all spoke in glowing terms of the progress he had made and of his loving nature. Sarah could see Linda looking increasingly ill at ease. Sarah wondered if all this praise only highlighted Linda's apparent inability to bond with the boy.

When the day came for their return, they made one final visit to the baby house. Alan went as translator, because Linda seemed uncomfortable with Sarah's ability to communicate with Vanya when she could not. Linda's parting words were these: She told him she loved him. She would return when a court date was set for the adoption hearing and bring him back to a new life in England. Vanya wanted to hear more about the room she was preparing for him. He asked her to tell him one more time about the bedside light, and to confirm that he would be able to switch it on and off himself. She embraced him for the first time in days, and left Vanya with his heart full of hope.

As she climbed into the car that was to take her to the airport, she was smiling at last. On her knees were two cakes, which she was taking as souvenirs of Russia.

Throughout the final days of her visit, Sarah had wanted to ask her bluntly, "Do you really want Vanya? It seems to us you feel a lot of antagonism toward him." But Sarah never said it. Thinking back, she says, "I am trying to work out why I kept silent while her behavior got worse and worse. Although her actions spoke otherwise, she insisted she was committed to the adoption. She had fought hard and gone through many hoops to get this far. The key issue was, what was Vanya's alternative? A slow death in a crib in an asylum. Perhaps that's why I said nothing. Linda was his only way out."

18
Christmas Pudding in July

July 1998

There was no word from Linda after she left. She did not call to say she and her family had got home safely. Nor did she call to ask after Vanya. There was just silence. But then, more than two weeks after Linda's humiliating meeting with Mrs. Morozova, the Russian bureaucracy ground into action and presented the latest list of demands—five more documents that Linda had to find.

Sarah tried for six days to get hold of Linda to tell her what was required of her, but her answering machine was always on. She kept dialing while furiously sorting out her family's possessions, which had accumulated over four years in Moscow. The packers were about to descend, and she knew from past experience they would sweep through the apartment like a tornado.

When she finally got hold of Linda, she tried her best to be upbeat.

"You're not going to believe this, Linda, but they're still harping on about the agency that did your home study."

"I thought we'd done that already," Linda snapped.

"Well now they need a document confirming the qualifications of the social worker who wrote it. Notarized and apostilled, of course."

"Of course."

"And there's still the problem of proving your earnings. They can't understand what self-employed means. Now they are suggesting that the social worker write a letter saying the information they got previously was incorrect, and you are in fact a nonworking housewife."

Sarah hurried on to the next point. "They are implying that the British Department of Health is incompetent. They say the legislation on adoption they provided is wrong. They want to see specific legislation on international adoption."

"Well what exactly do they want?"

"Grigory says any page will do so long as it seems to be on the subject." Linda had clearly heard enough, but Sarah had no choice but to finish the list.

"They also want a commitment from the local council to provide regular progress reports on the adoption. Can you believe this? Two years ago these same bureaucrats had been happy to lock him away in a place where no one gave a damn whether he lived or died."

There was silence on the end of phone, but there was still one more demand. She needed to get a new police report. The original one had been provided a year before and the Russians considered it out of date. This did provoke a response.

"Scotland Yard said it was valid for three years. Is that not good enough for them?"

"Maybe they think you've become gangsters." She heard a slight laugh.

"These demands could go on and on." Linda sounded exasperated. "This just proves that those women hate Grigory. They are taking revenge on him. I saw it with my own eyes. It could go on and on."

"I know this is hell. But look how well you dealt with British bureau-cracy. You can do the same with the Russians. I know you can." Linda refused to be buoyed up. She said she was exhausted. The cost of mak-ing and remaking the dossier had already eaten up all the money she had raised.

She did however find the strength to get hold of one of the docu-ments, confirmation of the social worker's qualifications. She drove through rush-hour traffic all the way to the airport to make sure it got to Moscow speedily. After that, she said she needed a break and could not do any more, but she vowed she was still committed to the adoption. Then there was silence again for two weeks.

Sarah and Alan's departure date was looming, and there were a mil-lion loose ends to tie up. Sarah was visiting Vanya as often as she could, doing what Adela's staff should have been doing—helping him to prac-tice walking and climbing ladders and having conversations with him and keeping his spirits up. He never stopped asking when the court date was going to be and when he was going to join his family in England.

One day Sarah brought him a lollipop.

"Can I crunch it?" he asked. Sarah said yes.

"No, you're wrong. Linda says I'm not allowed to crunch lollipops."

Linda was the center of his universe, the focus of his hopes, and a source of authority. She had not given him love, but she had shown him boundaries, and these he clung to.

"Call her, Sarah, and tell her I miss her, I miss her so much."

Sarah explained that Linda was having difficulty assembling all the adoption documents.

Vanya hung on her every word. "I keep thinking, how can I help Mummy? I wish all those documents could be ready by tomorrow. And if not tomorrow, then the day after." Vanya paused. "And then I will make a dossier for Julia so she can leave too."

It was clear he was turning over in his mind all that had happened during Linda's visit. Her absences, when she was said to be ill, were some-thing he still puzzled over. "Do you remember, she kept getting ill and then she got better all on her own?"

By contrast, back in England, Linda seemed to be focused entirely on her grandchildren and son. When Sarah finally got hold of her, she did not even ask a single question about Vanya or express any concern for him. She only talked about her family and her job.

Luckily, just when Sarah felt she could not cope on her own, three women with the right expertise came to the rescue. First there was Rachel, the clear-thinking lawyer and negotiator who had met Vanya twice and fallen for his charms. She immediately volunteered to hold Linda's hand in the struggle to get the documents. Crucially, she offered to be the one to phone Linda.

Then there was Ann, the social worker who had listened so patiently to Linda's complaints. She agreed to come to the baby house to give a professional opinion on Vanya's state of mind. She was able to confirm that Vanya was becoming traumatized at the lack of certainty over when he would be adopted. She said the lack of correspondence from the Fletchers to Vanya was worrying.

Finally there was Mary, an American psychologist and expert in adoption and fostering who zoomed around Russia like Batman, with a young Russian lawyer named Igor as her Robin, organizing medical visas for children in orphanages to go to America. She seemed to have superhero powers. Her visa had long run out, but she breezed through all the police document checks by pretending not to understand what they wanted until they gave up and let her go. Sarah bumped into Mary when they were both visiting Elvira, Vanya's friend from the hospital. She immediately offered to help with Vanya.

Just as Vanya's new support committee had worked out how to get hold of all the extra documents, Grigory telephoned. The packers descended and were all over the apartment like a plague of locusts. They were a miracle of efficiency but seemed to work without thinking. They almost packed up a dirty ashtray, butts and all.

Grigory dropped a bombshell. "I've got a court date," he announced with a new tone of authority in his voice. "The adoption hearing will be on July 7."

Sarah was stunned. "How on earth did you do that? It's a miracle."

"I've fallen out with those women in the ministry. They were never going to let the adoption go through. So now I'm moving to Plan B. I've bypassed them and gone straight to the judge."

Out of the corner of her eye, Sarah could see one of the packers loading her heaviest Le Creuset saucepan into a box full of glassware.

"But, Grigory, that date's only twelve days away. I don't think the extra documents will be ready in time."

"That doesn't matter. Forget them. The judge doesn't need them."

"But for God's sake, we've been moving heaven and earth to get hold of them, and now you say they're not necessary."

"Correct. It was those women who demanded the documents. The judge is in charge now, and she says she doesn't need them."

It all seemed too good to be true. How could these obstructive bureaucrats just be written out of the script, as in a comic strip? Grigory insisted the law was on his side. The judge was insistent on one thing only: Both adoptive parents had to be present at the hearing. If one was absent, it would be adjourned. Grigory told Sarah it was her job to convey this in the strongest terms to the Fletchers.

Sarah left a message on Linda's answering machine to give the amazing news of Grigory's coup. A court date had been set and the obstructive bureaucrats had been short-circuited. The hearing would just be a formality—the judge had already approved the documents. All her problems were over. All that she and George needed to do was to come out and attend the hearing. Then they could take Vanya home.

Sarah left the message in the morning, English time. There was no response all day, nor the next day. When she finally managed to get hold of her in the evening of the next day, Linda acknowledged that she had heard the message, but made it clear she did not want to talk. She was packing to go away for the weekend, as she needed a break. She would be back on Monday. That night Sarah confided to her diary her worst fear: Linda was not going to adopt Vanya.

Monday turned out to be a decisive day. The new, dynamic Grigory fired off a fax to Linda. Only two days before, the president of Russia had signed into law a new requirement that both adoptive parents attend the court hearing. That morning, Grigory had spoken to the judge, who had reminded him that the hearing would be adjourned if both parents did not appear in court. The judge had stressed that there was no way of getting around this requirement. Meanwhile, Alan persuaded British Airways to give the Fletchers free tickets to attend the court hearing and take Vanya home.

This time, they did not have to wait long for a reply. The fax machine burst into life just after 6:00 in the evening. It was a handwritten letter from Linda to the court. She said her eighteen-month-old granddaughter had broken her leg, and she had been assisting her daughter with looking after the other children. Additionally, as a self-employed person, she could not afford to cancel clients' appointments at short notice, as she had done when she came to visit Vanya in May. She would have to bring her fifteen-year-old son with her to Moscow, disrupting his education and adding further expense. She said she was ready to provide her husband with a power of attorney to represent her at the court hearing.

Vanya's support team found these excuses pathetic—the sort of reasons you gave for not attending a social occasion, not a once-in-a-lifetime event where the fate of a child was in the balance. Grigory snorted when he heard them. Clearly the family could no longer cope with this adoption.

Two days later, British Airways called wanting to know whether the Fletcher family was going to take up the offer of free tickets. They needed to know by noon British time. Rachel was deputized to contact Linda and tell her that it was decision time. As usual, she had to leave a message on the answering machine.

Linda's response a few hours later was full of bitterness and hurt. She refused to believe there was a deadline for the BA tickets. It was just a way of putting pressure on her. All her reasons for not coming to Moscow were valid and she had always said she could only come in September. It was midsummer, and all the kennels were full and there was no room for her dog. Her granddaughter was having trouble with the cast on her leg. Her husband would lose his job if he took more time off work. She felt she had been stripped naked by the home study, and there had been no time for those psychological wounds to heal. But despite all the delays, expenses, obstacles, her pain and suffering, and the pressure she was being put under, she said she was still committed to the adoption.

This response only complicated matters. She was not going to come to the hearing, but she was going ahead with the adoption. It made no sense.

Late that evening, a crisis meeting convened around Sarah's kitchen table to talk through what was happening and decide on a course of action. Mary, who had crossed the whole of Russia organizing adoptions of abandoned children and had adopted eight of her own, was clearly the expert. She was leaving the next morning to go back to the U.S., so she had to think fast.

The packers had stripped the kitchen bare, but Sarah found a Christmas pudding abandoned on a high shelf. They ate it with sour cream and lots of coffee.

Mary explained that the most important thing in any adoption was the bond between mother and child. If this worked, then everything else fell into place. So it was important to understand the motives of adoptive mothers. She took a piece of paper and divided it into two columns representing the two types of adoptive mother. Under Column A she wrote "selfish" and "I have a need and this child can fill it." Under Column B, she wrote, "selfless" and "This child has a need and I can fill it."

The Column B mothers were preferable: they had space in their hearts and their homes and their bank balances to help a needy child. Adoption was most likely to succeed with these mothers.

It was more problematical with mothers who were themselves needy and desired a child to validate themselves in some way. These were the mothers in Column A. To be honest, Mary said, everyone's motives were mixed. Sometimes it was hard to tell whether a mother was more type A or type B.

When Linda came on her first visit, she appeared to fall solidly into column B. She had all the skills to look after Vanya and was ready to open up her family to him. But when she came back a year later, she looked more and more as if she had drifted toward Column A.

"So what happened in that year to change her?" Mary asked, looking at Sarah, who said, "She never stops talking about her granddaughters now. She never mentioned them on her first visit."

"Why was that?"

"There had been some kind of falling out." Suddenly she got it. "But she got back on good terms with all members of her family."

"So there was a reconciliation?"

"Yes."

"There's your answer," said Mary. "Her need to adopt had disappeared. She now has her hands full with her granddaughters. She does not need him any longer."

Sarah recalled something she had done in May and felt guilty. She told Mary she had encouraged Vanya to show affection to Linda, and it had not been returned. Mary was not surprised. "He could not meet needs that were not there."

Rachel joined in. "You've forgotten something. Linda had not foreseen the effect that adopting Vanya would have on her teenage son. When she brought him out to Moscow, it was obvious Philip felt unhappy at being replaced."

"So why is she still saying she wants to continue?"

"They've committed a lot to this. They do not want to fail Vanya. But in their hearts, they no longer want to pursue it. It's become too difficult for them."

Ann suggested it would help to look at things from Linda's point of view. When she read Alan's article in the *Telegraph*, Linda thought she was responding to an appeal for help. So she felt it was Alan's duty to smooth the way for her and sort out all the problems that arose.

"But we had no choice but to help her," Sarah interjected. "She was so determined. And she couldn't afford an adoption agency."

"Yes, but look at the consequences of what you did," agreed Rachel. "Without you, they would not have got as far as they've got. They had an unrealistic idea of their own capabilities. In fact, when confronted with the obstacles, they don't really have the resources, the physical strength, or the time."

The question was what to do next. Sarah found a dusty bottle of blue liqueur, the last remains of the liquor cabinet, and offered it around.

Rachel advised that Sarah and Alan should do nothing more for the Fletchers. The best thing that could happen would be that neither of them turned up for the court hearing. There would be no adequate explanation, and that would be the end of it.

The issue now was Vanya's future. Rachel told the others about an idea that could save him from the asylum. She was going to approach Maria, a farsighted and highly motivated young Russian woman who had started up Russia's first foster-parent project. This was a historic initiative, literally the first attempt to stem the tide of children entering state institutions. Maria had never taken a child into her project who could not walk, and it was far from certain she would be allowed to take Vanya. But if she did accept him, he would get medical care in a home environment, and his foster mother would be paid and given support by a specialist team.

"It would be the perfect solution," said Ann.

"But hold on," said Rachel. "He can't be fostered so long as the adoption process is unresolved. If this is going to happen, Linda has to be persuaded to pull out."

The American psychologist Mary volunteered for this task. Alan gave her an international phone card and asked her to call Linda from the States. She said she would do it in any spare moments she had while organizing her daughter's wedding.

By now it was 3:00 A.M. Mary and Igor were the last to leave. They had a plane to catch in six hours. As dawn lightened the sky, Mary looked up and asked, "Is there any chance of seeing Vanya before we leave? We could go to Baby House 10 on the way to the airport."

"No. There's no time. We've missed enough planes already," insisted her young lawyer companion.

They did catch their plane, and Mary did find time to speak to Linda. She phoned Sarah five days after the all-night session to say that Linda had come within a hairsbreadth of saying she could not continue with the adoption.

They had spoken for more than an hour. Mary had told Linda she should think of her feelings, not her sense of duty. Bonding with a child was something that happened naturally or it did not. It could not be forced.

Linda had spoken about how she felt she had been pressured and manipulated. Mary had replied, No one is trying to push you or put you in a position where you push yourself into doing this. Linda had to get in touch with her real feelings. If there was no bonding, her life would be a strain every day, and the child would be the first to notice.

Linda had said that she was not worried about bonding. Vanya would just have to fit in like a newborn. But Mary had alluded to her long experience of adoption and said it was not like giving birth. It could only be successful if the mother could bond with the new child as firmly as with her natural children. By the end of the conversation, they had not reached a conclusion; but Mary was sure that Linda was close to withdrawing.

It took another long phone call, this time from Rachel, who used all her negotiating skills, for her to withdraw. Linda was in tears as the conversation went round and round. Rachel had an idea that might make Linda see her situation more clearly. Just as she was maneuvering the conversation around, she heard the sound of breaking glass in the kitchen and realized her five-year-old daughter had smashed a glass. Knowing she had shoes on, Rachel fought off her maternal instinct and pressed on. She said to Linda, "It's like when a couple is getting married and the wedding is already booked and one of them says they are having doubts. Would you advise them to go ahead?"

There was a pause. Linda said no.

"Well, you are in the same position."

Rachel sensed Linda was beginning to acknowledge the reality of her situation, and pressed home her advantage. She said other possibilities were opening up for Vanya. But it was Linda's interest in him that had kept him out of the asylum these past two years. Without her, Vanya would have been lost. But if she was not committed, it would be better to pull out.

The next day Linda sent a fax to Grigory asking him to withdraw her application from the Moscow court. That evening, Sarah and Alan were guests of honor at a farewell dinner at the British ambassador's residence. There was just time to write an important letter. They had been allowed to choose the guest list, and among the usual diplomats, journalists, and bankers was a sprinkling of pioneers of grassroots initiatives who more than anyone deserved an evening out. One of these was Maria, the director of the Our Family foster-parent project. In their letter, Alan and Sarah asked her formally to take Vanya in and find him a foster mother so that he could escape the fate of being sent back to an internat. "We realize that you do not normally take children from state institutions, but we beg you to make an exception for this child," they wrote. It was a long shot, but it was Vanya's best hope.

The evening was a great success. The guests dined at a long polished table, under glittering chandeliers and surrounded by vast portraits in gilt frames of past British foreign secretaries. After dinner there was coffee in the white-and-gold room, which had a magnificent view across the river to the sparkling domes of the Kremlin churches. Maria was delighted with the evening, and as she kissed her good night, Sarah pressed the letter into her hand. "I have a favor to ask of you. Read it when you get home."

By the time Sarah woke up the next morning, Maria had already responded by e-mail. She thanked her for referring to her "one of our children who would otherwise sink into darkness." Vanya's case, she wrote, would cause a "cascade of similar actions all around, and as a result, we will all be changed by this." She promised to do everything she could to help Vanya. But it would mean overcoming bureaucratic hurdles she had never dealt with before. She warned she could do nothing once he had been transferred to an internat. She would have to move quickly before it was too late to save him.

19

The Caged Bird

June–July 1998

It was a hot summer's day at the end of June. Vanya and Julia were alone. All the other children had been taken outside into the yard, but Vanya and Julia were too much trouble because they could not walk unaided. They were only taken outside when Sarah and her daughter, Catherine, came, or Vika's friend Alla or Olya or Julia's Granny Lucy, who came on Sundays and took them to play in the sandbox while she read them stories.

Vanya was telling Julia about all the things he had seen and done in Sarah and Alan's apartment when Linda and her family were staying. There was a dog, and at first he had been scared of the dog. Then Sarah had explained that the dog had lived on the street and people had been cruel to her and in fact she was more scared of him than he was of her. So he learned to be brave and sit still when she sniffed him. Then they became friends and she started to lick him. The dog got scared when he switched the Hoover on and used to run and hide under Catherine's bed.

There was so much to do an apartment. There was a cupboard full of tools, and he was allowed to open the boxes and handle all the nails and screws. There was a box of padlocks, and he could take the keys out and practice unlocking them. And there was a box of Christmas decorations full of shiny things. On Papa Jora's birthday, Mama Linda had let him decorate her hair with tinsel. She had bought a huge cake, and they had sat with Sarah and Alan and Catherine and drunk tea. They had invited Nellie in from the office. She was Russian, but she could speak English too. And the office was wonderful too. He told Julia that Alan was a journalist. Journalists were always on the telephone or writing on the computer. And Nellie had a computer too. It was like a television, but it had a mouse. Not a real mouse like the ones the cats in the yard catch. This mouse was like a toy car. You move it around with your hand. Nellie let him sit on her knee and play with it.

"I wish we could go there now," said Julia. "It's so boring here."

"I have to wait for Mama Linda to come back. She said she had to go back home to England and get my room ready. And then she would come back and get me. Now, Julia, you must ask me what my room is going to be like."

"Vanya, tell me what's going to be in your room," asked Julia obligingly. They played this game every day.

"Well, there will be a bed. A proper bed, like Catherine has, not a crib with bars. A bed you can slide out of when you want. You don't have to wait for someone to lift you out. And there will be a sheet and pillow case with cars on them. And a carpet."

"And will there be a light?" This was Vanya's favorite question. He took a deep breath before answering.

"There will be two lights. There will be a light on the ceiling with a switch by the door. Like we have here. But there will be another light on a little table by my bed. I can stretch out my hand to turn it on and off whenever I want. If I wake up in the night, I can switch it on and see things."

Julia was about to go on to the next stage of the game, when she had to ask him about the shower and the bath, when the door opened and in came Svetlana.

"Vanya, the court date's been set. It will be July sixth."

Vanya had heard the word "court" before and realized this was an important event. He had no idea when July was, but he could tell from the urgency in Svetlana's voice that it was soon. There was one thing he had to make sure of.

"So I won't be going to Internat 30?" he asked.

"No, Vanya. You're going to England."

Over the next few days, he kept hearing the word "court." Each time, it gave him a warm feeling inside. For the first time in his life, he actually looked forward to the long afternoon rest time, when he could indulge himself in imagining his future life. One thing he could not get straight. Linda had said they did not live in an apartment, but a house. What was a house? Why had she said the bedrooms were upstairs? What did upstairs mean? She said she had a cat who lived in the house and slept on her bed. What a strange thing. Everyone knew that cats were dirty and lived outside. And there was a dog. He knew about dogs. And a bird in a cage who could speak. He thought a lot about the bird. Why was it in a cage?

The next morning, when Sarah appeared, Vanya started to ask her all sorts of questions about England; but she did not seem to hear. She took him outside and made him practice walking. When he said he was tired, instead of letting him sit down and talk, she made him climb the ladder in the playground. Then she produced from her bag a toy hammer and nails. As he stood at the top of the ladder, she said, "Now you must mend the climbing frame." Vanya put all his concentration into holding the nail steady while he banged it into a hole in the metal bar at the top of the climbing frame. It was only later, during nap time, as he remembered the events of the morning, that he realized that Sarah had not answered any of his questions about Mama Linda.

The days went by, and he would ask every member of the staff he came across when the court was meeting. At first they would say numbers or words that he had not been taught, but he was reassured by their tone that it was going to happen soon. Then one day he asked, and the caregiver said, "tomorrow." That he understood. He would have his afternoon nap, and then in the evening he would sleep, and when he woke up it would be the court day. He was too excited to sleep that night. The morning came, and grumpy Galina was on duty. As he sat eating his porridge, he looked around to see if Galina had put out a coat and boots for him to wear to go to court. There was no sign of coat or boots. Then he remembered it was summer and he did not need a coat. He looked around for other signs that he was going to leave the baby house. Galina was her usual silent self. She dressed him in an old T-shirt and a patched pair of shorts and did not respond to his protestations that he needed something smarter to go to court. Hours passed and Galina took the other children outside, leaving him with Julia. Vanya could not take his eyes off the door, waiting for Adela or Svetlana to appear. His friend shot anxious glances at him but did not say anything.

When the door opened at last, it was Adela. There was a hard expression on her face. He had seen that expression once before, the day she told Vika's friend Alla, whose visits he so looked forward to, never to come again. "Today's the court date and they haven't appeared," Adela said.

Vanya's head spun. Could she be talking about Mama Linda and Papa Jora? It seemed she was. The next thing she said was, "The English are not coming."

Vanya said in a whisper. "Maybe they will come tomorrow."

"No, Vanya. Today's the court date. You must understand they are not coming. You're too old to stay here any longer. You'll have to go to an internat. You'll never have a mama."

When Adela had left, Julia stretched out a hand and put it on his. She whispered softly, "Don't cry, Vanya." But she was the one who had tears welling up in her eyes. Vanya's eyes remained dry. "She's wrong, you know. I'm sure of it," he said. "Mama Linda isn't coming, but another mama will come."

20
One of Us

July 1998

It was the day the court hearing was adjourned, and Sarah had to explain to Vanya why the Fletchers had betrayed him. As she walked to the baby house, she counted all the adults who had let him down in his short life—his poor birth mother, unable to fight the endlessly negative assessments of the Soviet doctors; Adela's deputy, who declared him unfit for adoption; Adela, too weak to stand up to her or to prevent his being sent to Filimonki; the director of the asylum, who refused to give him a chance; the "psycho-doctor" in Hospital No. 58, who didn't allow anyone to comfort him when he was lying all alone after major surgery; and finally, on that day in May when he had been all dressed up and waiting to be picked up from the baby house, Linda, who had stood him up.

Sarah felt that she and Alan had also let him down. They had befriended him and brought the Fletchers into his life, helped them get further than they were capable of in the adoption process, and been blind to their unsuitability as adoptive parents. They had carelessly introduced Vanya to the joys of home life, which he had embraced so enthusiastically. After this tantalizing glimpse of family life, he might never live outside institutions.

The night before, Sarah had had a long talk with Mary, the American psychologist, to prepare herself for breaking the news to Vanya. Her advice was that above all Sarah should not give Vanya the impression that the Fletchers had rejected him. It was better to lie than for a child to feel rejection.

Unusually, when Sarah arrived she found Vanya sitting on a bench. Someone must have taken pity on him and brought him outside. He was a lonely figure. She sat beside him with her speech all prepared. As usual, he said the most important thing first.

"Today's the court date, Sarah. They didn't come."

"I know. I'm so sorry." He looked at Sarah, waiting for an explanation.

"You see, Linda's granddaughter has broken her leg . . ."

"Where's her granddaughter?"

"In a hospital in England. That's why Linda didn't come."

As quick as a flash he said: "But Linda hasn't broken her leg, has she?"

"You see, Vanya, there's also no kennel for her dog, and she can't leave Philip with anyone—" Sarah couldn't continue. It was obvious that Vanya saw through these excuses. "Vanya, I am very cross with her. I feel she has treated you very badly."

"Sarah, don't say that. Linda is not a bad person. She is a good, kind person." On the day of the greatest disappointment of his life, Sarah could not believe he could be so forgiving, especially as he must know his only option now was going to an internat.

The next day, Sarah returned to the baby house to see if after the catastrophe of the Fletchers' withdrawal anything was left of the relationship she had built up with Adela over four years.

"For this mission I needed some support. I took Alan and a Prague cake. I had to stop Adela from sending Vanya off to an internat before

Maria could get the paperwork together for him to enter her project and, most importantly, find a foster mother.

"I half expected to find Adela standing at the top of the steps, barring the way and telling me never to come back. I knew she felt she had gone out on a limb for Vanya, and now the person we had introduced as his mama had let everyone down, leaving her exposed to reprimand. We followed her into her office, where I had had so many anxious conversations over the years.

"My strategy as always was to keep talking. I abased myself. It was as if I was crawling on my knees before her. I apologized for bringing this woman Linda into her life. We had been unable to persuade her to come for the court hearing, and now the adoption would not go ahead. I paid tribute to Adela's concern for Vanya, for recognizing his special qualities while all around, people treated him as an imbecile. I could see Alan unable to hide his surprise at this hypocritical torrent of half-truths.

"Adela had never seen a foreigner in sackcloth and ashes. She was used to foreigners rolling up in fancy cars and dispensing gifts. However good and humble their intentions, to her, they always embodied high status, wealth, and power. Her heart opened up. As we ate slices of the Prague cake and sipped our tea, I explained how Vanya now had a chance to go to Maria's project. Maria was a godly woman, a scientist who had been received into the Orthodox Church. Her project was new, but Adela should not be worried about this. I did not mention that Maria's project was partially funded by foreign money and used British expertise. I stressed that the project was still known by its old Soviet name of Children's Home No. 19 and was supported by the mayor of Moscow.

"The most important thing, I told her," Sarah says, "was not to send Vanya off to the internat. Once he was there, the authorities would not permit him to go to the project. So once again, I was counting on Adela's fortitude to keep Vanya for a few more weeks. I apologized that there would be paperwork to complete.

"As we finished our tea, it was clear we were still on speaking terms. Adela said 'God bless you' as we left, which we took as a sign that she would consider the fostering option."

Looking back a decade later, Sarah cannot believe she took on so much responsibility for Vanya's fate. "Not once did I get out the piece of paper where Adela told me to rescue Vanya from the internat. I should have shoved this note under her nose and said, 'Adela, you started all of this. Vika and Alan got him out of the asylum. Now it's up to you to shoulder your responsibilities and find him a future.' But I never did. I tiptoed around her like a mouse, bottling my anger and frustration. But if I had told her my true feelings, she would have banned me from the baby house and no one would have taken responsibility for Vanya's survival."

Sarah and Alan went to fetch Vanya from Group 6 and took him outside. It was a hot July day. Loving the male attention, he whooped with delight as Alan maneuvered him toward the climbing frame and encouraged him to go up the ladder. He seemed to grow in stature as he stood at the top. He craned his neck and pointed over the high steel gate to the bustling world outside.

"Uncle Sasha," he shouted in a commanding voice to one of the security guards lounging on the porch of the baby house reading a newspaper. "A car's coming. You must open the gate." The guard folded his newspaper and shuffled off to open the gate.

From his perch at the top of the climbing frame, Vanya no longer seemed part of the isolated world of the baby house and the bleak constrained lives of its inmates. Now that he could see over the high walls, he was at the heart of the new Moscow. The sounds of frenetic construction echoed all around as smart apartment blocks were thrown up on three sides of the baby house.

Alan yelled up to him, "Hold on tight. Don't let go."

Vanya unclasped a hand from the thick metal bar and held it up theatrically in the air. "You mean like this?" he teased, and pretended to wobble.

At that moment, both of them realized that Vanya was well on the way to being deinstitutionalized. Two weeks of being exposed to normal family life had had a dramatic effect on him. Having watched their restless daughter Catherine misbehave, he had a new role model.

The world of the baby house was even more bizarre than when Sarah had first tiptoed in four years ago. The sandbox—normally empty apart from twigs, leaves, and cats feces—was now buried under a vast pyramid of sand, after a truck had dumped its entire load there. The shabby genteel façade of the baby house was disfigured by a pile of coal spilling out of the winter fuel store. In a city fueled by gas, there wasn't a lump of coal anywhere else, but Adela's kingdom was frozen in a past era. Sarah recalled her first meeting with her, when she was covered in soot after wrestling with the ancient boiler.

A voice that was loud but also desperately seeking reassurance dragged her back to the present.

"Is my bed in England still ready for me?"

"Vanya, we'll talk about that later." She could not think of what else to say.

Seconds later, it was as though he had never revealed his innermost thoughts. He shouted, "Watch me leap off," as he slid awkwardly to the ground. When his leg got caught between the rungs and stuck out at a funny angle, he shouted, "Look, I've got a tail." His leg was exactly at the angle of a dog's tail.

As Sarah disentangled his leg, he surprised them again. "Where is Nellie? Is she waiting for me?"

Sarah and Alan had been dreading such a question since Linda's disappearance. He was clearly moving the focus of his ambitions from Linda to them, and this was his delicate way of saying he wanted to be back in their apartment. They had been very careful never to give him the impression that they were a possible adoptive family. The life of a foreign correspondent was unstable. Moving around the world was hard enough with two children and would have been impossible with a third, particularly one who had suffered so much neglect and needed stability.

Having got permission from the security guard, Alan made Vanya walk out of the gate to the car. "Do you remember when you took me to the psychologist?" he asked Sarah suddenly.

"Yes, I do."

"When I came back to the baby house, I burst into tears."

There was no mistaking the direction that Vanya wanted his life to take. This child who had been happy in the past with the smallest crumb of conversation was now actively trying to manipulate them. As he sat in the car, he asked Alan to turn it around so that he did not have to look at the baby house, which he now understood was a place of incarceration.

He spent a happy ten minutes sitting on Alan's lap in the driver's seat, figuring out all the controls. As he switched on the radio, he remarked casually, "They're singing in English." Then he asked: "Whose car is this?"

"It's Sarah's car."

"It's our car," said Vanya firmly. They had never heard him use the word "our" before. He had no possessions and he did not feel he belonged to his group or to the baby house. With the use of that single word came the realization that their family and the office of *The Daily Telegraph* were where he had chosen to belong, and this just as they were about to leave Moscow for good. He had more questions.

"Who are you leaving the car to?" His childish dream was obviously for the car to be left just outside the baby house, where it would be at his disposal.

Alan said another correspondent was coming and would use it.

"Will your flat be shut up?"

"No. The new correspondent will live there."

His voice sank to a whisper. "So you won't ever come back?"

"Yes we will, but not for a while."

The security guard banged on the car window. He had brought back a camera case dropped in the yard. It was time to return Vanya for lunch and the long afternoon nap. His legs appeared to stop working as he approached the entrance.

He was feeling anxious about the hammer and nails he had been playing with on the climbing frame and wanted to know where they were. He asked if Sarah could leave them with him, and he would find a hiding place for them. It was as though Vanya thought this was the last time he would see Alan and Sarah.

"The hammer and nails are in my bag. I'll bring them tomorrow."

His face lit up and he repeated the word tomorrow. Then he had another thought. "Are you sure Adela will let you in tomorrow?" Gone was the confident boy who behaved like he was master of his own fate. Now he knew he was once again at the mercy of a capricious old woman who had already banned several of his friends.

As they went past the kitchen, he seized an opportunity to delay his return to Group 6. He engaged the cook in a long conversation about why she was wearing an apron, a garment he had clearly never seen before, rather than a white coat, and asked her which locker she used. He then insisted Alan take him for a lengthy hand-washing in hot water before he joined the three-year-olds for soup and sleep.

The next day, Sarah kept her promise. With Catherine in tow, she brought the hammer and nails, as well as colored shapes and a board to nail them into, and a video camera. The idea was to take some footage of Vanya to show to more adoptive parents, even though she had no one in mind.

Vanya was sitting alone with Julia, while the other children were outside in the sunshine with Galina, the caregiver, who Vanya had indicated was mean-spirited and vindictive. There was only one corkboard, so Vanya and Julia had to share one. He enjoyed demonstrating to Julia the use of the hammer and nails.

As he tapped away, he said to Julia, "We've got another board at home." He turned to Sarah and said, "Do you remember, when I had a mama and we used to play at home? At home we had our nails."

Looking at the video now, almost ten years later, Sarah is struck by two things. "In the course of a night, entirely on his own, he had come to terms with his abandonment by the British family and consigned them to history. And his use of the word 'our' was very subtle—and painful to me. The word 'our' could only be at my flat, or in the car, anywhere but the baby house. They were 'our' nails when they were at home, but they lost this magical quality of belonging when they reached the baby house; then they were just nails.

"But I had told him that the flat was going to be occupied by other people. In short succession he had lost his mama and was about to lose his second family and the flat where he acted out his fantasies of working with tools. I realized we had given him a tantalizing look at the promised land, but he was to be cruelly deprived of the chance to set foot in it. I think any other child would have been destroyed by all these blows, but Vanya somehow never completely lost his assurance that things would come right in the end.

"I can barely dare to run through the tape now. I have come across a conversation which I would swear in a court of law never took place. But though it is wiped utterly from my memory, here it is, recorded on the tape."

Sarah: "We're going to Jerusalem soon."

Vanya: "With whom?"

Sarah: "There's me and Catherine and Alan."

Vanya: "And who else?"

Sarah: "And William, my son."

Vanya, in a tiny whisper: "And me too?"

"I do not know what I answered. The recording stops just as Vanya's face crumpled with the effort of asking for the impossible. Why did I press the stop button? Was I pretending to myself that he had never asked to come with us, as I could not live with the knowledge? The recording resumes with me changing the subject. 'What country do you live in now?'"

There is worse to come on the tape. Sarah had always prided herself on understanding with the utmost subtlety everything that Russians said. Here on the tape, she can see she made a gross mistake of comprehension that must have hit Vanya like a kick in the teeth. He was fascinated at the process of moving to a foreign land. Having no possessions of his own, he was intrigued that Catherine had all kinds of stuff that would miraculously follow her around the world.

"Has Catherine packed up her toys?"

"Yes. All her toys are on their way to Jerusalem."

"Who took them away?"

"They went in a truck and then they'll go by sea and I suppose another truck."

Vanya digested this information for a while and popped another of his surprising questions. "Are you taking the nails away?" he asked.

Sarah thought he was asking if she would take them home with her that afternoon, as she always did, since they would surely disappear as everything else had. "We'll probably take them, or they'll get lost," she replied casually.

"Looking at the tape, I can see he was asking a far bigger question: Were we taking the nails to Jerusalem? If I had understood, I would have answered that I would leave them behind with Vika for him. But then I was oblivious. I did not realize that I had just deprived him of those tiny brass nails, which to him, after the loss of his mama, his second family, his car, and his flat, were the most precious things remaining in the world—a reminder of the time when he was one of us."

Vanya said nothing, but Sarah can see on the tape that his confidence was dented. He seemed more aware of being a child in an institution. He warned her that they were in danger of being bawled out by the evil Galina for visiting him. Clearly the staff thought he had too many visitors and they were disrupting the smooth running of Group 6.

Sarah had brought a Milky Way chocolate bar, and Catherine divided it between him and Julia. Vanya insisted on eating it from the wrapper, not touching the chocolate. He asked anxiously: "Is it okay if I get my clothes dirty?" This was clearly a sin that merited a loud scolding.

Vanya decided it was time for a visit to the car; but there were two problems in the way, which he took it upon himself to resolve. He had to avoid their being shouted at by Galina, and he could not leave Julia all alone.

"I want to ask the guard for permission," he said. This was his way of insuring us against Galina's wrath. Years later, he described how Galina dragged Julia by her hair across the floor when she wet herself.

Even though that day everything in his life had been stripped from him piece by piece, he could not leave Julia behind. "We have to take

Julia with us," he insisted. "But you can't lead her by the hand. She has to be carried. And then we can sit in the car together." He could not think of Julia's being alone.

"It would be so boring for her on her own. We have to take her with us." And that is what they did.

The day had come for Sarah's final good-bye to Vanya. It was the morning of her departure and she had a surprise for him—a life storybook that she had made up of pictures she had taken of him: in the baby house, in Filimonki, in the hospital, and of all the people who had visited him, including Vika and her new baby, Stephen. She had sat up half the night writing the captions, becoming so obsessed that she forgot to pack the contents of her wardrobe. Luckily, a neighbor noticed all her clothes still hanging up, fetched a suitcase, and stuffed everything in it just as the car arrived to go to the airport.

It was the worst possible time to be leaving Moscow, with Vanya in limbo, Sarah recalls. "The timing was out of my hands. I may have thought I was a charity worker for the past four years; but in fact I was an accompanying spouse, with my visa and accommodation supplied by Alan's work. I could not stay."

Vanya was sitting on a bench, looking very appealing: The baby house had let his hair grow into a mass of brown curls. He was wearing Catherine's cast-off denim jeans. He had become the prince of the baby house—but one whose royal destiny had suddenly been taken away from him. He loved the album. Sarah had even stuck in some pictures of Andrei standing in front of a Christmas tree in Florida, the *Telegraph* office staff, and one of the dog.

They discussed each photo at length, both knowing that when they got to the last page, her visit would be over. "I was just reassuring him that Vika would visit when Stephen was big enough to be left with someone else—no one was permitted to bring a baby into the baby house—when I looked up. A couple was emerging from inside the baby house, the woman carrying a baby. They were clearly not Russian. It was rare to see new faces in Baby House 10, and Vanya and I stared at them shamelessly. The man whipped out a camera and got his wife to pose with the baby in front of the porch. They were talking in English, and as I strained my ears, I could hear they were Americans. I realized they had just adopted this child."

Someone had actually managed to adopt a child from Baby House 10. The only adoption Sarah knew of was Andrei's. The biggest American adoption agency working in Moscow had tried to work with Adela and given up. No one, it seemed, could cope with her eccentricities. They were not the usual type of adoptive couple; they did not exude wealth and privilege, they did not have perfect teeth and designer clothes, and they did not look like they had $30,000 to spare. But no one could fail to see their happiness at having taken possession of their new daughter, who was a typical baby-house product, with blotchy skin and unwashed hair.

"Excuse me," Sarah said. "Have you just adopted this little girl?"

"Yes. Isn't she gorgeous?"

They were happy to tell her the adoption had been arranged by a man who worked for the Russian Orthodox Church who had connections with their church in America. Sarah's first thought was, Why had Adela never mentioned this man? And why had she not enlisted his help in finding parents for Vanya after Linda had pulled out?

Sarah introduced this kind couple to Vanya. They were so moved by his story that they happily delayed bonding with their new daughter and ignored their impatient driver, who was holding the car door open for them and motioning for them to get inside. "As they gazed sympathetically at him, I let the whole story tumble out. I told them about how Vanya had been locked up in a mental asylum; and how, even when drugged and half-naked, he had managed to retain his humanity and send out a distress message to the outside world; how he had returned to the baby house a skeleton; and how after he appeared in a newspaper article, a British woman had vowed to save him and give him a life, but just last month she had cruelly let him down. And now he was abandoned and alone, with the threat of the asylum hanging over him once more. I told them about the morgue on the asylum grounds, waiting to receive its weekly consignment of children. Their eyes got bigger and bigger as I explained the Russian system of sending children with slight disabilities to wither away in asylums. I told them he had been diagnosed as an imbecile, even though he was an intelligent child with a bright personality, who made everyone he spoke to feel special. This became clear when he took it upon himself to ask them questions, with me translating. 'Is that your car?' he asked, and wanted to know where they intended to drive to and whether they were taking the little girl to live with them.

"I told them about his concern for other children—how he had saved Andrei by teaching him to speak, kept Elvira's spirits up in the hospital, and been like a caring brother to Julia. He deserved a family, I said. He had so much love to give."

The couple continued to listen, visibly shocked. Vanya waved as they drove off.

"I made my parting with Vanya low-key. I told him that my friends would continue to visit him. I did not tell him about my hopes that he would get into Maria's foster project. He had been disappointed often enough. I had always gone out of my way to show him I was his friend, not a mother. So on that final parting, I had to fight off my instinct to hold him close and hug him. I kissed him lightly on the top of his head, turned around, and walked out of the baby house to rush home and see to my own children's packing."

21
Candle Power
August–September 1998

Alan dragged his family off to Jerusalem in August, but Sarah's head and heart were still in Moscow. "I can remember my first weeks in Jerusalem, walking our Russian dog through the olive trees in the local park and thinking of Vanya languishing in the baby house. I watched my own children racing around on their bikes and getting brown in the sun and imagined Vanya deathly pale, waiting in vain for someone to take him into the yard. While my children were learning to appreciate fresh pita bread and plump black olives, Vanya was still on his diet of slop and gray omelet. My friends had all promised faithfully to make regular visits to him, but I knew that any of them could fall victim to one of Adela's moods and be banned."

Sarah started to imagine Vanya sharing their lives in Jerusalem. In Moscow, she had always killed these thoughts. For all the affection she felt toward him, she had never considered adoption. Instead, she had put her energies into helping Maria and others like her who believed that children should be in families, not institutions. But now that she was far from Russia, she was keenly aware of her continuing responsibility toward him.

Sarah was on the phone to Moscow every day. There was still a danger that Vanya could be slipped in among a consignment of five-year-olds to Internat 30. Any delay in the paperwork assigning him to Maria's foster project might be seized on by Adela to take the easy option. The word from the baby house was not encouraging. During one phone call, one of Adela's deputies praised the facilities at Internat 28, one of the best in Moscow, which she said would suit Vanya perfectly.

"Have you been there?" Sarah shot back. "It may be a nicer place than the others, but he would still be locked up."

Luckily, there was one member of staff who was willing to put herself out for Vanya. One day Svetlana, the woman who had accompanied Vanya to the asylum more than two years before, reported that Maria had called and told her what she had to do. It seemed she was willing to do it. The next day, Sarah called Svetlana at home. There was a note of pride in her voice as she announced that the department—the same women who had put so many obstacles in the way of Vanya's adoption—had agreed to send Vanya to be fostered. It seemed like a miracle. It took another four days for the precious letter of assignment to arrive at the baby house.

Rachel was true to her promise to stay in contact with Vanya. Before her first visit, Sarah reminded her to be sure to smile at the security guards, and asked her to thank them for their good-bye present to Sarah, a book of verse.

For the first time, Sarah dug out the book and read the dedication. Well thumbed and obviously much loved, it was a collection of poems by Yevtushenko, a cult poet who used to fill stadiums in the 1960s. Only in Russia, she thought, would a security guard make a gift of a forty-year-old book of poetry. It was signed by Vitaly, the chief security guard who had been officious, telling Sarah she could not take Vanya outside the gate. But here was a completely different Vitaly. His message was generous and warm. He thanked her for her concern for Russian invalid orphans and acknowledged her attempts to find Vanya a family and a better life "in conditions of economic crisis in Russia." As Sarah leafed through the musty yellowing pages in the bright Middle Eastern sunlight, she found some sympathy for the security guards. They had all been engineers and scientists, men held in high regard in Soviet society; but now they were cast aside. They had been washed up on the porch of the baby house, with their only status conferred by a cheap uniform.

As it turned out, Rachel never got a chance to pass on her message. The next day, she related how she had been greeted by a glowering guard who was in no mood to talk and only reluctantly let her inside.

She was made to wait in the corridor for 15 minutes until a doctor appeared to tell her that she had come at a time that did not suit the staff. After a further few minutes, a very small, stiff little figure in overalls and a red shirt appeared, looking rather serious.

Vanya stared at her for a few moments and then shouted "Rachel!" His first words were "I'm not going to England."

She told him she knew this already. She had been to see George and found him very sad. Or rather, she tried to say he was very sad, but could not think of the right word in Russian and ended up saying "muddy" instead. She hoped he had got the gist. He had certainly listened very carefully. "You know how Vanya goes completely still, alert and concentrating when you try to tell him something of significance. He does not miss much," she e-mailed.

Vanya asked Rachel what his life would be like in Maria's foster program. Would he have a brother there? She told him it would be like a big family. They played a game where he shut her repeatedly in a cupboard and went away. He particularly liked Rachel's pretending to cry. He then got called to lunch and she delivered him to a sour-faced younger woman looking after his group, who refused to acknowledge her. As usual, all the children were set in position on their chairs like little mannequins.

As Sarah read Rachel's e-mail, the glare of the sun was so bright she had to get up and close the shutters so that she could read the words on the screen. Rachel concluded: "They will miss Vanya when he goes, I think. With his loud voice and stoical interest and cheer, he positively shines out of the murk of the place. Everybody there looks like they fall into one of two groups, the bullies and the bullied. I'm afraid the place does not fill me with a feeling of warmth. But Vanya is looking forward to Maria's."

Sarah scanned the rest of the e-mail, barely taking in Rachel's description of a crisis developing in Moscow—lines of people patiently queuing outside the closed doors of banks; two middle-aged women on the street bashing each other over the head in a fight to get to the head of the queue at a currency exchange. She switched on the twenty-four-hour news channel. There was Moscow, with crowds besieging the banks, desperately trying to get their hands on their savings. It looked like a revolution was breaking out.

As she watched the mayhem on television, the phone rang. It was Alan saying the paper wanted him back in Moscow, and he was booked on the afternoon plane. Sarah's first thought was panic. "We had been in Jerusalem only ten days, and I did not have any money, my residence permit was not ready, and I had not driven the car and did not even know the route to Catherine's school. But at least, I thought, Alan could be in Moscow at the time of Vanya's transfer to a foster family."

The financial crash was the only item on the news. Russia was on the brink of bankruptcy. The ruble was plummeting in value. The banks had no money and had closed their doors. The camera showed a supermarket with bare shelves; apparently people had rushed in and scooped up whatever they could lay their hands on before their money lost all its value. Retirees with red banners and angry faces were shown gathering in the streets, shaking their fists and denouncing the capitalist crooks who had stolen all their savings. A horrible thought came to her: Maria and her foster families could not fail to be affected by all this turmoil. Maybe she would not be able to take in any new children. And Vanya would have to stay in Baby House 10.

This anxious thought recurred for the next four days. When Alan finally had time to visit Maria, it became clear that her commitment to rescuing Vanya was not in doubt. She told Alan that Vanya would be leaving the baby house in three days' time, on September 7, but the ministry required any child entering her program to undergo comprehensive medical tests. So Vanya would have to spend forty days in the orphans' hospital, the Morozovskaya, before he could be taken in by a foster family. This was heartbreaking news, but Maria promised that this time Vanya would not be alone. He would be under the supervision of a doctor attached to her fostering program, with whom Vanya had bonded when he was first introduced to Maria. This would give her time to find him a foster family.

Since the start of the crisis, Maria had not received any money to pay wages. Her foster family support team was starting to stockpile potatoes and canned goods for the winter. Even more worrying was a change in tone in the Moscow city authorities, who were demanding that she once again justify the existence of her program. Clearly the bureaucrats saw it as ripe for the axe.

Though Maria was ferociously efficient in her work, she was also a deeply convinced Christian, and the great crash brought out her mystical side. She told Alan she believed the crisis was not just a personal drama for people who had lost their savings, but a great trial for the Russian people whom God had singled out to serve His purposes. "We are forced again to wander in the desert in search of God's land," she said. "Only by passing this new test will we reach the New Jerusalem."

Alan squeezed in a visit to Vanya on the day he was due to leave the baby house. He was dressed to go out, but as usual no one had told him what was going to happen, and he was full of questions.

"Are you taking me to Maria's?" he asked.

"No. Maria will come and collect you herself."

"Will I have supper in the kitchen, like I did last time?"

Alan took a deep breath. "Vanya, I have to explain. You're not going to Maria's immediately. You have to go to a hospital first."

Vanya watched Alan's face intently as he processed this new information. "You mean Hospital 58? I don't want another operation." His face was white and he was close to tears.

"No, Vanya. Not Hospital No. 58. This is a new hospital. It's called the Morozovskaya. You remember that nice Dr. Zaitsev you met at Maria's? He works there. So you won't be alone."

Despite this shock, Vanya asked about Sarah, the children, and the *Telegraph* staff. As Alan got up to go, Vanya said, "I won't stop thinking about you."

"And I'll be thinking of you, and I'll be checking with Maria how you're getting on," said Alan, as he dashed off to catch the plane back to Israel.

In fact, Vanya sat all day waiting for the car. No one came for him. The next day, Maria sent one of her social workers to collect him. After a brief exchange of paperwork, Vanya's seven-year internment in Baby House 10 came to an end. He may have brightened the days of the staff and raised the odd smile, but ultimately his presence had become a burden. He was one less child to worry about. As the social worker carried him along the empty corridors and out into the yard, Vanya's gaze was firmly fixed ahead. None of the staff came out to wave him off, and he did not look back.

Thanks to the miracle of e-mail, over the next few weeks Sarah got regular updates from Moscow about Vanya. Under Maria's supervision, he had been transported to a different world from the one of neglect and abuse he had known for the past seven years. Maria asked for a list of all the Russians who had ever visited him so that she could tell them where to find him. Even though she was concerned that so many foreigners had come and gone in his life, she encouraged Rachel to continue coming to see him in the hospital. This had an added bonus—Vanya was her most effective Russian teacher.

It was clear that once again he had worked his charm on the hospital staff. Dr. Zaitsev told Rachel that he had nicknamed Vanya "the professor" because of all the clever things he said, in stark contrast to the baby house where, up until he left, the staff were sighing over him and calling him profoundly retarded.

Maria's progress reports on Vanya took on an increasingly gloomy tone as she worried about the state of Russia. She feared that the Communists were coming back to power. She wrote powerfully in English, her meaning reinforced by the use of some startlingly unexpected words. "My life here is always a race, and my telephone is roaring till late at night."

The long-term future of Vanya and other disabled children in her care was weighing on her mind. Before the crisis, she had thought that in fifteen years' time, when her foster mothers would be too old to look after their charges, Russia would have a fully developed system of care. But now she could see this was not going to happen, so the future of the disabled children was uncertain. She had always ruled out foreign adoption, but for these children she was now reluctantly looking into the possibility of finding homes for them abroad.

Sarah had never believed in the power of prayer, but under Maria's influence, she walked into the Old City of Jerusalem and lit candles in the Church of the Holy Sepulchre—one for Maria's program and one for Vanya. Jerusalem has a lot of churches, at least one for every Christian nation, and Sarah got into the habit of lighting a candle in each one. She asked for the help of the Russians, the Armenians, the Ethiopians, the Germans, the Syrians, and the Copts. She got so much in the habit that during a quick trip to England she found herself in Salisbury Cathedral searching around for a candle. To her shame, she realized that Anglicans do not light candles, but visitors were invited to fill in a prayer form. She wrote asking the congregation to pray for Vanya, and put the slip of paper in the box.

There was still no stability in Vanya's life. After what ended up being fifty days in the Morozovskaya hospital, he was transferred to a sanatorium. Then came the dispiriting news from Rachel that he would have to go to another hospital—presumably No. 58—for treatment on his knees because nobody in the baby house had bothered to do any exercises with him after his previous operations. The neglect had been so serious that the operation might have to be redone. Sarah sent back a blistering e-mail, written with all the clarity that distance confers. "What an idiotic system where kids from institutions are sent to hospital and operated on and nobody from the baby house ever visits or shows any interest in the child's progress. Yet each baby house has a masseuse and someone whose job is to do physical therapy but they do nothing and, what's more, feel no shame about their idleness."

The only people she had seen doing follow-up exercises with children in Hospital No. 58 were self-taught mothers. Yet Vanya's and Elvira's mothers were told to give up their children because there was nothing they could do for them and only the state orphanages could provide the necessary specialist care.

While all this was going on, Maria revealed she had two possible foster families for Vanya. One was a single mother, a "defectologist" who worked in an internat and had a teenage daughter, and the other was a family with two older sons. Maria said she would let Vanya choose.

Unbeknownst to anyone in Moscow or Jerusalem, there was a third contender. As Maria sat at her desk late in the evening—her favorite time, when all the social workers had gone home—and was weighing the suitability of the two candidates, another woman in another time zone was sitting at her kitchen table reading and re-reading an item in her church newsletter. She had picked up the newsletter the day before at the Russian Orthodox church of St. Nicholas in Bethlehem, Pennsylvania. During the service, a local couple had presented to the congregation the latest addition to their family, a little girl adopted from Baby House 10. The item in the newsletter was written by the adoptive couple, but it was not about their little girl. Under the headline AN IMPORTANT ANNOUNCE-MENT, it spoke of another child, a boy with the diagnosis of cerebral palsy whom they had met in the baby house. The boy was intelligent, cheerful, and kind; but he faced a bleak future. "This boy is so bright, it would be a shame to see this happen," they wrote. The couple invited parishioners to consider adopting him.

The woman's name was Paula Lahutsky, and her immediate thought was, "I can take him." She surprised herself with the force of her reaction. It seemed that her home was waiting for this boy. She had bought a single-story, ranch-type house for her father, a double amputee, whom she had looked after for the last four years of his life. It would be perfect for the boy.

For seventeen years, Paula, an unmarried woman, had worked as a school psychologist but had never had children of her own. She imagined how much she could do for this little boy. Her first reaction was to reach for the phone and speak to the couple who had written the announcement in the newsletter. But she stopped herself as she realized her heart was racing ahead of her mind. What would people think? They would ask each other, Who does she think she is? What makes her think she can give this boy the life he needs? By even considering this adoption, she was exposing herself to ridicule.

She hesitated for two weeks. She forced herself to think what this life-changing decision would entail. On the one hand, she had a comfortable and fulfilling life with a demanding job, a lot of friends, an extended family, and a close-knit church community. If she adopted a child from such a deprived background, all of that would have to take second place in her life. But then she thought how much she had to give, and there were Russian speakers in the community. But she would definitely need the support of those closest to her.

She decided to test the waters. She called around to her friends. One of her childhood pals, a man she had been to high school with and against whom she had competed for top grades at college, summed up all the reasons she should go ahead. "You work with kids with special needs, you live in a ranch house, you have Russian roots. The boy will feel completely at home. Paula, it's a no-brainer."

All this time, despite not having met the child or even seen a picture, inexplicably she could not get him out of her mind. One night she had a vivid dream. She saw clearly a small boy in a room full of cribs. He was looking directly at her through the bars. "Will you be my mother?" he asked.

After that, her desire to give him a home conquered her doubts. Her first phone call was to the adoptive couple, who encouraged her to proceed. They told her what an intelligent and appealing boy he was, and for the first time she heard his name, Vanya, short for Ivan, or John in

English. They explained they had used a man who worked for the Russian Orthodox Church to facilitate the adoption in Moscow. He was linked to the Orthodox Church in America. So Paula would have to call the headquarters of the Orthodox Church in New York.

Feeling nervous but uplifted by having made a decision, Paula dialed the New York number. A woman answered, and Paula explained her intentions. It soon became clear that Paula's enthusiasm was not matched by her contact on the other end of the line. The Church, the woman explained, might not be in favor of single-mother adoptions and there was a strong possibility she would not be approved. There had been a recent case where a single woman had adopted a child and it had ended in failure. Her application was bound to be judged in this light.

"Why should all children suffer because of one failed adoption?" Paula thought bitterly as she put the phone down.

22
Potentially Very Good News

November 1998–February 1999

As the year drew to a close, the weeks of meaningless tests in the orphans' hospital finally came to an end. Now it was time for Vanya to move in with his foster family. His new mama was called Sonya, a divorcée with a teenage daughter who had supported her family for years on the meager wages she earned as a defectologist in a children's internat, where her charges had all been labelled oligophrenics but were not physically disabled. Sonya had been chosen by Maria as someone who could look after Vanya in a family environment, begin his deinstutionalization, and increase his mobility.

His new family included Sonya's daughter and her mother, who came to live with them so that Vanya was never alone in the daytime. There was one disadvantage. Sonya lived on the fifth floor of an apartment block with no elevator. But she was a resourceful woman who had grown up at a time when everything was in short supply and people had to make the best of what they had. She turned the eight flights of stairs into a physical therapy exercise for Vanya.

When Vika came to visit, Sonya poured her a cup of tea and then immediately dressed Vanya in his outdoor clothes. She set the boy at the top of the stairs, his hand firmly grasping the handrail. Leaving the apartment door open, Sonya sat down at the tea table again, while Vanya made his slow progress to the ground floor. As Sonya and Vika ate their cake, they could hear Vanya bellowing greetings to the neighbors he met on the stairs, and the neighbors' less audible but warm response. By the time Sonya and Vika had finished their tea, Vanya had reached the bottom of the stairs, and they set off after him.

Sonya was utterly unlike Vika's churchy friends. She was a forceful woman from the provinces who had struggled, scrimping and saving, to make a life for herself in Moscow. She smoked, she dyed her hair, and she spoke with shocking bluntness. Sonya did not hide her disdain for "Bible-bashers."

Vika recalls, "I was shocked at first at the way Sonya corrected Vanya in front of me, telling him to sit up straight and not to slurp his tea. But I soon realized she was doing this for a good reason. She was drilling out of him his institutional habits and teaching him how to behave like a child brought up at home."

Despite her dim view of Christians, Sonya did not object to Vika's taking Vanya to church one Sunday. In the corner was an open coffin, with the corpse of an old man waiting for burial—a common practice in the Orthodox Church. Vanya asked Vika why he had died.

"He was sick," said Vika, without thinking. An expression of alarm crossed Vanya's face.

"Sick—that's what I am. Am I going to die?" he said. She had to explain that he was not sick; that was just something the staff at the baby house used to say about the children.

One thing concerned Vika: The television was always on in Sonya's apartment. "This was especially disturbing to me as I had not watched television in years and did not even own one. What's more, Sonya's mother—Vanya called her Baboulya—had introduced him to all her favorite soap operas.

"One day I heard Vanya and Baboulya discussing one of these soaps at great length. I realized that Vanya's life was lived almost exclusively indoors and through the television. Even with a loving foster family, this seemed to be all that Russia could offer him. He would be nine next birthday and I felt strongly he needed to start his education. All he was learning was the plots of silly TV programs."

For Sonya, fostering was a step up from her previous job, and better paid. Maria's staff looked after their foster families well, first visiting to find out all their needs and then checking up on them regularly and working hard to solve problems as they cropped up. They even helped with household repairs and replaced broken appliances.

But fostering Vanya did not just bring financial benefits. Vanya's presence provided a new equilibrium to her family and had a calming effect on the household. The original plan was for Vanya to spend a few months, or at most a year, with Sonya, Maria says. But quite unexpectedly Sonya became attached to him.

"Vanya was a very affectionate and grateful child who expressed his feelings openly and with great charm," Maria recalls. "He radiated enough warmth to melt the Arctic ice cap, so winning Sonya's heart was no problem. Her feelings for him—or rather the warmth she received from him—changed everything. She began to see him as part of her family."

Far away, beyond the ice cap, the strength of Vanya's charm was turning another life upside down. Paula refused to be put off from her ambition to adopt Vanya. She marshaled her arguments to put to the Church: She was an experienced school psychologist with many years of securing top-quality education for children with special needs. She was of Russian origin, a member of a Christian Orthodox Church, and understood Russian culture. She had a large extended family for Vanya to fit into. What better candidate to adopt him could there possibly be?

It took some time, but the Church eventually accepted her as a suitable parent and told their Moscow representative to go to Baby House 10. Paula knew she might have to wait quite a while, but this did not stop her jumping every time the phone rang. But when the phone call came, she could not at first take in what the Orthodox Church of America representative in New York was saying to her. The woman had to spell it out. "The boy has disappeared," she said. Apparently the church liaison had turned up at Baby House 10 expecting to find Vanya, but the elderly women who worked there had shrugged their shoulders and said he had left the baby house. What's more, they did not know where he had gone. One of them had told the church worker that she thought Vanya might be on his way to England.

Paula had been prepared for all kinds of surprises, but not this. Her head swam. The Orthodox Church representative continued talking. She related that the church worker in Moscow had said there were plenty of other children, "better ones," for her to adopt.

"Don't even tell me about them," Paula said with uncharacteristic bluntness. "I want him. I want Vanya. It has to be him." She told the woman firmly to keep looking.

Despite evidence that Vanya was not available and possibly on his way to England, Paula was resolute in her belief that he would be her son. She did not believe that an English couple was going to adopt him, and did not want to believe it. She was convinced that this was just an excuse not to look for the missing boy.

It took a long time for the mystery to be solved. Paula knew things moved slowly in Russia, but she hoped to have news of Vanya by Christmas, still a month away. She was not prepared for how totally Russia closes down over Christmas and New Year's. Under Communism, celebrating Christmas was banned, and the midwinter festivities focused on a godless New Year's holiday. But these days, the calendar is ransacked for ever more reasons to stop work. So toward the end of December, official life slows down while people prepare for the new year. The center of Moscow is filled with fir trees whose boughs, in line with the rampant capitalism of the age, are decked with gaudy chocolate bars or whatever the sponsor wants to advertise. Just when the hangover is about to clear, it is time for Russian Orthodox Christmas, celebrated on January 7. But the party is not over yet. On January 13 it is time to celebrate "Old New Year"—the beginning of the year according to the old Russian calendar abolished by the Communists. Despite the passing of the best part of a century since the old calendar disappeared, the feast of Old New Year is still treasured. So it was that almost three months passed before the church worker resumed his search for Vanya—three long months when Paula remained in limbo.

In Jerusalem, Sarah was unaware of the great hunt for Vanya until February, when she received an e-mail from Rachel so unexpected that she had to read it half a dozen times. With lawyerly caution, Rachel announced that she had "a bit of potentially very good news which I thought you might be interested in." Sarah scanned the rest and let out a shriek. An American woman, it appeared, was interested in adopting Vanya. She had apparently met him at Baby House 10.

Sarah's first reaction was incredulity. How had an American woman got past Adela to visit Baby House 10? She ran through her mind all the foreigners Adela had turned away. Then she thought of the American women who had joined in the music-therapy group, but at that time, Vanya was in the mental asylum. And the music-therapy group had been banned by the time he got back.

The more she thought about it, the more worried she became. After the experience of Linda, this might just be another recipe for heartbreak. "I thought of the cashmere-clad American would-be adoptive parents I had met in Moscow. They all had perfect teeth and they were looking for the perfect child. I thought of Vanya safely in Maria's care, and decided that the last thing he needed was to be yanked out and moved to America to live with a family that did not speak Russian and would not appreciate his gift for language. And they would probably rename him Duane or Bradley. Then I thought about Maria. The social services department had made her promise not to get involved in international adoption. This might put the future of her project in danger. In any case, Vanya was no longer in the adoption data bank, so how could he go abroad? Rachel's 'potentially very good news' seemed to me to be a disaster in the making."

Rachel's next e-mail added to the mystery. The woman who wanted to adopt Vanya was apparently an Orthodox nun of Russian ancestry. Nothing added up. Next she said the adoptive mother was a wealthy woman, living in her own house in a nice neighborhood, not in a nunnery. Anything, it seemed, was possible in America, even a millionaire nun.

All this had come to light after the church worker had called Maria to tell her that an American woman had approached him to adopt Vanya, and he had tracked the boy down to Hospital No. 58 and barged his way in and recorded a video. This was a bolt from the blue for Maria. Maria could not understand how this man had just gone blundering into Hospital 58 with a video camera. What had he told Vanya? she wondered. Whatever he had said was bound to confuse Vanya just as he was settling in to a new life. And what about Sonya? What had she heard?

When years later Sarah finally watched the video the church worker had made of Vanya, she was appalled. It was an in-your-face advertisement, with Vanya the product being sold. A pretty young doctor is presented as his personal physician, but she is obviously very nervous and does not seem to know much about his case at all. Gripping his walking frame, Vanya is made to set off down the corridor toward the camera. A born actor, he laughs happily into the lens. A game of checkers is staged between him and his best friend. Only the keenest of eyes could spot that both children are playing with white pieces.

The camera then focuses on the head of the department, who is full of praise for Vanya. "His intellect is unimpaired and he is very sociable," the doctor declares. He hopes Vanya will find a good family and go to school. At this point, Vanya, who so far has been a willing but mute star in this adoption advertisement, ruins the whole thing.

His voice is heard off camera, shrill and clear. "But I already have a family. I have a sister, and she goes to school."

The camera pans jerkily toward him. He smiles, and can tell the worker wants more. There is a pause and he says loudly and clearly in English, "Thank you." This goes down so well that he adds: "Good-bye."

Maria was outraged when she heard that the church worker had talked in front of Vanya about adoption without bothering to find out anything about his circumstances. But her reaction was mixed with relief. Maybe her prayers had been answered and there was indeed someone in America willing to give him a future. Now Maria had to break the news to Sonya before she heard it from someone else. Although she had continually reminded Sonya that Vanya's placement was only temporary, she feared the news would cause her a lot of heartbreak.

23
Ticket to Santa Barbara
March 1999

Vanya could not guess why Sonya was so angry when she hung up the phone. He had seen her angry before—Maria had sent a pair of crutches, but when they arrived they were scratched. She was cross they had not sent new ones for him. And then there was a time when she was short-changed at the market while buying a leather jacket. Or the time when her daughter had got a 3 for geography and Sonya knew she deserved a 5. But this time her anger was so much worse.

It had all started with the phone ringing in the hall. When Sonya picked it up, Vanya knew from the tone of her voice that it was Maria calling. Sonya was silent for a long period. It was most unlike her. The first question she asked was, "When is this going to happen?" There was another long silence. "But I thought you had chosen me. How do you know this woman is serious?"

After she put the phone down, she went into the kitchen muttering angrily. Vanya sat rigidly in his armchair, straining to hear what she was saying to herself. He wished Baboulya was there, but she had gone shopping. Through the open kitchen door, he heard Sonya opening and then slamming the drawer where she kept her cigarettes, and then the wheeze of the tap as she filled the kettle, and then the crash as she put it down on the stove.

After what seemed like a long time, he heard the key in the door. Baboulya had not had time to put down her bags before Sonya erupted. "You won't believe what those bitches have done. And all behind my back. They've gone to the Americans to find him a mother. Aren't I good enough? Haven't I shown them that I can look after him? I've even paid for you to come all the way to Moscow so that he's never alone. He loves it here."

From his listening post in the sitting room, Vanya seized on the key words. The first one was "America." Wasn't Santa Barbara in America? A TV image of bright sunshine, deep blue sea, and huge cars flashed through his mind. The next word that struck him was "mother." He had a mother, but was he going to have another one, an American one? Could you have two mothers?

Sonya was still pouring out her anger and hurt. "Will this American woman look after him like I do? And what about us? I gave up my job to look after him."

He heard Sonya picking up the shopping bags, and then Baboulya came into the sitting room, sat down beside him, and put her arms around him.

"Baboulya. What's happening? Am I going to America?"

"We don't know for sure, Vanya."

"Baboulya, if I do go, I won't leave you behind. I'll take you with me."

From that day on, the cozy atmosphere in the flat turned sour and tense. Sonya's angry mood never quite went away. Vanya found himself more and more alone. At mealtimes, when Baboulya always used to come and eat with him in the sitting room, he was now as often as not alone, all the others chattering away in the kitchen. He felt he was no longer part of the family.

When Rachel came to visit, Sonya did not invite her in. Rachel had to wait on the landing while Sonya dressed Vanya in his outdoor clothes. He would have liked to offer her tea, but he did not dare ask. Sometimes if he just opened his mouth, she would go mad. So he spoke less and less because everything he did say seemed to cause offense.

No mention was made again of America or the American mother, and Vanya did not feel he could ask about her. But he never forgot what he had heard.

24
An Evil Trick

March–June 1999

Paula had been given the video taken by the church worker, and throughout the spring, she watched it over and over. Each viewing strengthened her resolve to become this boy's mother. But she still felt a generalized anxiety and could not pinpoint the source. It was certainly not the mountain of paperwork—she dealt with that every day. Finally she realized what was upsetting her equilibrium. For some it might not seem like a problem, but for Paula it was. She was a timid driver when it came to long car journeys and finding her way around unknown cities. She would have to take time off work and drive to Philadelphia, a large city seventy miles away, and find the state immigration office, where she had to be fingerprinted and file an adoption application.

Help came in the most unlikely guise. Arriving home from school one day, Paula found her mailbox had been knocked over, and in it was a note of apology from the guilty driver, a woman called Stacey. A few hours later, there was a knock at the door; it was Stacey's husband, Greg, offering to pay for a new mailbox. Paula told him that was not necessary, but if he could fix it in the ground when she bought a new one, that would be helpful. She checked that she still had the phone number, which had been written by Stacey on a ticket stub for the Pennsylvania Turnpike.

"I drive the turnpike to Philadelphia every day," Greg said.

"Can I ask what you do?" asked Paula.

"I work for the government."

"Which department?"

"Immigration."

She explained that she was adopting a boy from Russia and was waiting for a summons to that very department. Seizing her moment, she asked him if she could ride with him when her appointment came through.

"Ma'am, you've been so good to me, I'll take the day off work to do that."

The next day the letter arrived, and Greg drove Paula to the immigration office. Thus it was that the problem of Paula's driving angst was resolved, thanks to the kindness of a stranger.

When Sarah heard that Vanya's adoption was going ahead, she felt she had to go back to Moscow and complete the life storybook that she had hastily thrown together in the days before she left for Jerusalem. She thought how important this album would be to give him a sense of self when inevitably—maybe in the distant future—he wanted to know more about where he had come from. Now the text needed to be translated into English.

But there was another, unexpected task she had been given. "When Maria heard that I was coming to Moscow, she asked me to talk to Vanya and prepare him for going to America," Sarah recalls. "This seemed an odd request. I had not seen him for a year, so why was she asking me and not his foster mother? I could not fathom this."

June is the best time of year in Moscow. Everything is moist, fresh, and full of life, unlike Jerusalem, with its bare, parched hills and the harsh sunlight bouncing off the stone-clad buildings. As she arrived in the center of Moscow, the intoxicating scent of the linden trees reminded her of past summers spent in Russia, which seemed to end almost as soon as they began.

Sarah decided to drop in and see Maria on her way to visit Vanya in his foster home. She took her a wooden cross from Bethlehem and noticed Maria had lost weight and looked pale and tired. It was obvious she was under a lot of strain.

"It's good you dropped by to see me before visiting Vanya," Maria said. "It's very important you do not say anything about going to America."

"But that's one of the reasons I came to Moscow. What's happened?" Sarah asked.

There had been a hitch. Six days before, Maria had been summoned to an urgent meeting with Mrs. Morozova, the woman who had forced Linda to wait for two hours outside her office while she took a leisurely lunch. Something in the tone used by Mrs. Morozova's secretary suggested the meeting was not going to be pleasant. Maria arrived to find the church worker who was dealing with Vanya's adoption already waiting in the corridor outside Mrs. Morozova's office. They were soon joined by a contingent from Baby House 10. Adela was in such a state of nerves that she was leaning on her legal assistant, Svetlana, who was whispering in her ear that everything would be all right and she had not done anything wrong. What happened next must have seemed like the confirmation of all Adela's worst fears.

Mrs. Morozova was sitting behind a great polished desk, with an assistant stooped at her elbow. She exploded, shouting and screaming at them and throwing papers around. Quickly identifying the weakest person, she focused her tirade on Adela.

How was it possible, she screamed, that a woman in America had found out about the boy from Baby House 10 and was now proposing to adopt him? How had this happened without Mrs. Morozova's knowledge? She would be launching an investigation to find out.

She thrust a pen and a blank sheet of paper at Adela. "You—now write a letter of resignation. Say you are resigning from your post as

head doctor of Baby House 10." Adela's hands were shaking and she was
crying as she picked up the pen and prepared to put an end to her thirty-
year career at the baby house.

Maria was not about to witness this bullying in silence. She reminded
Adela that she did not have to take orders from Mrs. Morozova. Adela
put down her pen, even more confused than before, her eyes cast down.

Then Mrs. Morozova turned screaming to Maria. "And now it turns
out this boy is in your care. How could it be that someone wants to adopt
a boy in your custody? Have you been advertising for adoptive parents
behind my back? Didn't you promise me not to have anything to do
with international adoption?"

Maria replied in a calm tone that she had played no role in finding
the adoptive mother.

"Then how did the American woman find out about this boy?"

Maria said she did not know. All she knew was that the American
woman assumed the child was in Baby House 10.

Mrs. Morozova was silent while she digested this information. This
allowed Maria to ask whether the adoption dossier had been approved.

Mrs. Morozova shot back, "The adoption cannot go ahead. The
child's documents are incomplete."

This puzzled Maria, as it was she who had put together all Vanya's
documents, including his medical records, put them all in order, and
handed them to the church worker.

Mrs. Morozova's assistant joined in. "You're very lax with documents.
You never have the right papers for your charges." The assistant disappeared and came back with Vanya's adoption dossier. "Look—it's incomplete."

Maria took hold of the dossier and started to leaf through it. Some
documents were indeed missing. She could only conclude that they had
been ripped out deliberately.

With Maria silenced, Mrs. Morozova turned her rage on the church
worker. "And you of all people, you should know how things are done.
Why didn't you do things the proper way?"

Mrs. Morozova waved the women out of her office so she could have a confidential conversation with the church worker. The assistant followed the women out and headed off down the corridor. Without pausing to think, Maria tiptoed at a discreet distance after her. Still undetected, she followed her up the stairs and right into her office. Sure enough, there on a desk were the missing documents, half concealed under a pile of papers. It appeared to Maria that the assistant had ripped them out before bringing the dossier down.

The woman gasped to see Maria standing behind her, but it was too late. Maria stretched out her hand to pick up the documents.

"I think these are the documents you couldn't find," Maria said.

"Oh, I must have forgotten them," the assistant replied brazenly.

Maria gave the assistant a scornful look and led the way back to Mrs. Morozova's office, clutching the missing documents to her breast.

Listening to this, Sarah was stunned at the cruelty of the bureaucrats trying to sabotage Vanya's future. It seemed to her that all they cared about was their position and their power. They didn't seem to give a thought to the children's welfare or, in Vanya's case, whether he lived or died.

With characteristic modesty, Maria says she did no more than anyone else would have done. But almost a decade later, the staff at Baby House 10 were still recalling with glee that wonderful day when the "indomitable" Maria had dared to stand up to the authorities.

Maria felt that, since now the authorities had been caught in a brazen act of sabotage, they would not prevent the adoption from going ahead. Their ludicrous suspicions that she and Adela were somehow involved in a secret child-selling ring had been allayed. But they were bound to slow the adoption down, to prove who was the boss. But as no one knew how long it would take, it would be better not to speak to Vanya about going to America. As it turned out, it would not have been possible anyway.

Rachel and Sarah climbed the stairs to Sonya's apartment in silence, not sure what sort of reception to expect. But Sonya welcomed them in, wearing a satin mini-robe for the occasion. Sarah felt touched that she had dressed up for her guests, but embarrassed for her that they had turned up in jeans and no makeup. They were not the sophisticated Western women she was expecting. They were shown into the sitting room, where Vanya, his foster sister, and Baboulya were sitting quietly. Sarah had brought Vanya a box of LEGOs, but it was left unopened on the table. He seemed very much on his guard.

Sarah sat down next to Sonya and tried to put her at her ease, and Rachel took a place beside Vanya, on the other side of the coffee table. Soon Sonya was recounting stories of her work in internats, how she had been mother to dozens of abandoned teenage girls. She brought out a box full of tragic letters from these girls pleading to come and live with her. She even got out photo albums of her childhood in the Caucasus.

She had clearly done heroic work with these desperate girls, but this was not what Sarah and Rachel had come for. As Sonya continued to talk, Vanya whispered to Rachel, "Let's go to the other room. I'll show you the kitchen." Sarah willed her friend to understand, but she could not make out what Vanya was saying. Sarah could only guess that he thought if he could get one of them alone, he might find out what was going to happen to him. As for Sonya, she said nothing about her life with Vanya or the progress he had made since coming to live with her, and the subject of his adoption never arose. She insisted on accompanying them on their walk around the neighborhood. In the end, Sarah never got a chance for a one-on-one chat with Vanya.

As she left, her only comfort was that his foster sister and grandmother seemed very fond of him. But neither Sarah nor Rachel could understand Sonya's behavior. She was suspicious of them and possessive of Vanya. Before coming to Moscow, Sarah had imagined herself with Vanya and Sonya, sticking photos of his months with his foster family into his album and chatting about his new life in America. She left not knowing what his future held.

25

A Prisoner of the Caucasus

June–July 1999

Vanya was curled up next to Baboulya on the sofa as they watched their favorite soap opera, *The Rich also Cry*. The rich man's wife was sneaking out of her mansion in the dead of night to meet her new friend, a waiter in the restaurant. Vanya noticed he brought the food to the tables, not like in McDonald's where you had to fetch it yourself. Vanya was pleased to see she was not going to leave behind her birthday present, a brand new sports car, even though she risked waking her husband. Baboulya and Vanya tensed as the garage door groaned open and the husband stirred in his sleep.

At that moment, the phone rang. Sonya had been resting in bed, and she staggered groggily into the hall to answer it. Vanya switched his attention from the fleeing wife and her sports car to Sonya. Sonya said little, but within seconds she had become fully alert.

"But we can't not go. My daughter is down there. I have to join her."

There was silence again. Then she said: "No, I'm not prepared to hang around in Moscow. I'll tell you what—I'll give you the phone number of our apartment in the south. You can call me if they ever set a court date."

Vanya's heart skipped a beat at the words "court date." He had had a court date with Linda. Now they were talking about another one. Was Linda coming back for him after all? Was he going to England?

He needed answers to these questions. Sonya had the answers, but she was not telling him anything. He was afraid to ask her; he knew she would shout at him. Now what was she doing? She was standing on a chair and angrily pulling down bags from a cupboard over the front door.

She stomped into the sitting room, turned off the television, and announced, "Mama, we're taking the evening train. You get the food ready. I'll pack." She did not even look at Vanya.

Soon Vanya was surrounded by frenetic activity. In the small sitting room, every patch of floor was taken up with a suitcase or a squashy zip-up bag. Sonya was darting between her bedroom and the sitting room, carrying armfuls of clothes.

Baboulya was in the kitchen. "Do we really have to catch the train this evening?" she pleaded. "Couldn't we go in a couple in days so we have time to pack properly?"

"No. It has to be today," Sonya said. Vanya saw she had the look in her eye that meant she had made up her mind and would not be swayed.

Baboulya came into sitting room, her hair awry and still dressed in her cotton nightshirt.

"But I've got all this food to cook for the journey and I haven't packed my clothes. And look at Vanya—he's not even dressed." Sonya ignored her as she strained at the zipper of an overstuffed bag.

Vanya had never been on a train before. That evening they spilled out of a taxi at the Kazan station and into a tide of people. Nobody made way for his stroller, and Sonya forced it through an unyielding crowd of people dragging cumbersome pieces of baggage. All the time she was saying to her mother, "Come on, come on, we mustn't miss the train." As Sonya pressed ahead, Baboulya lagged behind, burdened by two heavy bags. When they reached the train, a woman in uniform told them off for being late. As Sonya passed the stroller to her, Vanya looked down and had a thrill of excitement to see the giant steel wheels below him. They had barely got their bags inside when the train jolted and began moving out of the station.

Vanya was delighted to see they had their own little room, with two sets of bunk beds. Baboulya settled him on one of the lower bunks as she and Sonya dragged in the bags. There was a rattling outside the door, and the woman in uniform brought in three glasses of tea and two lumps of sugar each. For the first time since the phone call, Sonya looked relaxed, and encouraged Vanya to help himself to sugar. Baboulya unpacked a picnic, and they all peeled hard-boiled eggs and ate them with black bread.

Vanya was not used to sleeping on a bunk, and as the train lurched and swayed he fell on the floor at least three times. After a whole day of watching the countryside and a second night of falling out of his bunk, they arrived at their destination, the station at Mineralnye Vody, where Sonya had spent her childhood.

In Moscow, Vanya's life had been mostly indoors in front of the television. But here life was dramatically different. To Vanya's relief, Sonya's mood improved and she even started to smile again. One thing he could not understand was why they kept moving from relative to relative. They would spend two days in Baboulya's flat and then move to Sonya's brother's place and then after two more days, without warning, they would be back at Baboulya's.

The days had a strict regimen. Every morning, Sonya woke him and took him for treatment in a big building in a park, with white columns outside. The treatment would start in a hot room where they wrapped Vanya's legs tightly in towels as hot as he could bear. When he objected, Sonya told him to bear it because this treatment would cure him and he would walk. He put up with the heat even though he felt his legs were on fire.

If that was not enough, when the cloths were removed, she took him to another room, where he had to lie on a bench with his feet in the air, attached to a massaging machine. It was very painful, but Sonya said he had to bear it because it would stretch his feet.

When that was over, a fat woman in a white coat gave him a big injection in his bottom, as they used to do in Filimonki. The injection did not make him sleepy, but it upset his stomach and he had to sit on the lavatory for two hours afterward. Even at home—wherever that happened to be—Sonya would put him in metal leg braces, with a hinge at the knee. Once again Sonya ignored his pleas to be allowed to rest and told him the braces would straighten his legs. She clearly believed all of these treatments would help him.

In the afternoon, he would be set free from Sonya's treatment regimen. He was allowed to play in a sandbox under the trees with his cars.

Sometimes his foster sister would sit next to him and make sand castles or roads for his cars. Then she would take him in his stroller to buy an ice cream on the promenade, from where they could see the snow-capped Caucasus mountains.

But one day everything changed again. It was a balmy evening. Vanya was in the sandbox outside Sonya's brother's flat. He was singing to himself as he lined up all his cars on the edge of the sandbox. He imagined himself as the driver of the lead car in a rally through the mountains. He looked up to see Sonya striding toward him, a furious look on her face. She stood over him.

"Vanya, I've got something important to tell you. Two women are on their way here from Moscow. They're coming to take you away from me. They're going to give you to another woman and she'll beat you." She paused for breath. "You've got to stop them."

She swooped down on his line of cars and grabbed two handfuls of them.

"This is what you must do when they come." She hurled the cars one by one into the sandbox. "You must throw your toys at them. You must tell them to go away. If you behave badly enough, they won't want to take you. If you go to live with this woman, it won't be like living with me. She'll be nasty to you and beat you."

Vanya could not take in what she was saying. No one had ever suggested he behave badly before. All his life he had tried to understand people and to please them. He remembered guiltily the one time he had misbehaved in the baby house. Vika had told him about camels and how they spat. He had pretended to be a camel and practiced spitting, and the staff at the baby house had scolded him. He felt bad when he remembered how he was caught spitting. He didn't want to have that feeling again.

But Sonya had said he would be beaten. Memories of his time in Filimonki flashed into his brain. Children were dragged across the floor into a room next to his. The door was slammed shut, but he could still hear the sound of their shrieks as they were beaten. He was always worried that he had done something wrong and it would be his turn next.

Vanya quietly collected up his cars and set them back in their places on the edge of the sandbox while Sonya sat silent and brooding.

She suddenly burst out, "After all I've done for you, and all the treatment I've organized for you, I'm left with nothing. Instead of insulting me, they should be thanking me."

Sonya went back inside. Vanya continued playing with his cars, but his thoughts were on the extraordinary things that Sonya had said. Who were these women who were coming for him? They must be bad women, like Galina in the baby house who used to pull Julia's hair. Why didn't they want him to stay with Sonya? It seemed Sonya did love him after all, even though he had made her angry so often. It was obvious from what she had just said that she needed him. Poor Sonya.

He forced himself to imagine throwing toys at the women as she had told him to do. That would make them not like him. And they would not want to take him. And he would not be beaten. And he could stay with Sonya and she would not be sad.

Try as he might, he could not imagine himself throwing toys at anyone. He had another thought. Perhaps if the women gave Sonya lots of presents, she would be happy and she would not miss him so much. That's what she needed. A suitcase full of lovely things. That would make her happy.

26
A White Lie

July–August 1999

The court date for Vanya's adoption was finally set for July 30, and the church worker instructed Paula to arrive in Moscow two days before. Paula thought there was too little time between her arrival and the court date, but the church worker had been insistent that there was no need for her to come any earlier. He explained that the law required her to have three meetings with Vanya before appearing in front of the judge. She would go to meet Vanya straight from the airport, then she would see him again the next day, and then the third time in the morning before the court appearance. When she pointed out that she had to be in court at 10:00 A.M., and shouldn't she come a day earlier, he dismissed her concerns. "You'll be getting up early."

The daunting journey to Moscow was made easier by the fact that she would have friends at every step. Two close friends drove her early in the morning to JFK airport in New York and waved good-bye, promising to be waiting for her when she returned with her son.

Emerging into the arrivals hall at Moscow airport, she was gripped by panic at the press of people crowding around her. The hall was so packed that it seemed impossible to force a way through with her suitcases. A picture of her Russian grandfather traveling in the opposite direction formed in her head. He must have battled though similar crowds almost a century before, she thought, to get a berth on a ship to America. In 1914, at the age of seventeen, he had left his native Ukraine to make his fortune in the American coal fields. He had never returned. But here she was, his granddaughter, making the journey for him.

She pulled herself back to the present and scrutinized the sea of Russian faces. They were all a blur. Her gaze was drawn to a blond beard on a youthful face, which broke into a warm smile of greeting. It was Alexei, a young deacon who had lodged with her for three years—at first on his own and then with his wife, Maria—while he studied at an Orthodox seminary in Pennsylvania.

"Paula. Welcome to Moscow."

She found herself enveloped in a bear hug. Alexei wrestled her suitcase from her, locked his free arm around hers, and pulled her through the crowd and outside into what seemed to her like a construction site with cars parked at every angle.

"Alexei, I'm so grateful you're here to meet me," she said as Alexei started the engine. "Without you, I couldn't have done this. You and your wife are like family."

"We are not like family," he said ponderously. "We *are* family."

As Alexei piloted the car through the swirling traffic to Moscow, she shrank back in her seat at the sight of the smashed wrecks of vehicles beside the road. Cars were passing them on both sides, cutting in ahead of them, and the traffic seemed to have no rules at all. The Pennsylvania Turnpike seemed positively sedate compared with the Leningrad Highway.

The church worker had given Alexei an address in the center of Moscow, which she assumed to be Baby House 10. He had promised he would be waiting for them. So when they drew up outside an old house in a narrow winding street, she thought this must be the building within whose walls Vanya had spent his whole life. As Alexei parked the car half on the pavement, her eyes were scouring the street for the man who was going to take her to see her son. There was only one person on the street, a man in a dark suit and white shirt carrying an attaché case. With his short haircut and clean-shaven face, he did not look like a church type. In fact, he looked like he was in business. But while Paula and Alexei were getting out of the car, the man approached, and after a perfunctory greeting, muttered, "I'm going inside. Wait for me here."

Paula was pleasantly surprised at how pretty the buildings were. There was a smart new bank, and a church nearby. But there was no sound of children's voices. The place seemed deserted. As the minutes ticked by, she began to feel anxious. She asked Alexei what he thought could be going on.

She focused on the door, awaiting the appearance of the boy she already thought of as her son John. But when the door opened, the church worker was alone.

"You must come inside."

Paula reached over to the backseat for the bag of presents she had brought. She and Alexei followed the church worker into the building. Her first thought was, Why are there no children around? It was completely quiet. Something was clearly wrong. They found themselves in an office piled high with books and files, and brightly colored wooden ornaments on the shelves. The church worker introduced them to a slim, pale young woman with a great pyramid of curls.

"Paula, this is Maria. She will explain the situation."

In perfect English, in a low but authoritative voice, Maria explained that Vanya was not in the building. He was with his foster mother, 1,000 miles to the south.

"Foster mother! What foster mother?" Paula burst out. She struggled to comprehend. She looked at her surroundings and something clicked. "This isn't Baby House 10, is it?"

Maria's pale face broke into a smile. "No, this is not a baby house.

This is the Our Family foster project. Vanya left the baby house a year ago. He's living with one of my foster mothers."

Paula felt her world crumbling. She turned to the church worker. "Why didn't you tell me he had a foster mother all this time? Why didn't you tell me he wasn't in the baby house?"

The church worker showed no contrition. "I didn't want to bother you with all the details."

"And now I find out he's not even in Moscow!"

He shrugged, apparently indifferent to Paula's growing anguish. "What about the court hearing? It's the day after tomorrow. What are we going to do?"

The church worker insisted it was business as usual. "We can't change the court date. The hearing has to go ahead. We'll sort something out."

Paula gazed at him in mute incomprehension at his detached reaction to the mounting crisis.

Maria stepped in to reassure her. "Don't worry, Paula. I'll fly down and get Vanya. But it won't be until after the court hearing. It'll be okay, because Vanya doesn't have to be in court."

Paula instinctively knew she could trust this young woman, but nothing could stop her feeling more deeply disappointed than she had ever felt in her life. Back in the car, she broke down in sobs. The nine months of anticipation, the mountains of paperwork, the rearranging of her life, and then the long journey through eight time zones had ended in nothing. The boy was gone. Through her sobs, she told Alexei she felt heartsick. She had so counted on seeing John that day. She felt like a mother leaving the maternity hospital with empty arms.

The next thirty-six hours would have been impossible to bear if she had not had the support of Alexei and his wife. She kept her feelings of anxiety at bay by playing with their baby, going to church, and reminiscing about the time when they lived together in America. But every so often, fear would steal upon her. What was she going to say to the judge?

She woke on the morning of the court hearing after an almost sleepless night. She was about to stand up in court and testify that she had seen John three times and had bonded with him. She pictured herself being led away in handcuffs for deceiving the judge. Then she thought about the video. How many times had she watched it? At least 300. She knew every gesture, every expression of her little boy. She smiled to herself as she recalled how he said "thank you" at the end in thickly accented English.

Later that day, when the judge asked Paula to describe her relationship with the boy, she replied without hesitation, "Loving." The judge approved the application. They boy was hers. Now all she had to do was find him.

27

Unforgiven

August 1999

Vanya was by himself in the sandbox, still unaware that after all the years of waiting and longing, he had just acquired a mother. All he knew was that two evil women were coming to take him away from his mama, and give him to another mama, who would beat him. It was his job to scare them away by throwing his toys at them.

As the light began to fade, a car drove up. He stared intently as two women climbed out and saw there was something familiar about them. As they approached, he saw one was Maria, immediately recognizable with her pyramid of curls, and the other was Irina, who had come to visit him several times at Sonya's apartment. Surely these could not be the evil women that Sonya was talking about?

They sat down on either side of him and asked him where his cars were going. As he explained to them about the rally through the mountains, he realized these must be the women, and he felt guilty that he was not doing what Sonya had asked him to do. He felt anxious that she might suddenly appear and see him being friendly.

"Here's one to add to the race," said Irina, pulling out a brand-new toy car from her bag. It was so shiny and new that Vanya placed it at the head of the rally. It was obviously going to be the winner.

He felt a stab of guilt that he had taken the car. He should have thrown it in their faces as Sonya had demanded. But now it was too late.

"You should give Sonya a big suitcase of presents," he blurted out. "That's what she needs."

The women did not react to this. They asked him gently where Sonya was, but she was already striding toward them.

Upstairs in her brother's apartment, Sonya made tea for everyone without saying a word. The women drank their tea in silence, while Vanya played with his cars in the living room. Maria's soft but insistent voice broke the silence.

"But surely you understand. This is Vanya's only chance. There's nothing for him in Russia. You know yourself, you've worked in an internat. Children like Vanya are kept in cribs. In America, he'll get an education."

"You think I haven't done my best for him? He's a different child now. He's part of our family. He's not like a child from an institution anymore. And look how much his walking has improved. I've been taking him for treatment on his legs, and the latest vitamin therapy, every day. I'm not just here on holiday, you know."

"We're very grateful for all you've done for him. You took him in when we were desperate . . ."

"Yes, and it wasn't easy. I had to bring my mother to live with us in Moscow so that Vanya would always have company."

"But Sonya, this is his one great opportunity. You know yourself that there is no school in Russia that would take him."

"You just don't understand." Sonya's voice rose and there was the sound of a chair scraping back. "You're taking away my son."

Vanya caught a glimpse of Sonya's grief-stricken face as she stormed into the sitting room to grab her cigarettes and made for the front door, slamming it behind her.

Vanya looked down at the car in his hand, the shiny new one that Irina had given him. He put it down on the ground. It was no longer the rally leader. He smashed it into another car, with all his force. He was dimly aware of Irina crouching on the floor beside him.

"What's the car doing, Vanya? It seems to have had a crash."

"It's a police car, and it's coming to arrest us all and take us away."

"But nobody's done anything wrong. No one is going to jail. But we're taking you to Moscow tomorrow where someone is waiting for you."

Vanya returned to smashing his cars. The new car was completely out of control. It crashed head on into a table leg, then reversed and smashed into it again. Its shiny paint was chipped. He left it a wreck and went on to do the same with the other cars. Bang and smash they went.

That evening, after the women had gone to spend the night in the other flat, Sonya vented her anger on Vanya.

"Why didn't you do what I said? Why didn't you throw your toys at them and drive them away? I told you what to do." Her face was contorted with rage and she was bellowing at him. "I thought you loved me, but you're a deceitful boy. You let me down."

Something snapped inside Vanya. He had to say something to make her stop. He felt again the hurt of the months since she had cooled toward him. "I don't love you. I want to go with Maria tomorrow."

As soon as the words were out of his mouth, he regretted what he had said. Sonya left the room. An hour later she came back with a suitcase. She silently put everything he owned in it—his clothes and his precious cars. She helped him into bed, still not speaking to him. Nor did she kiss him good night. She turned out the light.

He barely slept that night. Sonya came to wake him when it was barely light. She was still silent. He took a deep breath. "You know I love you. I'm sorry I said what I did. I'll miss you, Sonya."

He waited for her to respond, but she did not. As he was finishing his porridge, the doorbell rang. Sonya picked up his suitcase, grabbed his coat, and took him downstairs to the waiting car. She put him on the backseat and shut the door. She did not even say good-bye.

A decade later, as Vanya looks back on his nine-year-old self, his voice still betrays the pain and hurt of that moment of parting. "I wanted so much to make peace with Sonya and heal the wounds before I left," he says, "but she would not accept my apology." As for Sonya, even now, when asked to talk about Vanya, she can barely breathe. It seems as if emotion is restricting her throat.

At the airport, Vanya had no time to dwell on his parting with Sonya. He was mesmerized by the sight of aircraft of all sizes and excited when they headed across the tarmac to the biggest one, the flight to Moscow. But once on the plane, he was overwhelmed by thoughts of the family he had abandoned—the only family he had ever known.

Throughout the flight, he tormented a big teddy bear. He held the bear by the ears and beat his knee against it. The unfortunate bear was the focus of all his anxiety. Once again he was leaving behind all that was familiar and heading into the unknown. These feelings were compounded by grief and anger at Sonya, who had rejected his attempt at reconciliation and refused to come to the airport and say good-bye to him.

By the time they began their descent, trauma had completely numbed him. Maria carried him down the steps from the plane and onto the tarmac. He was so exhausted that he could barely register the features of the smiling woman who was there to greet him, the person he had overcome so many obstacles to find.

"Hi, I'm your mother," she said, in American-accented Russian.

For the first time in his life, Vanya was speechless.

In the car on the way to Moscow, Vanya sat on the backseat, between Paula and Irina. The church worker was driving, with Maria in the passenger seat beside him. When he found his voice, it was to talk to the driver. As ever, he did not pass up an opportunity to talk to a man about cars. Having discovered what type of car it was and who owned it, he suddenly, without pausing, turned to Paula and asked her: "Will you beat me?" These were the first words he said to his mother. Paula did not understand his question. Maria translated. Paula still looked puzzled. Then her faced changed.

"Oh, no," she replied, visibly shocked.

He leaned toward her and they embraced. After that there was no need for translation. "When I witnessed this moment of acceptance when he began to trust his new mother, I wanted to cry from happiness," Irina recalls.

What Vanya really needed at that time was to go somewhere quiet and comfortable to continue bonding with his mother. But it was not to be. The church worker was obliged that day to attend a celebratory feast at the Church of the Archangel Michael in Moscow. He did not explain why he was taking his passengers to have lunch with a lot of bishops in these, the crucial first hours of Vanya and Paula's life together. But Paula guessed at the reason—he would not have to organize lunch for his charges.

The Church of the Archangel Michael was no ordinary church. It was one of the most famous in Russia thanks to appearing in a much-loved film, *The Irony of Fate*, where the director daringly contrasted its timeless beauty with the grim monotony of Soviet life. Even for the non-religious, the church with its five gold domes and bright red exterior was a symbol of hope.

When they arrived, the feast had already begun. Bishops in their black robes and long beards were digging into buckwheat bliny and red caviar, pickled herring, and an array of cold meats. Before they were shown their table, Vanya told Maria he needed the toilet. Maria asked him who he would like to take him. Without hesitating, Vanya said, "Mama." Paula could not believe that within an hour of meeting, he had identified her as the one who would provide for his needs.

The church worker showed his guests to a table with a good view of the feasting priests. The women were given glasses of Georgian wine and Vanya had a glass of water. Soon, in the Russian tradition, the toasts began, as one bishop after another got to his feet and raised a glass of vodka to the health of the assembled party. Vanya was so fascinated by this ritual that he somehow put aside the trauma of the past twenty-four hours. He ignored the food piled high on his plate and watched the bishop on the table to his right stand up, propose a flowery toast, and then sit down amid a downing of shots of vodka. Vanya felt sure it was now his turn to speak on behalf of his table of women. He picked up his glass in one hand and pressed down on the table with the other, trying to raise himself up. Just in time, Paula realized what he was trying to do. This small child was so quick at picking up social cues that he was already trying to be one of the guys—or in this case, the bishops. She put a loving hand on his shoulder and said, "There'll be time for that, plenty of time, when you're older."

28
Reunited
March 2007

So far, Vanya's remarkable story has been told by the people who became close to him in the 1990s—Vika and Sarah—and by Vanya himself. My role as the author has been to collect their stories and put them together into a narrative. But the story does not end with Vanya's getting on a plane to America. Now it is time for me to emerge from the shadows and do a bit of sleuthing to discover what even the people closest to Vanya did not know about his past.

I had always wondered what happened to this extraordinary child who, naked and powerless, had refused to be defeated by the cruel Russian orphanage system and had touched the lives of so many people. Unexpectedly, in early 2007, after a long journalistic career, I found myself with time to find out what had happened to Vanya. It was time for a reunion in America.

Thus it was that in March 2007, Sarah and I drove up to a single-story house enveloped in a thick blanket of late spring snow. This was not Santa Barbara—real or imagined—but Bethlehem, Pennsylvania.

Standing by the door, supported on crutches, was a handsome young man with sparkling white teeth and a rather austere haircut. Sarah could not stop herself greeting him as she had done when visiting him in Baby House 10 all those years ago. The words *"Privet Vanya"* just slipped out. The young man looked puzzled. It was eight years since anyone had greeted him in Russian or called him Vanya. Now he was John Lahutsky, high school student and youth leader in his Scout troop.

His mother, Paula, greeted us warmly, and in minutes we felt we had known her all our lives. In honor of her Slavic heritage, the front room was decorated with brightly colored Russian folk art.

It was obvious that John and Paula were very close. When asked how they felt at their first meeting at Moscow airport, they replied in unison, "I was terrified"—and both laughed.

John learned to speak English fluently within three months of arriving in the U.S., and almost as quickly forgot his Russian. I was touched he had transferred his style of speech from Russian into English. He still had the endearing habit of pausing while he searched for exactly the right word. Recalling the appalling conditions he was kept in in the Filimonki mental asylum, he searched for the words to describe the bare mattress he had to lie on twenty-four hours a day. "It was made of . . . fabricated leather." Nothing could better describe the texture of the cheap synthetic material covering a rectangle of foam.

Nowadays, John travels to school every day on the bus. His favorite subject is history, but he finds math difficult because simple mathematical techniques are acquired early in life, when he was locked in a silent room.

For the first time, while we sipped ice tea, we heard Paula's story, how her life had changed forever when, in September 1998, she was reading her parish newsletter and came across an item written by a couple who had just adopted a little girl from Russia.

What Paula told us solved the mystery of how she had found out about Vanya. This was the couple who, emerging from Baby House 10 with their newly adopted daughter in July, had bumped into Vanya and Sarah on a bench outside in the yard. Vanya had made such an impression that they could not get him out of their minds and felt compelled to act. The item they wrote had the same effect on Paula.

Paula told us that throughout the two weeks Vanya spent with her in Moscow after their first meeting at the airport, he remained in an extremely delicate state and very tearful.

As we filled her in on the background, Paula understood how terrified he had been that she too would reject him. We all agreed that his state was hardly surprising since, despite all his efforts to bond with two previous "mothers," he had not been taken to England and he had been excluded from the warmth of his foster family. Like all abandoned children, he had got used to taking responsibility for his own fate, and when the two mothers turned their backs on him, he blamed himself.

John recalled one of the bitterest memories of his time in Baby House 10, which haunted him like a recurring nightmare. He kept seeing the face of Adela leaning over his crib on the day Linda had failed to come to court. Her gentle features were transformed into a witch's snarl and her meek voice became Baba Yaga's evil cackle, endlessly taunting him: "They haven't come for you. You'll never leave now."

At the time, Paula had only a vague inkling of all the trauma Vanya had been through. One of the problems was that Vanya had not been prepared for what was going to happen to him. During the nine months it took Paula to complete the adoption, no one actually took Vanya aside and explained to him that he was going to America. This is not as surprising as it sounds. Maria, Vanya's official guardian, had no contact with Paula until she arrived in Moscow. She did not even know the date Paula was arriving. Given the obstructiveness of the authorities and Vanya's betrayal by Linda, the psychologist on Maria's staff thought it better to say nothing until the adoption was a certainty. By that time, of course, it had already happened.

But the person who had done most to save Vanya could not share in the joy of his adoption. The reason was simple: Vika had taken her baby out of the city to spend the summer in the fresh air of the countryside, living in a wooden house with no phone. Thus it was that Vika did not have a chance to say good-bye, hug him and hold him and wish him luck in his new life. Neither did her group of friends who had invested so much time in visiting him. For Vika, when Vanya disappeared from Moscow, it was as if he had died.

To this day Maria regrets it was not possible for Vika and Paula to meet. Vika could have told her the story of Vanya's early years and helped her understand all the trauma her son had been through. "To an extent we were all excluded in one way or another from the adoption process. What happened is an example of how Russian law is not child-centered. The social services and the courts consider children as commodities that can be moved here and there without any human touch or consideration of their feelings."

During the two weeks that Paula had to wait in Moscow for the adoption to be confirmed, Vanya remained in a state of acute distress. This might have overwhelmed another mother, but Paula was a school psychologist and she persevered through all the tears. Once back in Pennsylvania, Vanya was finally convinced that there would be no more rejection. One day, he came back into the house after playing in the yard and felt confident enough to say, "You are my beloved mama."

We spent two days with John and Paula, reminiscing about the past. Not surprisingly, these memories were deeply painful to John and raised some unsettling questions.

John made clear he still feels very bitter about his falling out with Sonya, and it is his memories of this distressing period that inspire the previous chapters. We told John that he is not the only one who has painful memories. The experience left a deep wound in Sonya, which also has not healed. Her recollection of the months they spent together is dramatically different from his. The course of events left her feeling betrayed and bereft because, despite everything that happened, he has a place in her heart.

On the second day, he began to ask more focused questions about his life in Russia as he struggled to make sense of the treatment he had received there.

Why, he wondered, had Adela—who appeared to be a good person—allowed him to be sent to a mental asylum? "I think she must have been afraid of the Communists," he ventured.

He wanted to know what had happened to his parents. "There are rumors in the documents they were abusing alcohol," he said delicately. He was also aware he had an older half-brother, Vadim, and a sister, Olga, born in 1985, who at the time of his leaving Russia was in an orphanage.

The hardest question to answer was the one he found most difficult to ask. He asked Sarah, "When you told Vika of the terrible conditions I was kept in in the mental asylum, did she rush to report it to the police?" He was too polite to put the question bluntly: Why didn't you get me out of there immediately? Why did you leave me there suffering for nine months?

It was clear this was an American talking. In John's mind, a report of child abuse should mobilize the police and the social services to mount a rescue operation, with helicopters and guns at the ready. It was hard to explain that his treatment in Russia was not against the law, but the routine fate of children diagnosed as oligophrenics.

Providing a fuller answer to John's delicately posed question was the stimulus for writing this book. The question as to the fate of his family would require some old-fashioned knocking on doors.

Before parting, Sarah felt it was time for two people who a decade ago had been so close to be reunited. She reached for her cell phone and called a Moscow number. When a cheery voice answered, Sarah said, "There's someone here who wants to speak to you."

"Vika, it's John here."

He could not get another word in. He was deafened by an unstoppable torrent of Russian. His face took on a panicked look. Then he pulled himself together and said firmly, "Vika," several times, until there was silence on the line. Then he said something in English he knew she could not fail to understand: "Vika, I love you very much."

29
A Bit of Sleuthing

May 2007

A few weeks after that reunion in Bethlehem, I was back in Moscow, standing on a narrow metro platform with trains crashing through the station on either side of me. Every ninety seconds, they arrived from opposite directions, their screeching brakes and clattering doors perfectly synchronized, like machines on a giant factory floor. I could not leave the platform because I was waiting for a young woman whose lack of punctuality had exasperated me a decade ago. Ten years ago, Vika had guided me to a little boy hidden away behind high walls. Today I needed her skills again.

I wondered if I would recognize her. Back then she had been a poor student, embarrassed to ask me to buy her a meat pasty to sustain her. Now she was in her mid-thirties, respectably married and mother of three children. As the trains continued to smash my eardrums, I took out from my jacket pocket a single sheet of paper—the record, dated November 27,

1991, of the arrival of a baby boy, Vanya Pastukhov, in a Moscow orphanage. Next to his name was a one-line address. It appeared to be a
village, but somehow inside the city of Moscow. It was most confusing,
but this photocopy was my only clue, my pirate's treasure map. It was all
I had to help me trace one family in a city of 12 million. When the entry
was made in the register, Moscow was the capital of a superpower, the
U.S.S.R., which ceased to exist within months. The city itself was being
bulldozed and rebuilt even as I waited. The chances of finding anyone at
that old address were, I thought, slim in the extreme.

When Vika skipped off the train, she looked scarcely older than the
day of our first meeting eleven years before. Tall and slim, she showed
no sign of having been through three pregnancies. Her enthusiasm for
the task I had set her was undimmed by having three boys at home, all
the more so as this was a rare outing from the relentless burdens of moth-
erhood. Over the hellish noise, she explained the lengths she had gone to
escape. The youngest was ill and was parked with grandma; the eldest
had a headache and was home alone.

We headed to the surface, to be faced with a teeming mass of humanity. Amid the buses, trams, and minibuses, there were stalls selling everything under the sun. There was a great struggle to survive, like in a
city in Africa or Asia. I had a flashback to Communist times, when re-
tail was a question of putting the customers off, not drawing them in. I
remembered a furniture store around the corner from where I lived, with
a much-prized display cabinet in the window. On it was stuck a label:
THIS ITEM IS NOT AVAILABLE.

We found some taxis pulled up on the pavement, some wheezing La-
das with a band of leather-jacketed and gold-toothed cutthroats leaning
on them. The pudgiest one seemed to be the first in line. I showed him
the address, and he asked for 400 rubles. We agreed on 300. He bumped
off the pavement, and soon we were heading toward fancier parts.

It was a totally different Moscow from the one I had left behind nine
years before.

I remembered coming to this part of town to nose around the house
where Solzhenitsyn, the famously reclusive dissident writer, had chosen

to live on his return from exile. I remembered only wooded hillsides and an unspoiled river. Now on the Moscow riverbank there were four fantastical tower blocks with bright orange balconies and a make-believe lighthouse. On the top of each tower there appeared to be two Greek temples and a coliseum, to add tone.

"They're for the superrich. They can moor their yachts outside," the driver explained. All the poor people who used to live there had been rehoused, causing a lot of local resentment, so that this piece of make-believe Miami could rise on the banks of the Moscow River.

With undisguised schadenfreude the driver continued, "The builders broke all the technical rules. I read about it in the newspapers. The towers are built on marshy ground. If the electricity is cut off for an hour, the basements will flood."

"It's a good thing you didn't buy a penthouse there," I said. He laughed and we became friends.

We drove over the eight lanes of traffic of the outer ring road, and in an instant we had moved from city to countryside. We were now among tumbledown single-story houses with rusting tin roofs, drunken windows decorated with painted fretwork, and yards full of rusting cars. Amid these wooden peasant homes, mini-castles of brick were poking their turrets above the birch trees—more residences for the rich, which were incongruously known as cottages.

Vika and I looked at the address again. It was just a street name and a string of numbers: 2nd Myakininsky Street, 2-2-7. It looked like all the streets had the same name, and were numbered first, second, third, and so on. So we were looking for house number 2 on the second street. And house number 2 must be made up of several buildings, and we needed the second building. And in that building we were looking for flat 7.

The village seemed to have only one road, but there were no street names, no numbers, and no one to ask. None of the buildings looked big enough to have seven flats in them.

Vika had scoured the village in 1996 to track down Vanya's birth mother, but she did not recognize any of the buildings now. At the end of the road, I saw a concrete gatehouse guarding the entrance to a development of fancy new houses with plenty of space to park 4x4s out-side. I got out of the taxi to ask directions, but it was like trying to get into the Green Zone in Baghdad. I could not go up to the gatehouse but had to shout through a high steel fence.

"Is this second Myakininsky Street?"

"It might be," said the guard.

"So where would Number 2 be?"

He pointed to the other side of the road. We drove by the village bus stop and up a steep sandy road toward the top of the hill. Without a word of complaint, the driver gunned the ancient Lada over mounds of sand and around great potholes, refusing our offers to get out and walk. We came to a halt by a giant concrete wall cutting a swath through the forest. It was already twice as high as me, and its supports suggested it would be twice as high again when finished. From behind the wall came the sound of bulldozers and shouting workmen.

The road was cut by a great steel gate. I got out and tried to squeeze around the end of the concrete barrier, but at that moment the gate opened and two men emerged. One was short, jolly, and round, the other tall and intellectual-looking with glasses and a comb-over. I showed them the ad-dress and they did a comic doubles act.

"It's been bulldozed," said the first.

"It's still standing," said the second, just as confidently.

"Bulldozed."

"Still standing."

They argued furiously as they pointed to the other side of the wall. All the houses had been cleared away except for one. Perhaps this was the one we were looking for. At least, I thought, there's a 50-50 chance that Vanya's first home still exists.

I asked, "What are they building behind the wall?"

"They're building *taunhauzy*," said the egghead.

"What on earth are they?"

"You know—like cottages, but bigger."

The light dawned. Vanya's old home was being demolished to be re-placed by town houses. If a new Russian cottage was the size of a Disneyland castle, then the town houses must rival Buckingham Palace. No wonder a twelve-foot wall was not high enough to shield them from the envious eyes of the poor.

"Who is going to live there?" asked Vika, appalled at the destruction of the forest.

"The common people, of course," the guard joked, aping the pompous manner of a Soviet announcer. "Under Russian capitalism, comrade, the poor are protected from the tyranny of the rich!"

The guard was now unstoppable. "Take a look at that wall. It's as big as the one the Americans are building in Baghdad between the Sunnis and the Shiites."

He told us to go down the hill and come back up another way and we would find the entrance to the building site. We did as he told us and came to a guard post with two uniformed security men. I showed them the address. One replied, "I've never heard of it. Go and ask the grannies in the village."

Vika was totally confused. Back down the hill, we came across an old woman, the postal mistress no less. The driver, now a willing partner in the quest, hailed her. She said she had no idea where the address was. We sat in the car in silence, not knowing where to try next. Half the morning was gone, and no result.

"I don't think we'll find anyone here," I said gloomily to Vika. "We'll probably have to come back in the evening. Maybe everyone is planting potatoes."

"Something will turn up," she said. She was supposed to go to her son's piano concert in the evening, so the idea of returning later was not welcome.

As I sank in gloom, Vika suddenly leaped out of the car. She had seen a woman peering from behind a half-open gate and had rushed to accost her.

"Can you help us?" she asked. "We're looking for the family of a boy called Vanya who used to live here. The mother's name is Natasha."

"I know who she is. I knew the family," said the woman. "Come in."

We got out of the car. Our helper was dressed in a sky-blue polo shirt, and she introduced herself as Nadia, the village elder. Her family had lived here since the seventeenth century. She had recently retired from what she coyly described as state security—in other words, the KGB. Vika was delighted to see the walls of her neat wooden house were decorated with religious icons and Orthodox crosses.

"The person I knew best was the boy's grandmother, Tatyana. She was a painter-decorator," she said. Like all the people who lived in the settlement up on top of the hill—she pointed to where the bulldozers were at work—Tatyana worked in a complex of holiday homes down the road in Rublyovo, the next village.

Nadia's husband butted in. "That's where the Communist party bigwigs used to come for a good time."

She told us Vanya's grandmother was a hard worker, a great cook, and a demon for cleanliness. She and her husband, Ivan, lived happily together and spent hours tending their vegetable plot. Just yesterday, she said, she was following Tatyana's recipe for pickled pepper salad.

Tatyana did not have a child until she was nearly forty when, to her surprise, she gave birth to a girl, Natasha. Nadia did not seem very keen to say anything more about Vanya's mother.

Vika pressed her, "When did things start to go wrong?"

"Natasha was spoiled rotten. She was born to an older mother, her only child," Nadia said. "Tatyana died when Natasha was pregnant with Vanya. In fact, both she and her husband died in quick succession, and Natasha couldn't cope with three children without her parents' support."

Nadia said Natasha's older boy, Vadim—Vanya's half-brother—had been in her son's class at school, but she believed he was now in jail.

She broke off our conversation to consult with her husband. They had been intending to catch the village bus to get blood tests done at the doctor's. Having established they had missed the bus, she said they would go another day. "For a good deed, you can put anything off."

She told us all the residents of the settlement had recently been moved on to make way for the new town houses. With true KGB efficiency she called a friend in the administration who might be able to tell us the whereabouts of Vanya's family, but she was not in her office. A secretary said she might be back after lunch at 2:00—in two hours—and we should call back. Nadia then found the cell phone number of a neighbor who had known the family better. There was no reply from her.

She was still determined to do something to help us. She led us up the hill back to the wall and pointed to the building behind it. "If you climb a tree you can see the building where the family lived."

Standing on a mound of rubble, we could just make out the top of an old Soviet apartment block, the one where Vanya's family used to live. It was the last building standing, its destruction delayed for a reason that I could not yet fathom.

It began to rain. We ignored it and took pictures. Nadia's cell phone rang. It was the former neighbor, Oxana, returning her call. Vika spoke to her, taking notes as raindrops splashed on my notebook.

I asked Nadia how it was she had popped her head out of the gate just at the moment we had run out of ideas where to look. "My guardian angel is never far away and puts me where I should be to help people."

My KGB angel, I thought to myself.

Vika finished the call. Oxana, the neighbor, remembered Vanya as a baby. Though premature and weak, he had the most wonderfully expressive eyes. She had never forgotten those eyes, which said, I want everything, the whole world. She had assumed he had died long ago in an institution.

She told us the reason why Vanya's old home was still standing while the other buildings had already been demolished. It was all because of Vanya's older half-brother, Vadim, who was still registered as living there, even though he had served his prison term and disappeared. Under old Communist law, no property could be redeveloped until the registered residents were rehoused. Thus it stood empty, waiting for Vadim to appear and sign away his "living space."

Oxana thought she could help us find Vanya's older sister, Olga. She had given Vika the number of another neighbor, Aida, who might have a contact number for her.

Vika and I got back into the car out of the driving rain. We felt utterly drained. I had even forgotten that I had left my glasses on the roof of the car. Luckily, my new friend the driver had rescued them. After bidding farewell to our KGB angel, we headed back to the metro station. The driver accepted 1,000 rubles.

We had a late lunch in a horrid barnlike restaurant above a new shopping center. Despite the strain of the day, Vika had not lost her endearing quality of making the best of everything and enthusiastically made her choices from the exotic dishes on the menu. She asked what was in the Caucasian salad. The waiter said he did not know, so she ordered it anyway.

While we waited for the waiter to bring us tiramisu, I could not resist teasing Vika: "It seems KGB people have guardian angels. Perhaps we've been wrong about the KGB all these years."

"Not at all. It was Vanya's guardian angel who led us to her."

"She was so helpful, perhaps she was the angel, and just pretending to be a KGB agent."

I handed Vika my phone. She had proved herself to be a sensitive cold caller, and I did not want to put people off with my foreign accent. This time, the phone calls went smoothly. Oxana had called Aida and she was expecting Vika's call. Aida gave Vika the number of Olga's husband, Farid. He in turn gave Vika his home number. A minute later, Vika was speaking to Vanya's sister.

She was resting at home. She apologized for not inviting us to come by but said they had just moved, and the place was a mess. We agreed to meet the next day at the metro nearest to Vika's house. I promised I would bring a cake and a newspaper to identify myself.

"How will we recognize you?" I asked.

"You can't miss me. I'm very pregnant."

30

The Sister's Tale

May–October 2007

Early the next morning, I left the hotel for a fancy bakery I had spotted the night before. The prospect of meeting John's sister was so daunting that I was glad to carry out a simple mechanical task like buying a cake. The statistics—even the official ones—on the fate of children brought up in state institutions and then released into society at the age of eighteen offered little hope. These vulnerable young adults were targeted by drug dealers, human traffickers, and pimps and, as often as not, ended up on the street as prostitutes, alcoholics, and drug addicts. But we had promised John to find out about his family and could not let him down.

As I negotiated my way through the pack of stray dogs that lived around the hotel, I counted 400 rubles in my pocket, surely enough for the most expensive cake in Moscow. The bakery was already full of well-dressed Muscovites buying croissants and baguettes. As I scanned the display, I realized I was completely out of touch. The cheapest cake was 700 rubles, about £15.

I slunk out of the shop past the rich Russian ladies, each with a full hand of credit cards from gold to black, to find a cash machine. I ended up spending 800 rubles on a small flan with an over-the-top decoration of exotic fruit—kumquats, cape gooseberries, and even a slab of grapefruit.

Sarah and I arrived early at the metro station. As there was only one exit, the agreement with Olga was to meet at street level. Standing erect beside a column was a slight young woman with long straight light-brown hair, and a pale face. She was obviously pregnant and holding a cake box. We greeted her. She was softly spoken and simply dressed, in fact, the total opposite of most young Russian women—no high heels, no short skirt, no makeup. She had a very Russian face, with high cheekbones. Later she showed us pictures of herself with bleached blond hair, but she said it did not suit her and she would not do it again. Although she seemed delicate and vulnerable and in need of protection, she said she was happy to walk to Vika's. We each took an arm as she crossed the busy road.

Vika was in a state of great excitement, her three boys bouncing around the apartment. Vika and Sarah could not wait to tell Olga their memories of her brother, but first we had to hear her story. She sat down at the kitchen table, straight-backed and with great poise, like a ballerina. From her bag she pulled out a worn newspaper clipping. I recognized the article, which *Izvestia* had run based on the story I had written a decade ago about Vanya's going to England.

"The director of the orphanage came up to me one day and said, 'This must be about your brother.' So I always thought that my brother was in England," she said. She told us that only the previous month, she and Farid had been watching a popular television show, *Wait for Me,* where viewers write in and ask for help in finding long-lost relatives. "I thought maybe they could find Vanya, but I didn't know his birth date or his new surname."

She told the story of her early life and the breakup of her family with a quiet dignity, not shying away from the painful details but clinging to some happy memories. Only one thing betrayed the fact that she had been brought up in institutions—never having been given choices in childhood, she could not make up her mind between the fruit teas she was offered or decide between the kumquat flan and the bird's milk cake she had brought.

She remembered living with her mother, Natasha, and father, Anatoly, in her father's apartment. But the best times were when she visited her grandparents. She always knew her mother loved her, but she would leave her with them for longer and longer periods. She loved going with her grandfather to his vegetable plot. She remembered her grandfather planting apple trees—one for her and one for her older half-brother, Vadim, who lived permanently with her grandparents. Life changed dramatically when she was four years old, when first her grandfather died and then her grandmother followed him to the grave. Vadim went to live with his father, but he never recovered from the loss of his grandmother, and as he grew up he got into more and more serious trouble with the police. Olga was whisked off to a children's home.

While she was in state care, her mother got pregnant with Vanya, and her parents decided to change their lives. Her father sold his flat and they moved into her grandparents' old apartment, determined to turn over a new leaf. They gave up drinking and persuaded a neighbor to testify that they were now fit parents and should be allowed to take Olga home from the orphanage. To celebrate her return to the family, they bought a dog, a Newfoundland, like the one who looked after the children in *Peter Pan*. They called her Irma, and Olga became very attached to her.

Her mother, she recalled, was very strict. Meals were served to a rigid timetable, and when her friends were playing outside, she was kept in for an afternoon rest. Her mother was popular with all the neighbors—until she started drinking again.

She recalled that her father, a cook by trade, used to make the family a wonderful dish of potatoes and mushrooms. Her parents started to argue. Then one day, her father brought her home from day care, opened the door, and she immediately sensed that the apartment was strangely silent. There was an empty space in the living room where Irma's bed used to be. She ran into the kitchen. There was no sign of the dog bowl.

"Where's Irma, Daddy?"

"We couldn't afford to feed her. She's gone to a good home. Forget about her."

Worse was to come. Her parents had a terrible row after her mother had been drinking. She has a memory of her father standing over her, with Vanya in his arms, and he is asking, "Who do you want to live with, with Mummy or Daddy?" Thinking of his cooking, she replied, "With you, Daddy."

Not long after that, she recalled, her mother left home, and her father went after her, locking the door behind him. It got dark and she was alone in the flat with Vanya. She remembered crawling onto the window sill and calling out to the neighbors that she was hungry. One of them climbed in and rescued her. Only hours later did her rescuer think to ask where Vanya was. She said he was fine, she had been popping bits of bread in his mouth all day to stop him getting hungry, and he was lying on the floor. So the neighbor had had to rescue him too.

The next day, the police came to take them away, and that was the last she saw of her brother. She was five and he was one. Because of the age difference, she and her brother were split up. She went back to the children's home and he to a baby house.

While she was at the children's home, a couple came to take her out. They took her to their dacha and asked her to do a drawing of the pink and white church near the children's home. They promised to come back to see her again—she now understands they were considering adopting her—but they never did. "I guess they're still on their way," she laughed.

When she turned six, she was put before a medical-psychological commission to decide whether she was fit to go to a normal school. One of the tests was to identify a tree. Hedging her bets, she said: "It's an oaky maple." She failed the test, was labeled "cretin," and transferred to an orphanage for the mentally retarded, where only the most limited education was offered.

Then she did something truly remarkable. She managed to convince the teachers how clever she was. She took on the role of classroom assistant. Through sheer determination and with no outside support, she got herself transferred to Orphanage No. 15, where she would receive an education.

A year after she arrived, another extraordinary thing happened. The orphanage was turned into a circus school, under the patronage of the superstar of the Moscow State Circus, the clown and movie actor Yuri Nikulin. All the children were put through strenuous tests, and she was selected to become an acrobat. She trained to stand on her hands and balance on different objects. During a performance, when she was handstanding on two columns of bricks and removing them one by one, she lost her balance and fell off the narrow stage. She ended up in a hospital, having major back surgery, and her career as an acrobat was over. She was thirteen.

Had she not fallen, she would have gone into the Moscow circus institute and traveled the world, but instead they sent her to learn how to sell wine and spirits. She curled her nose at the idea; both she and her husband were teetotalers.

It was time to ask her what happened to her mother. In 1997, when she was twelve and Vanya was back in Baby House 10 recovering from his ordeal in the mental asylum, she decided to initiate contact with her mother, whom she had not seen for six years. She wrote a letter to her and sent it to their old home. "Where are you? Why don't you come and see me? I love you very much."

Natasha was not living in the old apartment. She had let it out to a succession of ever more unreliable tenants, who trashed the place. The day Olga's letter arrived, she happened to be checking the flat, and picked up the mail. She came to see her daughter the very next weekend. From then on, she visited Olga regularly, sometimes bringing with her the new man in her life, an older man who had first courted her when she was only seventeen. He was introduced to her as Uncle Volodya.

Under his influence, Natasha stopped drinking and they petitioned for Olga to come and live with them. By early October of the following year, about the time Vanya was entering the foster program, everything was arranged. Natasha would come and pick up her daughter and take her home on Saturday, October 10. The day before, Olga began to feel uneasy and called her mother to remind her. Natasha replied, "Of course, darling. How could I forget? I've been to the market and bought you a new outfit. You can't go around in those orphanage clothes."

The next day Olga sat, clutching her only possessions—a favorite pencil and some school exercise books—and waited for her mother to appear. Hours passed. She went to the phone and called home. A man answered, but it was not Uncle Volodya.

"Can I speak to my mama?" she asked.

The voice replied, "You've lost your mama."

We were shocked into silence. Only Olga sat composed.

Sipping her tea, she said her mother had been taken ill the night before. The ambulance took a long time to arrive, and she died in the hospital.

By a cruel twist of fate, she turned eighteen and was released from the orphanage at the same time as Vadim was released from prison. With the death of his grandmother when he was seven, Vadim had become a troubled boy. He began to steal bread and then was caught trying to steal a car. He was labeled as a "social deviant" and, at the age of only twelve, he was sentenced to four years in a young-offenders prison. He never recovered from the experience of being locked away with much older criminals, and had been in and out of prison ever since.

So Olga and her troubled brother ended up together in their mother's apartment, the one we had glimpsed over the high wall the day before. The half-brother and -sister's relationship soured when Vadim's former cellmates came to stay. Vadim's behavior became threatening. Luckily, she had already met Farid, who was working as a foreman on a building site. He told Vadim to pack up his stuff and never come near his half-sister again. When the developers came to rehouse the residents, Olga demanded a one-room apartment in Moscow, away from her half-brother, which she now shares with Farid.

No one knew what to say. Sarah got out the latest photos of John—a formal school portrait and some in his Scout uniform. Olga's face lit up at the sight of her brother, and she sat staring at the photos, gobbling them up with her eyes.

"He looks so American. Just like Arnold Schwarzenegger," she exclaimed.

"But much more cultured," said Vika, appalled at the idea.

"He's got Mother's curls," she said, looking at an earlier photo. She said she had once complained to her mother that she had inherited her sticking-out ears, but not her curly hair to hide them.

The photos meant a lot to her. Until her mother's death, Olga did not have a single family photo. When she had been allowed out of the orphanage to attend her mother's funeral, she had found her mother's identity card, pulled off the picture, and put it in her pocket. Until now, that was the sum total of her family album.

I could not help noticing the extraordinary similarity between the characters of Olga and John. Both had struggled to overcome their terrible background, finding drive and focus within themselves. Both had developed strong moral values and a sense of self-worth unusual in children brought up in soulless institutions.

Not surprisingly, John was delighted to hear that we had discovered his long-lost sister. He was even more delighted to be told a month later that she had given birth to a baby girl, Karina, his niece.

Throughout the summer, there were inconclusive attempts to get brother and sister to speak to each other, which always foundered on the time difference and the need for an interpreter.

Finally in October, Sarah found herself back in Moscow, sitting with Olga and Farid and holding Karina on her knee, anxiously waiting for the phone to ring. Back in Pennsylvania, John had come home early from school, after telling everyone he was about to speak to his sister from whom he had been parted when he was a baby.

The great reunion turned out to be a technical minefield. They all stood in the narrow hallway, taking turns holding the baby. Farid put on the speaker phone; but the old Russian telephone lines were not up to the task, and no one could make out what John was saying. With Sarah passing the receiver around, John had to say everything twice—once so his relatives could hear his voice and a second time for the translation.

Despite this laborious method, some communication got through. Olga reminded John of their early childhood—Irma the dog, trudging through the snow with their father into the forest to chop down a fir tree for their New Year's decorations, and their father's tasty fried potatoes.

She had something to say that had been weighing on her conscience all these years. Baby Vanya was lying on the sofa and their mother had told her to watch him and make sure he did not fall off. But she had turned away to put a record on, and he had plopped on to the floor. "Please forgive me. I was only little."

Paula said, "I feel like I have gained a daughter and a son-in-law."

Farid issued a flowery invitation to John and Paula to come and visit his extended family in the north Caucasus, where they were assured of a warm welcome.

Finally it was John's turn to speak to Farid. There was one of his ominous pauses, and at last he said, "Farid, make sure you take good care of my sister."

As Olga accompanied Sarah to the bus stop, she was hugging herself and laughing as she repeated John's words.

31

The Vanya Effect

September 2009

All the people involved in John's journey have found their lives changed—some in small ways, some dramatically.

Vika says, "Vanya has an amazing and rare gift that saved his life— the gift of connecting with people. He immediately remembers your name and knows how to talk to you. Talking to him is a treat for the soul.

"Because of him, I found talents within me I didn't know I had. I learned how to organize people and how to deal with people in authority.

"Through my small efforts, and the efforts of others, God was able to create a miracle. To me, Vanya was a litmus paper to show whether people were good or indifferent."

Recently a man rang the number of Vika's old apartment. The caller wanted to speak to Vika to apologize for the abusive phone calls he had made to her in 1997. He said he had been forced to make the calls, and was full of remorse.

Sarah continues to support Action for Russia's Children (ARC), the charity she cofounded that helps Russian grassroots initiatives fighting to keep children out of state institutions. In 1999 she went to Buckingham Palace to receive a medal, the MBE, from Queen Elizabeth, for services to the welfare of disadvantaged children in Moscow. She is still angry at Alan for dragging her away from Russia.

Emily Spry, the English student who visited Vanya when he was in Hospital No. 58, returned to Oxford University to study English literature, but felt her vocation was to become a doctor. She has just started working in pediatrics.

Elvira, the raven-haired girl who was befriended by Vanya in Hospital No. 58, was found by adoptive parents in America just before she was due to be sent to an internat for the ineducable. She lives in Oklahoma and is now called Elena. An eleventh grader, she likes to study science and is learning to play the guitar and piano. Her favorite authors are J. R. R. Tolkien and C. S. Lewis. She considers Jesus the most important influence in her life.

Andrei, the friend Vanya taught to speak in Baby House 10, left Moscow in 1997 to live in Florida where his father was manager of a five-star hotel. In 1999, the family felt cwalled by God to return to Russia. They still live in Moscow, and have taken more than twenty children from disadvantaged backgrounds into their care. Andrei and his father have regularly visited Baby House 10.

Vladimir Putin, President of Russia 2000–2008 and now prime minister, declared in 2006 his wish that all abandoned children should be placed in families and not in institutions. But there are still more than 800,000 children in the care of the Russian state—a greater number than at the end of World War II when much of the USSR lay in ruins.

Maria Ternovskaya, the founder of Russia's first foster-parent project, is continuing her work in the face of growing hostility from the bureaucracy. Despite her 95 percent success rate in placing the most disturbed and abused children with foster families, the Russian parliament has outlawed the form of fostering she pioneered. Despite official harassment, she refuses to give up.

Rachel Smith returned to Britain in 1999 and works as London secretary for ARC. She has not given up trying to learn Russian.

Masha, the little girl in Group 2 of Baby House 10 who was so loved by Vika, died shortly after her transfer to Internat 30.

Valeria, the blue girl who got a heart operation thanks to Sarah and Alan's intervention, died two years later. She had never been the center of anyone's universe.

Dima, the boy who swam through his urine in the Filimonki mental asylum, died at age ten.

Slava, the disturbed boy who attacked Vanya, is locked away in an institution. A request to see him in 2007 was rejected.

Anna, the little girl with the bright personality who got the first wheelchair in Baby House 10, was transferred to Internat 28. A lively seventeen-year-old, in 2007 she was spending her days on one floor of the institution, making things out of beads and waiting to be transferred to a home for the elderly, where she would spend the rest of her days.

Adela, the head doctor of Baby House 10, survived the trouble caused by Vanya's unauthorized adoption and died while still in her post. Her funeral was held at the baby house. The coal-fired boiler has gone, but the regime is unchanged, with the children still tethered in their baby walkers.

The elderly deaf caregiver in Baby House 10 who gave Sarah a sweet during John's valedictory tour was murdered in the stairwell of her home in 2006.

Grigory, the lawyer who denounced corrupt practices in international adoption, was arrested in May 1999 and charged with baby trafficking. He was held for three years, almost all of it in solitary confinement, and refused access to books, exercise, visits, or packages. After six months, just as he felt he was about to go out of his mind, he had a religious experience on the anniversary of his mother's death and found the strength to continue. His case came to court four times, with him conducting his own defense, and was thrown out each time by the judge for lack of evidence. In April 2002 he was released, without apology, and is now a well-known defense lawyer. He has acted in some high-profile human rights cases, but he is particularly proud that some of his former enemies—including a public prosecutor, a prison governor, and secret service agents—have asked him to defend them. After his treatment in prison, all Russian lawyers have learned not to challenge the bureaucracy in international adoption. He remembers Adela with fondness and gratitude. Despite extreme pressure, she refused to cooperate with the authorities in concocting evidence against him in the baby-selling case, seriously weakening the prosecution's case against him.

Valentina (Auntie Valentina) retired from the baby house in 2000. Shown pictures of John in America, she wept with joy.

The teenagers who looked after Vanya in Filimonki are still the victims of the abuse of psychiatry. They are still in the same institution, which is now surrounded by a high wall with barbed wire. Now in their mid-twenties, they are denied all rights. Some of them are allowed out to work in the local chicken factory.

Sonya, Vanya's foster mother, is now the loving guardian of Julia, the girl who provided companionship to Vanya in his last months at the baby house.

Dr. Ronald Swanger, the New York pediatrician who visited Baby House 10, now lives in retirement in Florida. He volunteers for a children's advocacy center.

Sergei Koloskov, the pianist turned parental rights activist who brought the state of children in the Filimonki mental asylum to the attention of the world and passed on Vanya's cry for help, now serves as an expert advisor for the Russian ombudsmen for human rights. This allows him to inspect children's institutions throughout the country.

He said recently, "In every internat we always find one or two Vanyas, children who are obviously intelligent. Among the screams and complete silence, there is one boy or girl who is able to converse with us and begs us for a toy.

"There are still 5,000 children in Russia who live in what is called permanent bed regime, that is, they are condemned to spend their whole life cycle in bed.

"I think that if a normal person goes just once to one of these institutions, he is left with a wound that will never heal. I feel I cannot stop this work until this injustice ends."

The grand piano at his home is now almost invisible, hidden under piles of documents—the files of children and young adults in state care whom he is trying to help.

There is one more person who has not yet found a place in this narrative—an eleven-year-girl in Children's Home No. 31. She does not remember her pretty, curly-haired mother who died when she was only eight months old. Until recently, an elderly man with a walking stick, her father, used to visit her, but he has not been seen for a while. The girl is called Tatyana, after her grandmother, and has her mother's fine features, including the sticking-out ears.

Since she arrived at the children's home, a number of Russian couples wishing to adopt have come to look at her, but they have been put off by her medical record, which describes her as a "child invalid." In fact, her only medical problem was a heart complaint, which was corrected long ago.

I did not get a chance to meet her, but I am told that, unusually for a child brought up in an institution, she is articulate, lively, and demanding of the affection of the staff, and no one who comes into contact with her forgets her.

EPILOGUE
The Boy from Bethlehem

September 2009

It's been ten years since I came to America. I only have to look at the picture Alan took of me on the grounds of the internat in 1996 to see how far I've come. He put a baseball cap on my head, to hide my shaved head, but I will never ever live down the shame of it. It's a Red Sox hat. Of all the teams, why the Red Sox? *I'm a Yankees fan.* Sometimes I support the Phillies because I live in Pennsylvania, but I never ever root for the Red Sox. I hope New England will forgive me.

Today I'm a student at Freedom High School in Bethlehem, Pennsylvania, where history is my favorite subject. I get up every morning at 5:45 to catch a school bus and that's no treat, believe me. But however tired I am, I never ever have an afternoon nap. In Russia, I wasted too much of my life in bed, and now I always feel like I have so much catching up to do.

When my mom brought me to America, I was nine and a half years old, but I was put into first grade. I didn't speak English, and had to learn it quickly. I was lucky, though, because I made a friend in day care. His name was Danny. He was my age, but he was already in fourth grade. Danny taught me, as I taught Andrei in Russia. Andrei learned to speak Russian from me, and I learned to speak English from Danny. For two years of day care we talked every day, before and after school. He was the first person to invite me to a birthday party and ask me to a sleep over at his house. After all this time, Danny is still one of my very best friends.

Mom tells me that when I learned English in those early days, my favorite word was "our." Never having owned anything, I loved to talk of "our car" and "our house." "Everything is ours," I would say, to reassure myself that it wasn't all going to be taken away.

My mom can talk for hours about all kinds of things that happened in those early months. For instance, she gave me a toolbox, which became my most treasured possession. Now, she understands that the happiest moments in my life in Russia were when I was playing with the hammer and nails. She reminds me that I loved to play in the snow and get wet and dirty, which I had never been allowed to do. Very soon after I arrived in America, she took me to a wildlife park. I was unsettled by the sight of cages and the animals behind bars. I kept asking, "Why is that animal behind bars?" Not everything scared me or reminded me of the bad times in Russia. Mom always talks about an incident that happened at Disney World. Tigger stepped out of character (something that's strictly forbidden in the world of Disney) to whisper to my mom, "God bless him." I think God heard Tigger's prayer.

One day in third grade, something happened that I knew would broaden my horizons. There was a school assembly to encourage boys to join the Cub Scouts. I wasn't even sure what joining Cub Scouts would be like, but it sounded like there would be exciting activities, such as camping out. After school that day, I told my mom about it and asked her if I could join the Cubs. She wasn't certain that the Cub Scouts would be able to accommodate my disabilities and seemed reluctant to let me join. I said to her, "Mom, give to me a chance." (My English still had a few traces of Russian then). After that, she couldn't refuse me.

As I was finishing my time in Cub Scouts, the boys in my den all had to decide which of several nearby Boy Scout troops to join. We went to look at at least four troops. But there was one that made a big impression on me. While most of the boys decided to join a particular troop together, I made a different decision. For me, it had to be Troop 362. For me, it was the best troop I had found so far. I could tell it was a well-organized troop with a lot to offer.

This worried my mom. She thought I wouldn't be comfortable on my own. "Don't you want to be with all your friends?" she asked.

But I insisted. "Mom, don't you dare try to talk me out of this."

That was five years ago. Mom often tells me, "I have to admit it, John, you were so right when you selected Troop 362." Through the troop, I have formed good friendships, explored the outdoors, and acquired important skills for life. The thing I like the most is that they never made a big deal about my disability. Through my membership in the Boy Scouts, I've matured over the past five years and acquired some solid leadership skills.

In 2006, I had to undergo what's known as an "ordeal" if I wanted to advance to the Ordeal Level of the Order of the Arrow, a sort of Boy Scout honor society. The ordeal I had to go through was that I had to spend a night in the forest alone. I would have no phone and no flashlight. Even though I need a device like a walker or crutches to help me get around, I was treated like everyone else. The only thing I was allowed to have was a sleeping bag and tarp to keep me warm and dry. They also gave me an orange and an egg to eat for breakfast. It took forever to convince my mom, but I finally got her to agree that I could go through this trial, and off I went with the other Scouts to the night of our Ordeal. It was about 11:00 o'clock, raining and dark when we arrived. An older Scout dropped me off, and there I was, all by myself in the middle of the woods in the dark. There was nowhere dry to sleep, and the tarp was no good at keeping the rain out. By morning, my clothes were soaking wet and I had hardly slept a wink. My mom swears she didn't sleep a wink either, worrying about me all night long. When the sun came up, I ate the egg and the orange while I waited for someone to pick me up. I survived my ordeal, passed the test, and became a member of the Order of the Arrow. Since then, I've gone on and am proud to say that I've become a brotherhood member of the Order of the Arrow.

Mom and I worship at St. Paul Orthodox Church in Emmaus, Pennsylvania. This church is one of the clearest links with my past. My Russian certificate of baptism, signed by the priest who came to Baby House 10 on Tuesdays, is one of the few things I have brought from Russia that counts for something in America. I go to Sunday School there and used to be an altar boy. It's a small church, but filled with wonderful people. In fact, I can always count on them to buy popcorn from me when I raise money for the Boy Scouts every year.

Besides church, school, and Scouts, coming to the United States has given me the opportunity to see things I would never have seen in Russia and develop tons of other interests including a love of vintage television shows and old movies. I have seen every James Bond movie, and when I had to dress up at school one day in 2003, I chose to go as 007, in a home-made tuxedo. I love J. K. Rowling's entire Harry Potter series, I like watching sports—Philadelphia Eagles football, Penn State football, baseball, and golf. I'm one of Tiger Woods's biggest fans.

My family is a great blessing. When my mom brought me to the United States, I became part of a wonderful extended family, living close by here in Pennsylvania and as far away as Texas and California. The "family" also includes a group of my mom's friends who all love me and are very good to me. I also have to say that my family in the United States wouldn't be complete without my dog, Jambo, named because we got him just before a Boy Scout Jamboree. My family, though, doesn't stop at the U.S. borders. I'll never forget the day I was lying in the bathtub and Mom yelled through the door that Alan had found my sister Olga. I hadn't seen her since I was one and she was six and we were taken away and put in separate institutions. When I finally got to hear her voice, I cried. It seemed like so many parts of my family were coming together.

Of course, the biggest blessing in my life is my mom. I wouldn't be who I am today without her. All the time I was in Russia, everything I said and did was a cry: Give to me a chance. My mom has given me a chance. Our relationship is the best in the world. She loves me, supports me, encourages me, and guides me. She loves me for who I am and is proud of me. When I have a problem, I come to her with it. I can't imagine what my life would be like without her. She tells me she can't imagine her life if she didn't have me. We know God brought us together, and we thank Him for this every day.

I'm lucky. I have a great life, but I haven't forgotten my past. How could I? I am very grateful to all the people who helped save me while I was in Russia. Some of them have not been mentioned in the book. If we included all of them, the book would have been in several volumes. I hope they will all have the strength and courage to continue their work so that children will no longer suffer as I did.

It is my hope and prayer that this book will put an end to the evil system that locks children away behind high walls in inhuman conditions. My dream is that, someday, all these institutions will be closed down. All children should live in families. I want them all to have a chance.

How This Book Came
to Be Written

The genesis of this book lies in an interview given by John and Paula to their local newspaper in May 2006. When Alan and Sarah read it, they realized that John knew very little of the extraordinary story of his early years. This prompted Alan and Sarah to rummage through boxes of jumbled-up papers, notebooks, and photographs dating back to their time in Moscow. There was enough information to establish a basic timeline for the events of John's life in Russia. Over the course of two years this timeline grew into a spreadsheet with 310 dated entries. Sarah's photographs brought the timeline to life. But first they had to be sorted: The pictures had long ago become divorced from their negatives. In the end, she scanned more than 1,000 negatives. Clues in the pictures—such as the number of candles on a birthday cake—settled which year they were taken. A hoarder by nature, Sarah had kept all her notebooks and diaries, and when these were unearthed from the bottoms of plastic crates, they added another dimension to the story: There were scraps of conversations with John and reports of the anxious debates by John's supporters over what to do after the failure of the British adoption. Alan's diary, written on an obsolete personal organizer with a volatile memory, had been wiped out by a flat battery. But a backup found on an old computer brought it back to life, confirming a host of dates and recording notes of conversations with Adela, Vika, and other people involved.

Some home videos of John—taken in 1998 with the aim of finding him a family but never used for that purpose—provided a faithful record of his final months in the baby house. Those tapes provide much of the material in chapter 20, including comments he made that were so poignant they had been excised from human memory. A dormant Compuserve Internet account, which should have been closed years before, provided a treasure of e-mails covering 1998 and 1999, illuminating a period that otherwise would have been hard to recall. Among publicly available material, a documentary film by Manon Loizeau, *Growing Up in a Strait Jacket,* jogged memories about the Filimonki asylum. The camera even caught, for the most fleeting moment, John aged six bouncing up and down in his crib to attract attention.

John's recollections are practically nonexistent before 1996. From then on they get gradually clearer and fuller, so that by 1999—the period when he was being fostered—his memories are intense and deeply painful. Paula, not surprisingly, has vivid memories of her life-changing decision to adopt John, and the barely believable sequence of events that unfolded as she arrived in Moscow.

In 2007, at Alan and Sarah's reunion with John in Bethlehem, he asked a series of questions that required three research trips to Moscow to answer. Vika was typically enthusiastic in unearthing the past. Maria Ternovskaya and her staff, including Irina Schipilova and Maria Kalinina, were generous with their time. John's sister, Olga, explained the family history, as did former neighbors. Almost everyone who knew John in Russia—once they had got over their shock at seeing a photograph of him as he is now—was keen to add to the picture of a child who would not give up. Past members of staff of the baby house provided a depth of understanding of the working of this institution.

Many people helped to explain the hidden workings of the Soviet medical and child care system, with its baby houses, children's homes, and internats. These include Sergei Koloskov, president of the Down's Syndrome Association; Boris Altshuler, director of the children's rights charity Right of Child; Anna Bitova and Roman Dimenshtein of the Centre for Curative Pedagogics; Svyatoslav Dovbnya, pediatric neurologist, and Tatiana Morozova, consultant psychologist, of Early Intervention Institute in St. Petersburg; Dr. Ronald Swanger, the retired New York pediatrician; and Dr. Stewart Britten of HealthProm. No list of acknowledgments would be complete without Caroline Cox, whose book *Trajectories of Despair* exposed the widespread misdiagnosis of children in Russia and whose fund-raising allowed the establishment of Maria Ternovskaya's foster program, Our Family.

The book could not have been written without the recollections of former Moscow residents Ann Kitson, Fay Roberts, and Rachel Smith, all of whom provided vital insights into John's life and the lives of other children in state care. Emily Spry brought to life Vanya's time in hospital. Video footage of children in Baby House 10 taken by Viv Frost proved invaluable in re-creating Group 2 and Group 6.

All the events in the book happened in the manner described and as close to the date indicated as it is possible to ascertain. As for the conversations in the book, they are based on interviews with the main characters and all other available information. These conversations are reconstructed: There is no pretense that this dialogue is a verbatim record.

Some of the individuals have had their identities disguised in order to protect their privacy. In a few cases conversations that continued over several days have been compressed in order not to weary the reader.

The story of John's rescue is a complicated one with a big cast of characters: It is not a sprint, but a relay. Many people who deserve a mention have been left out in order not to complicate the narrative. In some cases characters are composites: the boy called Ilya in the Filimonki asylum represents three teenagers—sent there as punishment for running away from children's homes—who showed uncommon kindness to John in appalling circumstances.

The evidence for almost all the events in the book relies on a participant or a witness. There are some things that indisputably happened for which there is no witness: One of these is John's assessment by the Psycho-Medical Pedagogical Commission from Hospital No. 6, described in chapter 3. Many people helped with information on how these assessments are carried out, including a psychologist, a speech therapist, and a caregiver in a children's home. Olga provided details of her own experience of the same assessment process. The pictures that John were asked to identify are taken from Soviet preschool books.

As ever with human memory, different people's recollections do not always tally. Sometimes they even contradict. The decision on which version to include rests entirely with the authors. No responsibility lies with the people who kindly cooperated in the writing of the book.

The purpose of this book is not to divide people into good and evil. Rather, it is to measure humanity by a different scale, from indifferent to caring. As Vika said, Vanya was the litmus paper. Many people, far more than can be mentioned here, cared for Vanya. Apologies to them that their efforts are not publicly recognized. But if this book reduces, even slightly, the ranks of the indifferent, it will have succeeded.